I0824298

SHORE, FOREST AND BEYOND

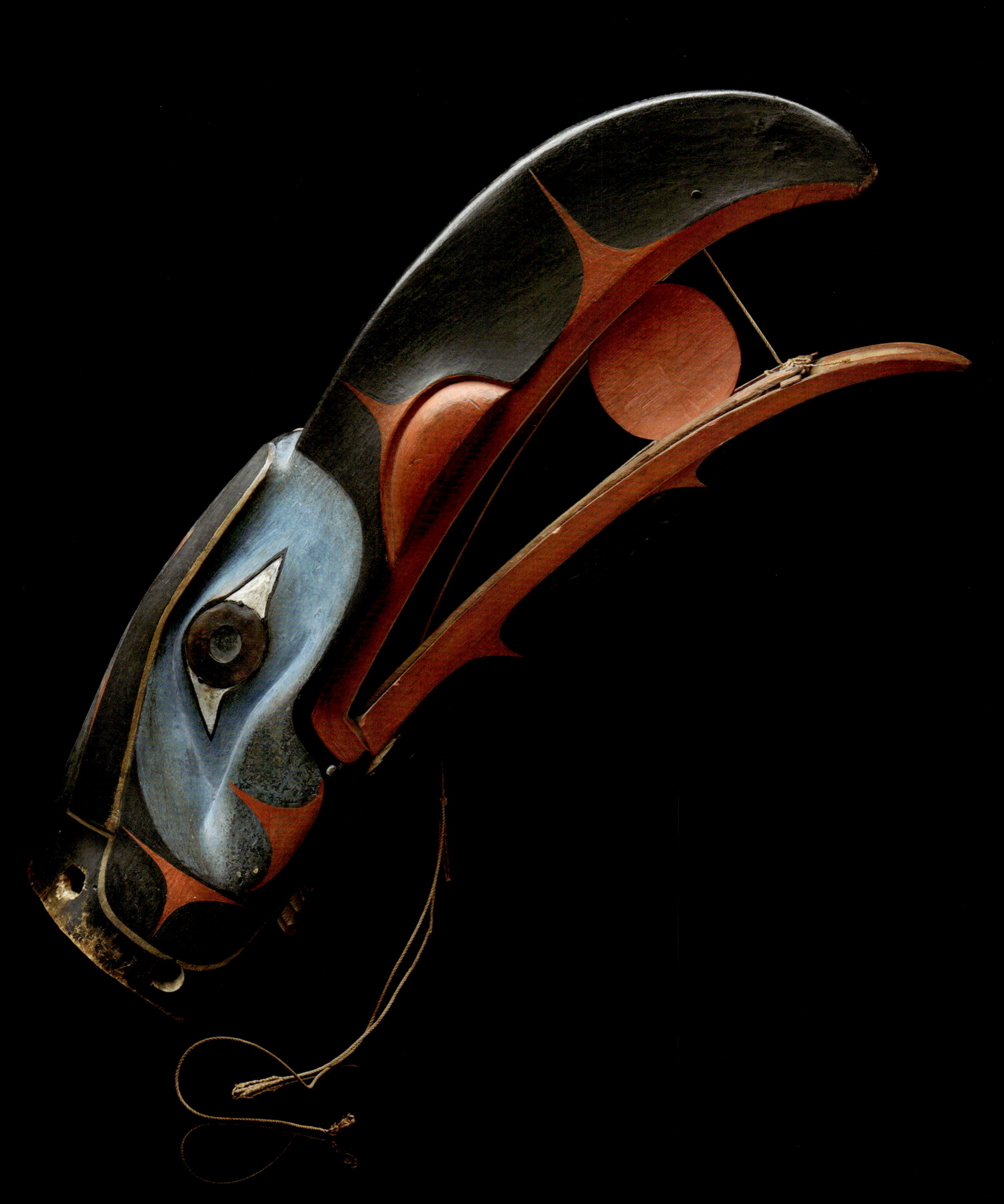

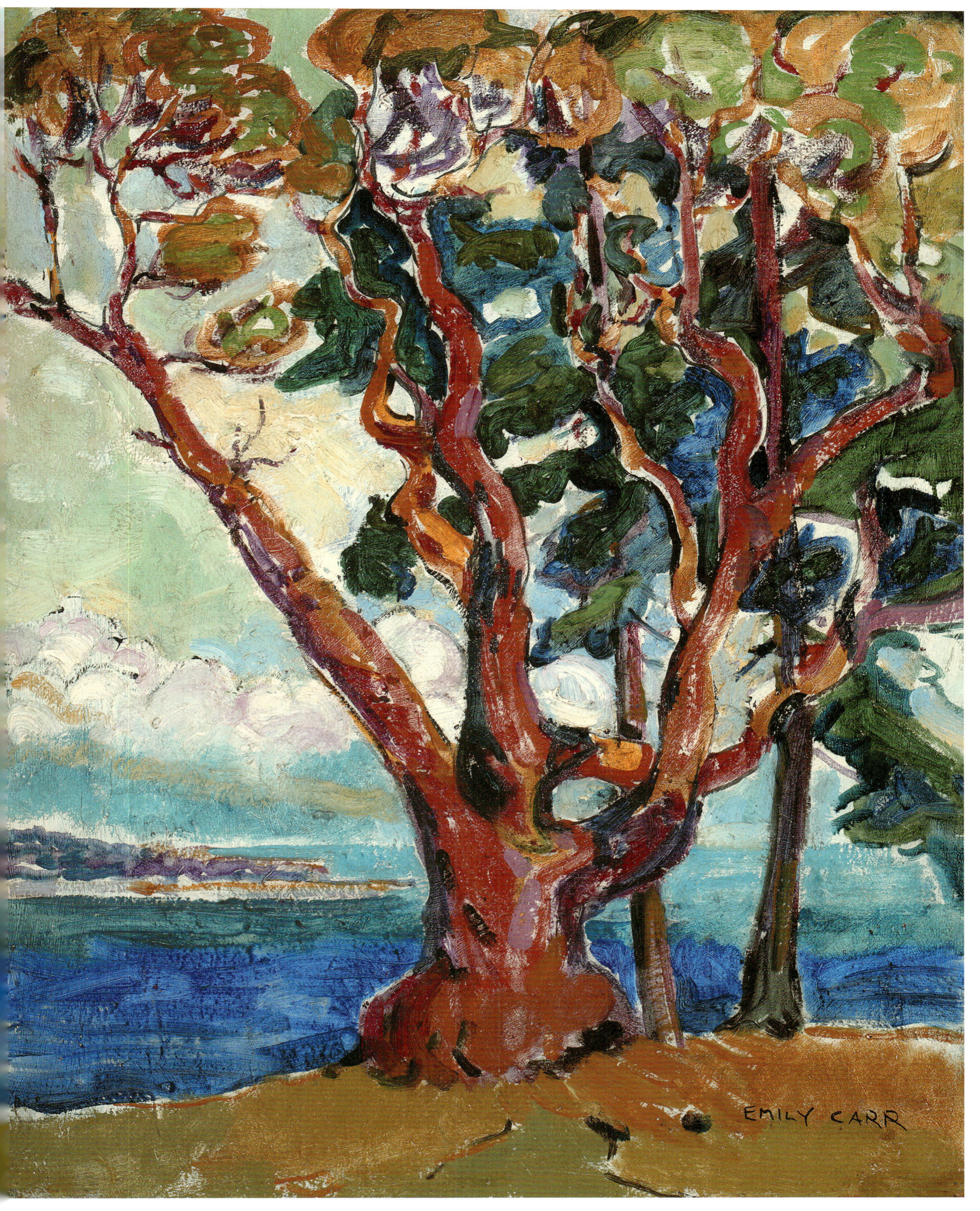
EMILY CARR

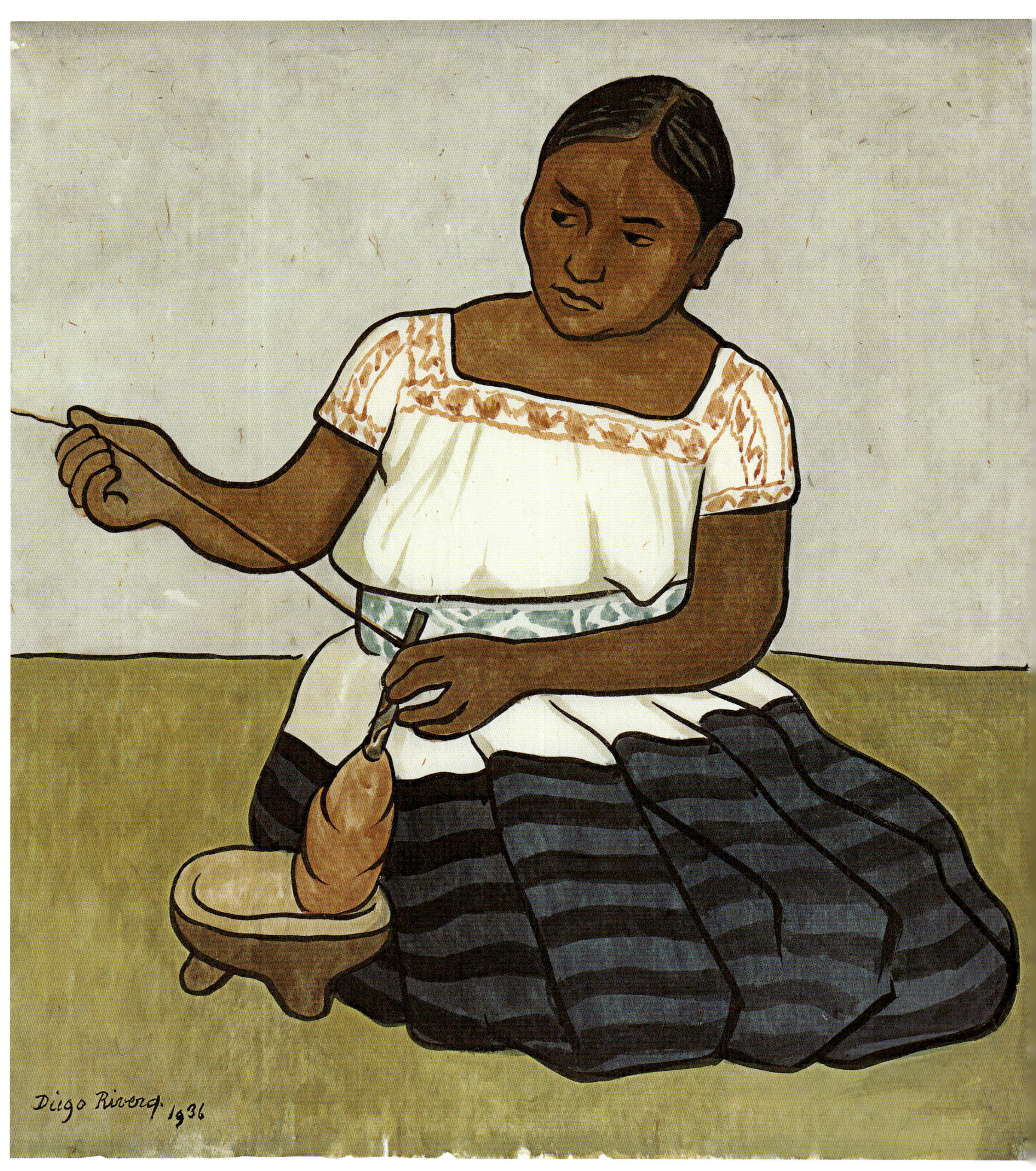
Diego Rivera 1936

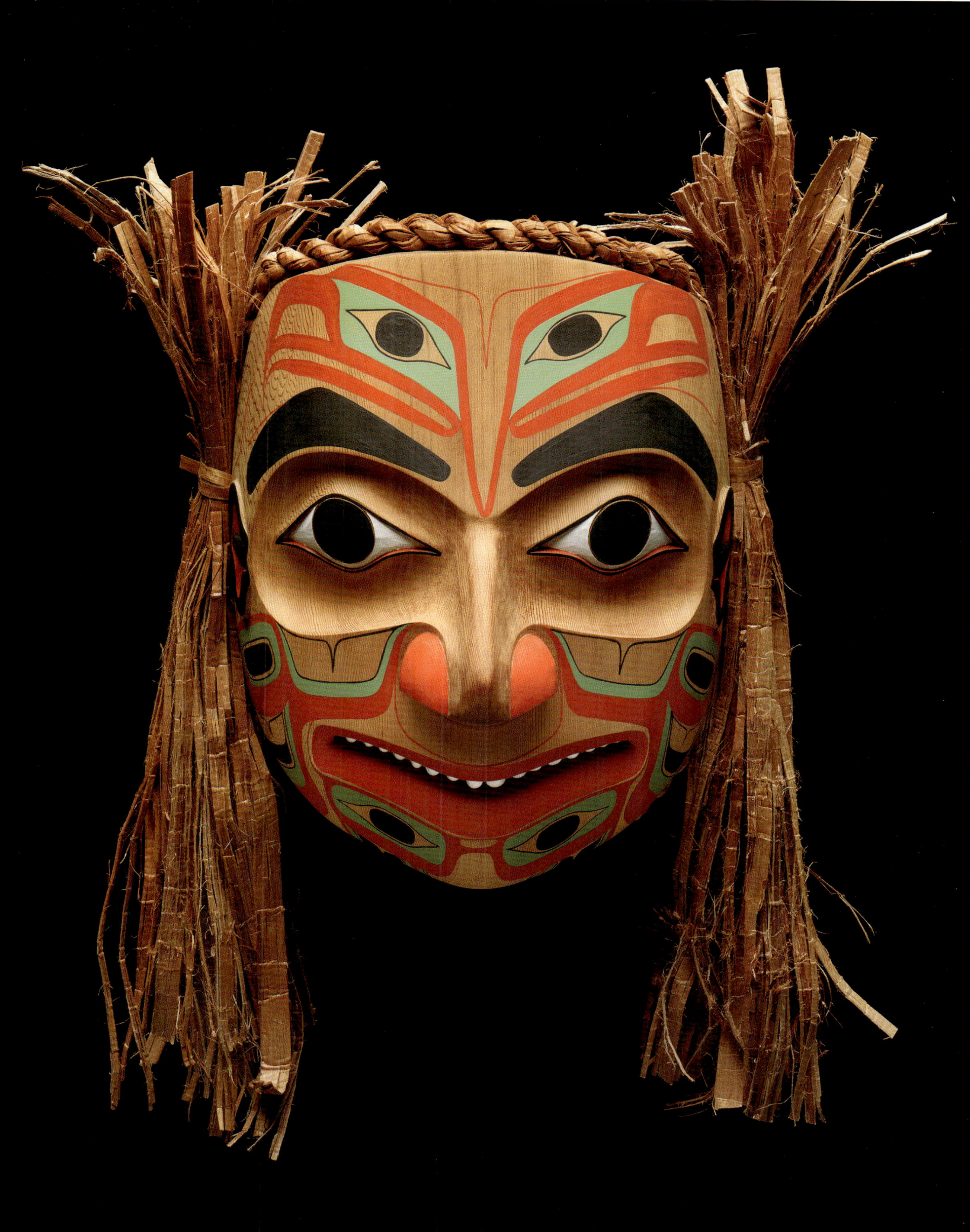

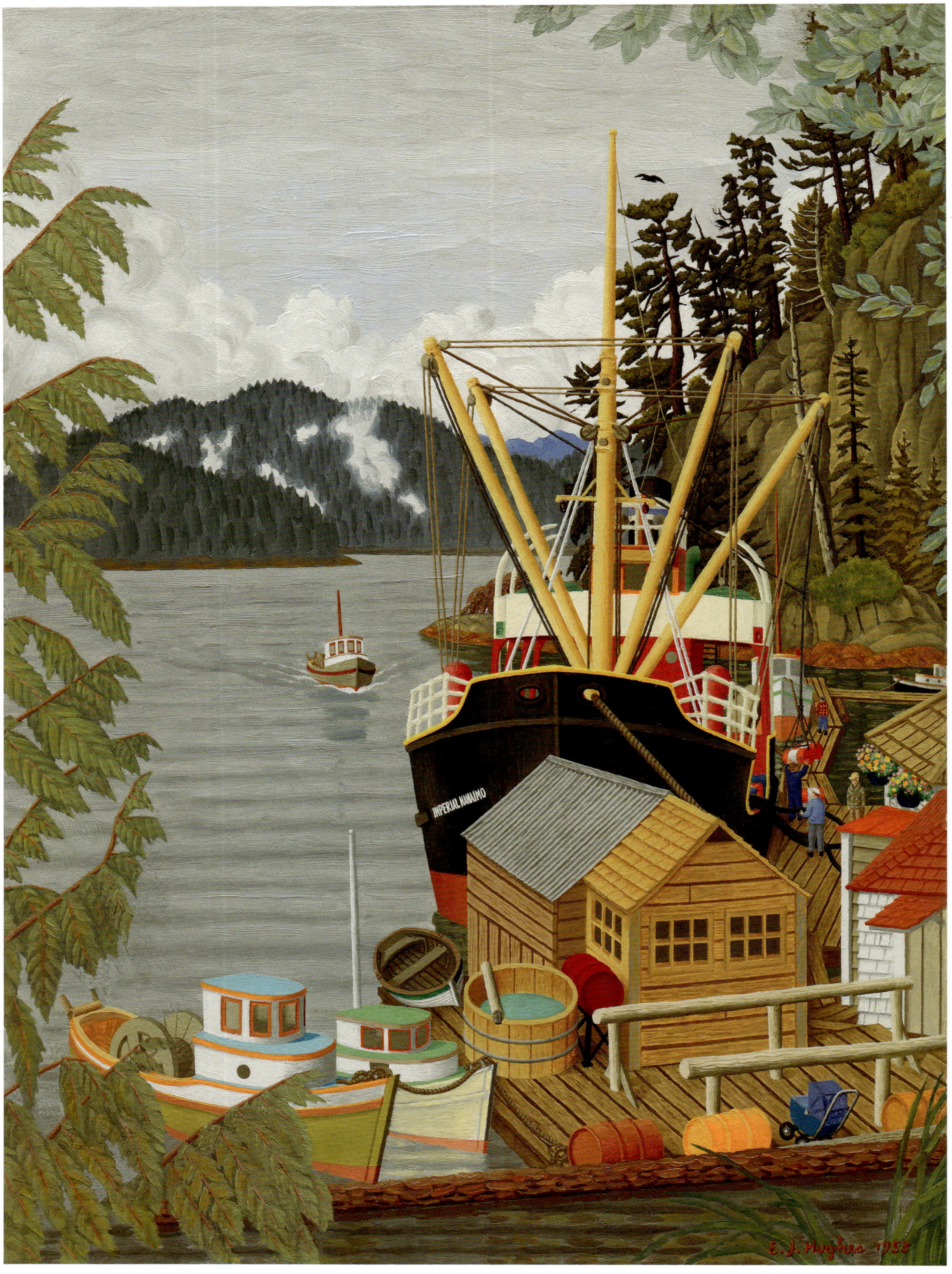
IMPERIAL NANAIMO
E. J. Hughes 1953

SHORE, FOREST AND BEYOND

ART FROM THE AUDAIN COLLECTION

Douglas & McIntyre
D&M PUBLISHERS INC.
Vancouver/Toronto/Berkeley

Vancouver Art Gallery
Vancouver

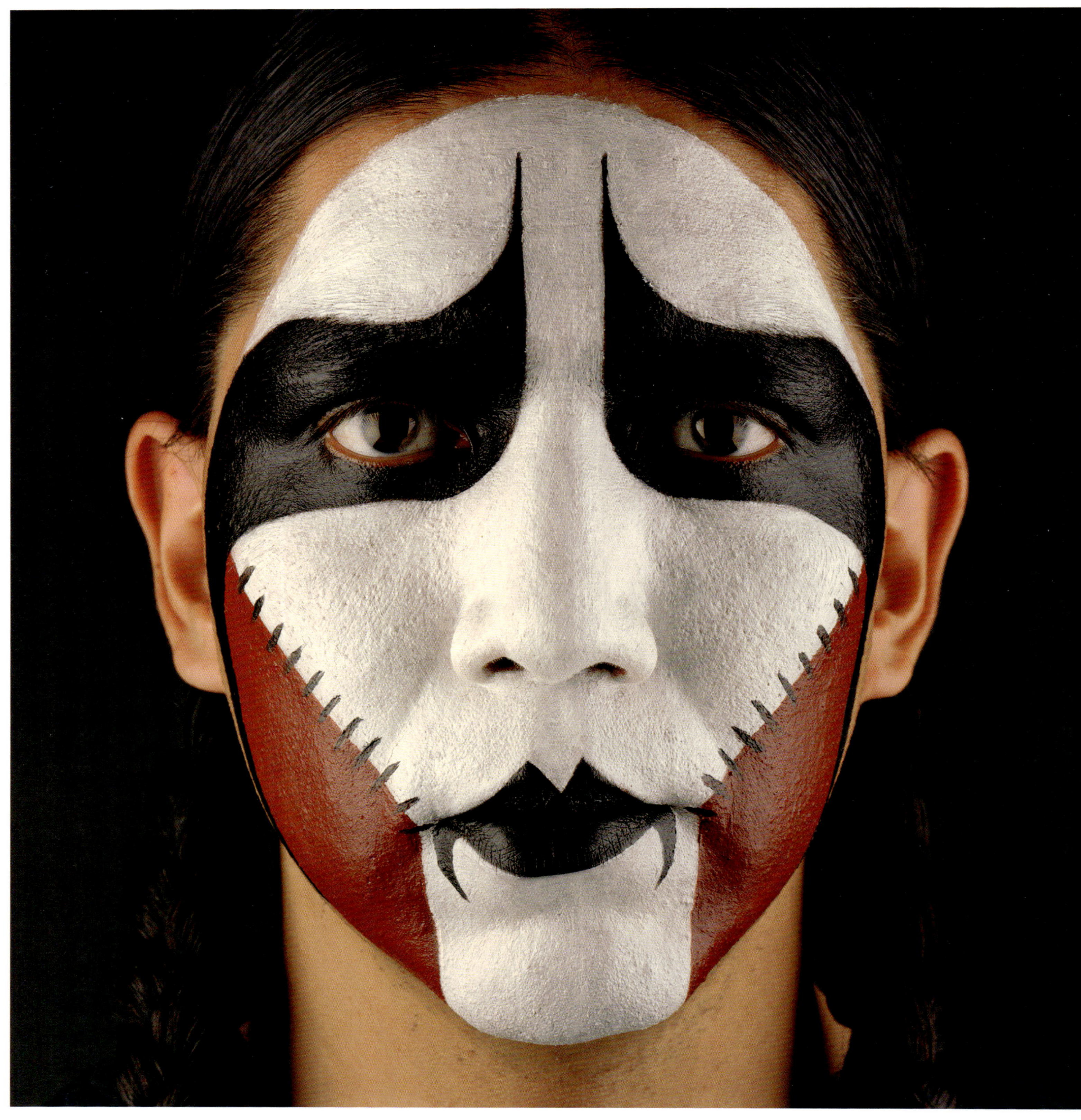

Dana Claxton
Paint Up #1 2010

CONTENTS

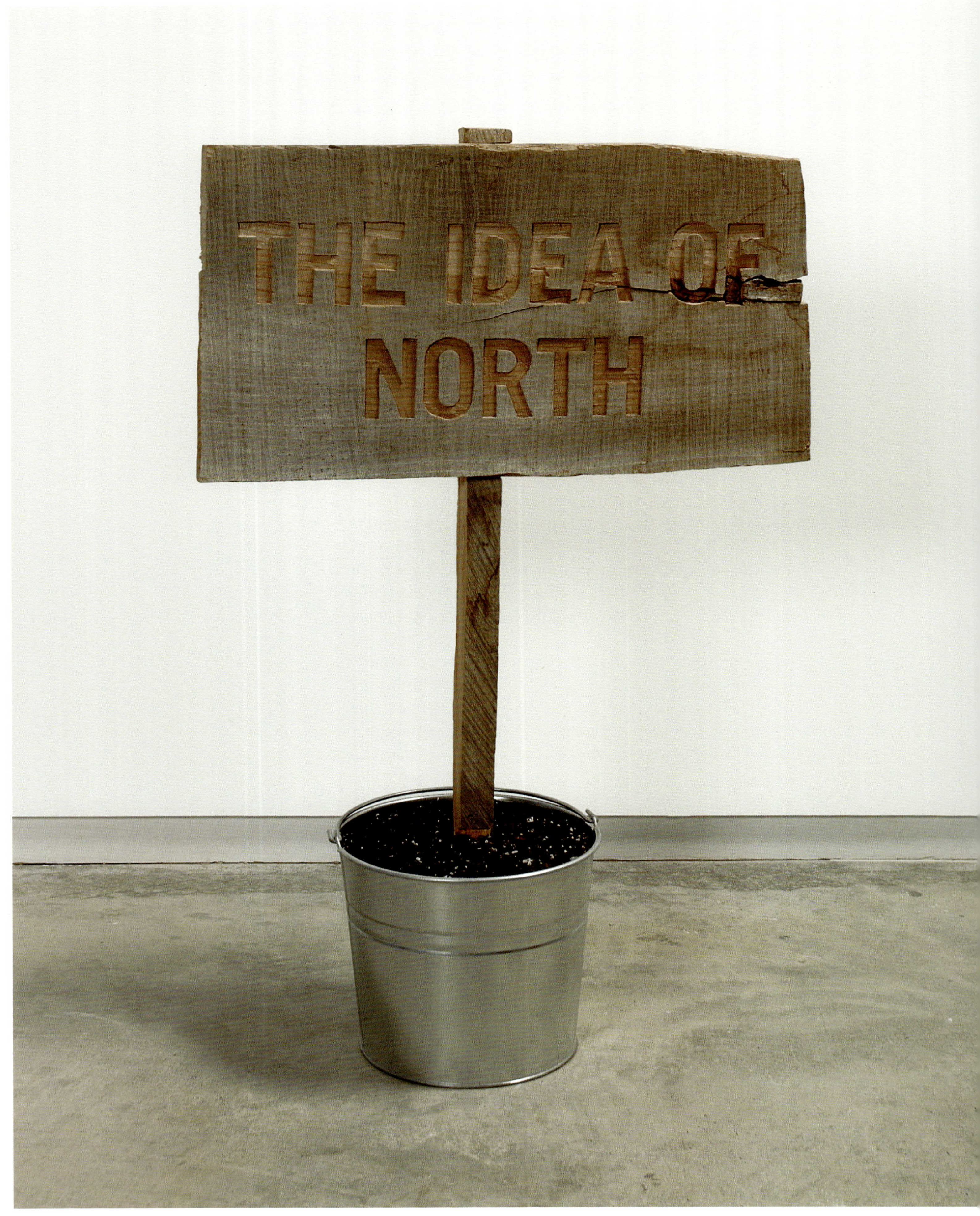
THE IDEA OF
NORTH

FOREWORD

MICHAEL AUDAIN AND YOSHIKO KARASAWA are an indelible presence in the cultural life of British Columbia. While interested in art from many parts of the world, they have an inexhaustible passion for the art of this region. For the Audains, art is far more than an avocation; it gives meaning and richness to life. They also believe sincerely that art can make a fundamental difference in the lives of individuals, and this has led them to support numerous visual art projects in British Columbia and other parts of Canada.

When I approached the Audains several years ago with the idea of exhibiting the highlights of their collection, they were initially somewhat reluctant to share the results of a private passion with a wider public, perhaps because Michael consistently downplays the significance of his contributions, whether as an advisor, collector or philanthropist. The collection is, however, truly remarkable for both the quality and scope of its holdings, and the Vancouver Art Gallery is therefore very honoured to present this first public exhibition recognizing its extraordinary character.

Over the last quarter century, the Audains have formed one of the most distinguished collections of art in Canada. Firmly rooted in the visual history and contemporary art practices of this province, the collection and this exhibition bring together exceptional examples of work by artists of First Nations and Euro- and Asian-Canadian ancestry. The best of nineteenth-century indigenous art, particularly an unparalleled group of masks, gives deep meaning and context to contemporary works by First Nations artists. The profound achievements of Emily Carr, represented here in a singularly spectacular fashion, provide context for the achievements of other Modernists who worked in British Columbia, such as Lawren Harris, B.C. Binning and, later, Jack Shadbolt, Claude Breeze, Gordon Smith and others. In more recent decades, Vancouver has developed into an internationally renowned centre for photo-based practices, and the Audains have fervently embraced this work.

Theirs is a collection marked by personal passion, notable as well in the assembly of works by the Mexican artists Diego Rivera, José Clemente Orozco, David Alfaro Siqueiros and Rufino Tamayo. These leading Mexican Modernists (whom Mr. Audain has admired since he took a bus trip as a student to see the murals of Mexico City) have produced art which is informed by a profound social consciousness. Such

facing
Ron Terada
The Idea of North 2007

work is rarely seen in Canada, and the Audain collection contains, to the best of our knowledge, the most important group of Mexican Modernist works in this country.

The exhibition also features art donated by the Audains to the Vancouver Art Gallery, including work by Stan Douglas, Rodney Graham, Jock Macdonald, Scott McFarland, Jeff Wall and Etienne Zack. In each case, the Gallery's holdings have been substantially enhanced through their generous donations. Indeed, it is through the philanthropic gestures of collectors such as the Audains that public museums are able to build and enrich their permanent collections; a recent demonstration of this generosity is their gift of a group of nineteenth-century First Nations objects. The Gallery has long sought to build a modest, but representative, collection of historical First Nations art to more completely tell the story of the art in this region. This major gift, which includes work by Haida, Heiltsuk, Nuu-chah-nulth and Tlingit artists, represents a very significant beginning for which the Gallery is profoundly grateful.

The Audains are unique in the sheer depth and breadth of their philanthropy; beyond their passion for collecting, they have been important benefactors to the cultural life of this country. For example, the Vancouver Art Gallery, the University of British Columbia, the Bill Reid Gallery of Northwest Coast Art, the National Gallery of Canada, the Museum of Anthropology at UBC, Artists for Kids and many other organizations have benefited significantly from their extraordinary support. At the Vancouver Art Gallery and National Gallery of Canada, Michael has funded curatorial chairs and acquisition endowments. In 2004, he endowed the annual Audain Prize at the Vancouver Art Gallery, which recognizes lifetime achievement in the visual arts for artists from British Columbia.

Mr. Audain and Ms. Karasawa have also served on many community boards: Ms. Karasawa was instrumental in establishing the National Nikkei Museum and Heritage Centre and is active on the board of the Vancouver Opera, while Mr. Audain is the chair of the Vancouver Art Gallery Foundation and a member of the Gallery's board of trustees, as well as the chair of the board of trustees of the National Gallery of Canada. Mr. Audain's notable public service and philanthropy have been recognized by honorary degrees from Simon Fraser University, the University of Victoria and Emily Carr University of Art and Design; a Distinguished Service Award from the British Columbia Museums Association; the Edmund C. Bovey Award from Business for the Arts; as well as appointments to the Order of British Columbia and the Order of Canada.

A project of this magnitude requires the Herculean efforts of many individuals. My sincerest thanks go to Gallery staff, particularly Ian Thom, Senior Curator—Historical, and Grant Arnold, the Audain Curator of British Columbia Art, for their wholehearted commitment to all aspects of *Shore, Forest and Beyond*. In addition we are very grateful to the Honourable Gordon Campbell, Jessica Berlanga Taylor with Julia Soto Martínez, and Charlotte Townsend-Gault for enlightening readers with their texts. The exhibition has been generously sponsored by Scotiabank; we are very appreciative of their continuing commitment to the Gallery and their impressive, expansive support of the arts in this country. The accompanying book has been financially supported by the Jack and Doris Shadbolt Endowment for Research and Publications. I would also

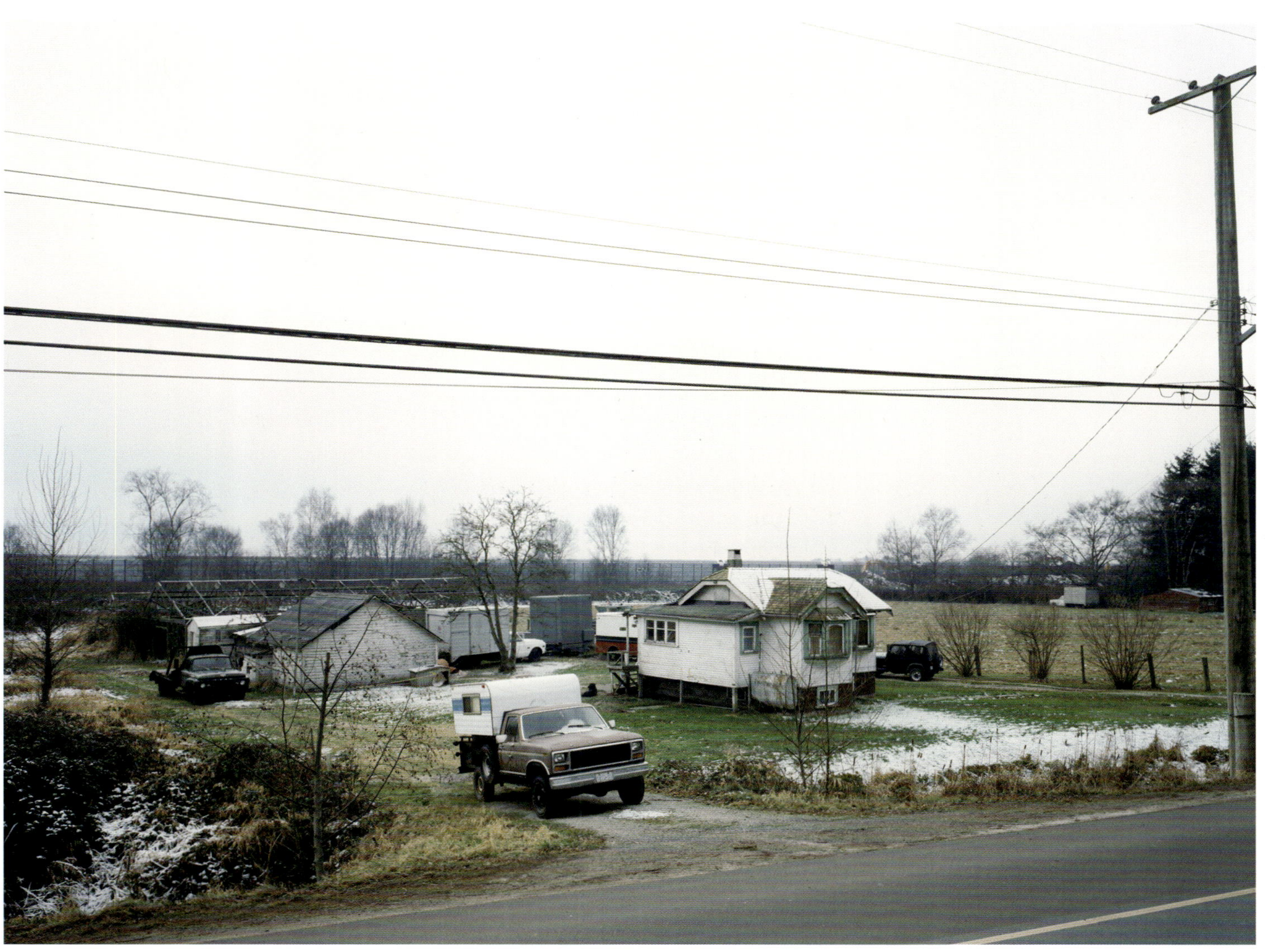

like to acknowledge our partnership with Douglas & McIntyre and thank in particular Scott McIntyre and Peter Cocking.

Shore, Forest and Beyond beautifully illustrates the Audains' long-term engagement with the outstanding visual artists of British Columbia. On behalf of the Vancouver Art Gallery, I would like to express my sincere gratitude to Michael Audain and Yoshiko Karasawa, who have set the highest standards for philanthropy and cultural leadership in this country. Their support of the Gallery has been unparalleled, and their most recent gift not only marks a historic moment for the Gallery's collection but also recognizes the unique artistic legacy and patrimony of this very special region.

KATHLEEN S. BARTELS
Director, Vancouver Art Gallery

Jeff Wall
River Road 1994

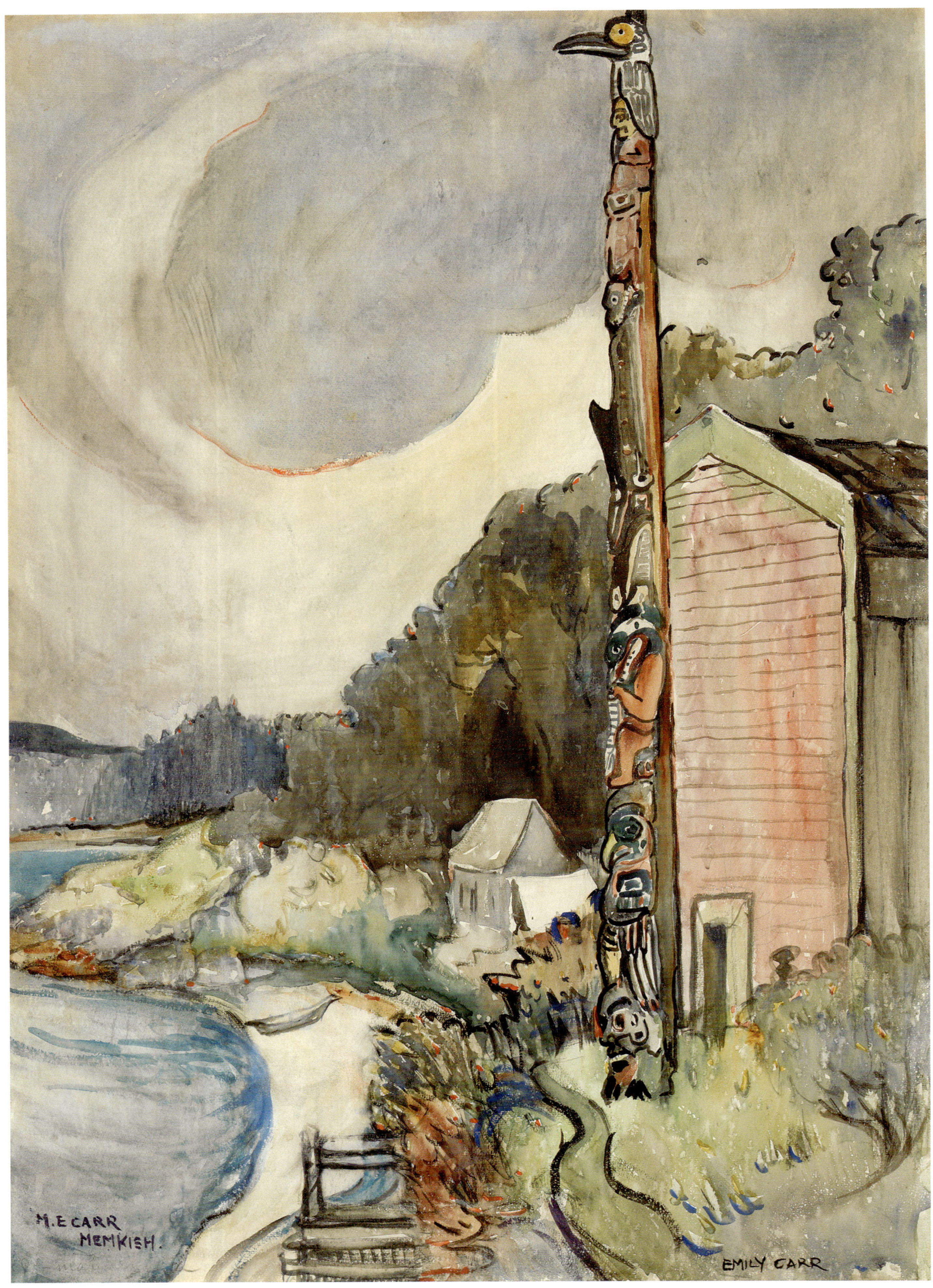
M.E CARR
MEMKISH.
EMILY CARR

INTRODUCTION

IAN THOM

"Living with art has been one of the great joys of my life."
MICHAEL AUDAIN

IN HIS ENGAGING comments which follow this introduction, about the collection that he and his wife, Yoshiko Karasawa, have assembled, Michael Audain notes that he has never purported to be a serious art collector. Such a disarming statement might raise the question of why this exhibition has come about. Clearly the Vancouver Art Gallery believes that due to their range, quality and visual power, many aspects of the Audain holdings deserve to be exhibited and, in fact, many of these objects have already appeared in a variety of public places in Canada and abroad. Although Mr. Audain does not consider himself a serious collector, others do. Why? Even a brief conversation with him reveals that he is passionate about art.

All collections reflect, to some degree, the character of their owners. In part, what distinguishes a significant and aesthetically meaningful art collection from mere acquisitions is the owners' willingness to challenge themselves and their assumptions about the world. From the works they have assembled, it is clear that Mr. Audain and Ms. Karasawa have never avoided the demands that art can make on the viewer. They are acutely conscious of how the objects they have chosen might speak to each other and thus inform a larger conversation about British Columbia and the world.

Mr. Audain had a striking epiphany about the work of Emily Carr. He moved from seeing her work as "scary" to appreciating her as an artist who can be compared, in her relationship to the Other, to Paul Gauguin—a very considerable shift! How does a shift like this occur? Through a level of engagement that requires really looking at art and, from that point, eliciting meaning for oneself. The Audains have made art an integral part of their lives. They have engaged with the world of artists, galleries, museums and other collectors, but most crucially, they have engaged with the very private act of looking. This looking has nurtured, delighted, informed and enriched them both.

Michael Audain says that he has never had a "grand plan"; instead, the collection grew as opportunity and funds allowed. In this respect it is not unlike others, but several aspects of this collection make it worthy of special attention. It encompasses

facing
Emily Carr
Memkish 1912

major works by virtually every significant British Columbia Modernist (B.C. Binning, Lawren Harris, E.J. Hughes, Jack Shadbolt, Gordon Smith and Takao Tanabe, to name just a few), and the Emily Carr paintings are, to my knowledge, the finest grouping in private hands. Also remarkable are the holdings of historical and contemporary First Nations work, including wonderful examples by anonymous master carvers of the nineteenth century and contemporary artists such as Sonny Assu, Robert Davidson, Jim Hart, Brian Jungen, Marianne Nicolson, Bill Reid and Lawrence Paul Yuxweluptun.

The collection's concentration on the art of this province, both First Nations and non–First Nations, is especially noteworthy. While this grouping is not encyclopaedic—no collection ever is—it does reflect what Mr. Audain describes as the strong visual arts tradition that evolved here. When viewing these works, we are able to trace that inspiring history over several hundred years. The high quality of the art, the choice of major works (major, that is, in ambition and often in scale), the in-depth representation of individual artists within the collection and the encouragement of artistic exploration rather than predictability in commissioned works also stand out. It takes an important level of commitment to trust that an artist will produce extraordinary things, to know that it might be a good thing if the commissioner doesn't immediately understand the result.

This sense of adventure is evident everywhere in the collection, which encompasses imagery as diverse as that of Emily Carr, Charles Edenshaw, Diego Rivera and Jeff Wall. Contemporary art can often be difficult for non-artists to understand but the Audains have not shied away from it in their acquisition of works by contemporary photo-based artists such as Stan Douglas, Rodney Graham, Jeff Wall and sometimes disquieting paintings by Claude Breeze and Attila Richard Lukacs. Mr. Audain was, by his own admission, initially intimidated by the work of contemporary photographers but he has clearly embraced the vital creative practices of many living B.C. artists in photography and other media.

Shore, Forest and Beyond: Art from the Audain Collection cannot represent the full range of the collection's works; indeed, one of the challenges for this museum has been to keep up with the pace at which the inventory changes and grows while still giving our audience a good sense of its form. Clearly there is a strong emphasis on the art and artists of this region, but we have also found it important to include the Mexican Modernist works the Audains have assembled over the last decade, an aspect of the collection that is also, to our knowledge, unique within Canada. These artworks include significant examples of the work of José Clemente Orozco, Diego Rivera, David Alfaro Siqueiros and Rufino Tamayo. Mr. Audain's interest in this work stems from his life experience but, interestingly, a number of British Columbia artists represented in the collection, such as E.J. Hughes and Jack Shadbolt, also reveal connections to Mexican Modernism in their work.

I would suggest that one of the things that makes this collection interesting is the fact that it is so personal. Great private collections, many of which have formed the basis of museum holdings around the world, are significant partly because they create visual conversations that might not be seen in more conventional encyclopaedic

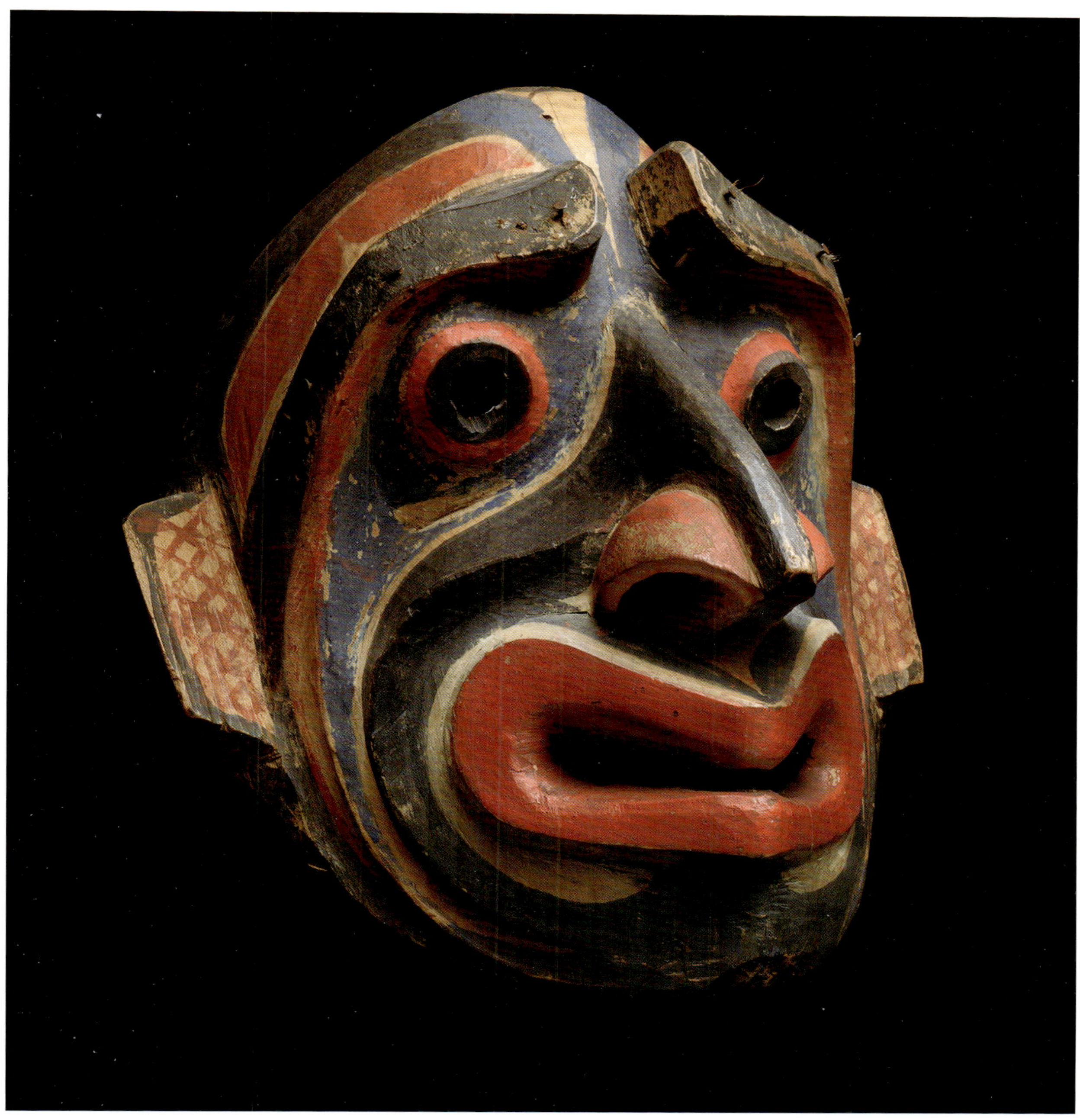

collections. History is made through individual stories and actions. Whether private or institutional, collections evolve as a series of personal decisions that tell a distinctive story.

We believe that the narrative of this particular collection, to be revealed as the reader moves through the book, is remarkable and deserving of our attention. The Vancouver Art Gallery is delighted that Michael Audain and Yoshiko Karasawa have kindly consented to share it with the larger world.

Kwakwa̱ka̱'wakw Artist
Human Face Ridicule Mask
c. 1880

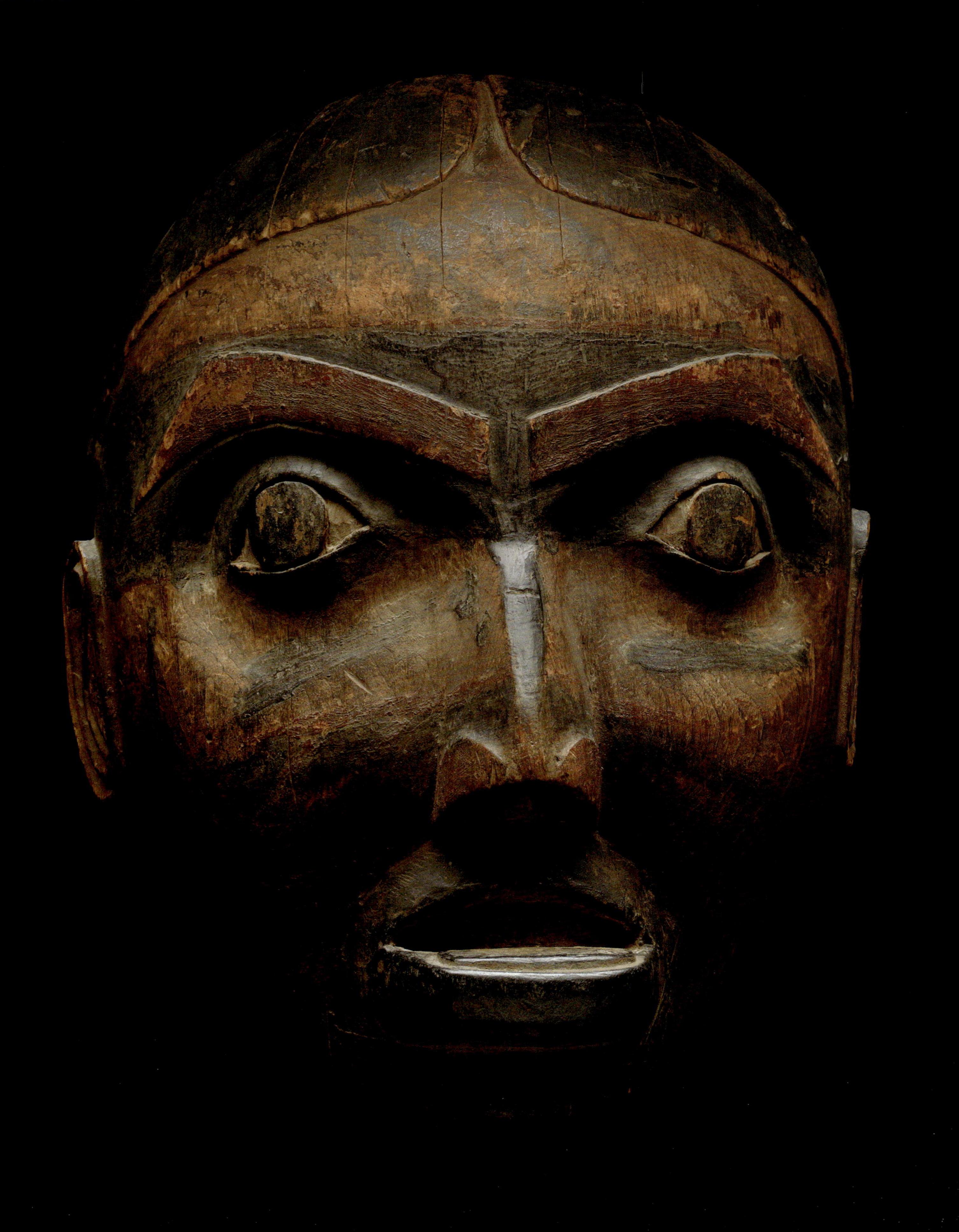

SOME REFLECTIONS

MICHAEL AUDAIN

I AM OFTEN ASKED how I started collecting art. I did it like most people, by buying one picture at a time. In the early 1960s I would buy small pictures by Vancouver artists who were just getting established—bill bissett and Michael Morris come to mind. The main thing was that they had to be priced under fifty dollars.

At home, my parents were not particularly interested in art. Heads of various sheep, elk and moose decorated the walls, and the side tables were strewn with photos of family horses and dogs. There is only one picture that I recall from a house we occupied when I was about thirteen, a Scandinavian-like painting of what looked like arbutus trees. When I asked my stepmother how it came into her possession, she said that it was a gift from a friend who had bought it at a jumble sale.

At the various schools I attended, all eleven of them, I was hopeless at drawing and painting. It's true that I enjoyed a photography course as part of my air cadet training, but it had to do with reconnaissance photos from high-flying aircraft. At my last boarding school I believe I was considered rather peculiar when, instead of taping up pin-up photos of Marilyn Monroe or hockey heroes like most boys, I decorated the inside of my locker door with prints of Dutch old masters that came my way through a student membership from New York's Metropolitan Museum of Art.

Young families usually don't have much surplus cash, and my first wife, Tunya, and I were certainly in that category, living in a series of houses with second-hand furniture from the Salvation Army and other thrift shops. Nevertheless, by the 1970s, whenever I was in Toronto I would drop by the Isaacs Gallery and pick up the odd picture. I could only muster up the courage to buy something expensive after a good lunch lubricated by the cocktails we used to consume in those days. Fortunately, Av Isaacs and his artists were very generous in extending credit. For instance, when I bought a large William Kurelek painting from Av he got the artist to agree to let me pay fifty dollars a month over a couple of years.

I bought art simply because I wanted pictures to hang on the wall. I noticed what a difference a picture could make to the ambience of a room, and indeed how shifting work around could change a room's whole feeling. Tunya, who had studied at the Art Students League in New York, was supportive and seemed quite content to make do

facing
Haida Artist
Female Portrait Mask 1840–60

with old mattresses on the floor covered by Indian bedspreads. Nor did our children complain about the neighbours having newer cars than our family.

Even today I buy art in order to live with it at home or in the office, never to store it away in a vault. In fact, living with art has been one of the great joys of my life. It is a private pleasure, however, and not one I have an urge to inflict on other people. Nor is the prestige of showing off a recognizable object on the wall a motivation. Unlike many generous art collectors whose homes I have visited, Yoshi and I have never had any desire to open our home to tour groups. If friends visit and ignore the pictures, that is perfectly fine with us. If, however, guests seem to have a genuine interest in art, then we are happy to escort them around.

I never intended to be a serious art collector, and have never acquired an object because it would help build a first-rate collection. Nor do intellectual questions come into it. I buy based on emotion, because I am fascinated with an object that I simply cannot live without. Although I often end up acquiring two or three works by an artist who particularly interests me, it's more for fear that a single one might get too lonely.

Actually, I have always resisted the art collector label. You see, the Audains for generations were in the Indian Army and my father lived in India as a child. Besides having a British governor, chief justice and chief of police, under the Raj each state had an official called "the collector" who was responsible for raising taxes. As this chap was generally despised by both whites and Indians alike, answering to the title of collector is something I have never relished. I have just picked up art objects when they became available, as long as I could more or less afford them.

BRITISH COLUMBIA

The artworks that we have at home were primarily created by British Columbians over the last two hundred years. Why the focus on this province? From the age of nine I lived mostly on the B.C. coast, usually only a few metres from the seashore. Our family has deep roots here; my grandchildren are seventh-generation British Columbians.

While it is true that I have lived for periods in other parts of the world, B.C. is where I feel most at home. It's where I can walk in the forest, know the names of all the wildlife and flora plus put my fishing line overboard and be fairly confident about what species of fish I might hook... if any.

I am a proud Canadian; however, I know enough about the country to appreciate that we are a land of strong regionalists. Thus, my identification with B.C. and its strong visual arts tradition stretching from ancient times up to today may explain my focus on its artists.

NORTHWEST COAST

Our British Columbia collection starts at the beginning, with the art of the First Nations of the Northwest Coast, which more than one leading expert has declared to be among the most sophisticated of any Aboriginal people. Although we have acquired these works fairly recently, my respect for Native art goes back to my youth when I was a frequent visitor to the Cowichan Reserve near Duncan on Vancouver Island.

facing
Emily Carr
Quiet 1942

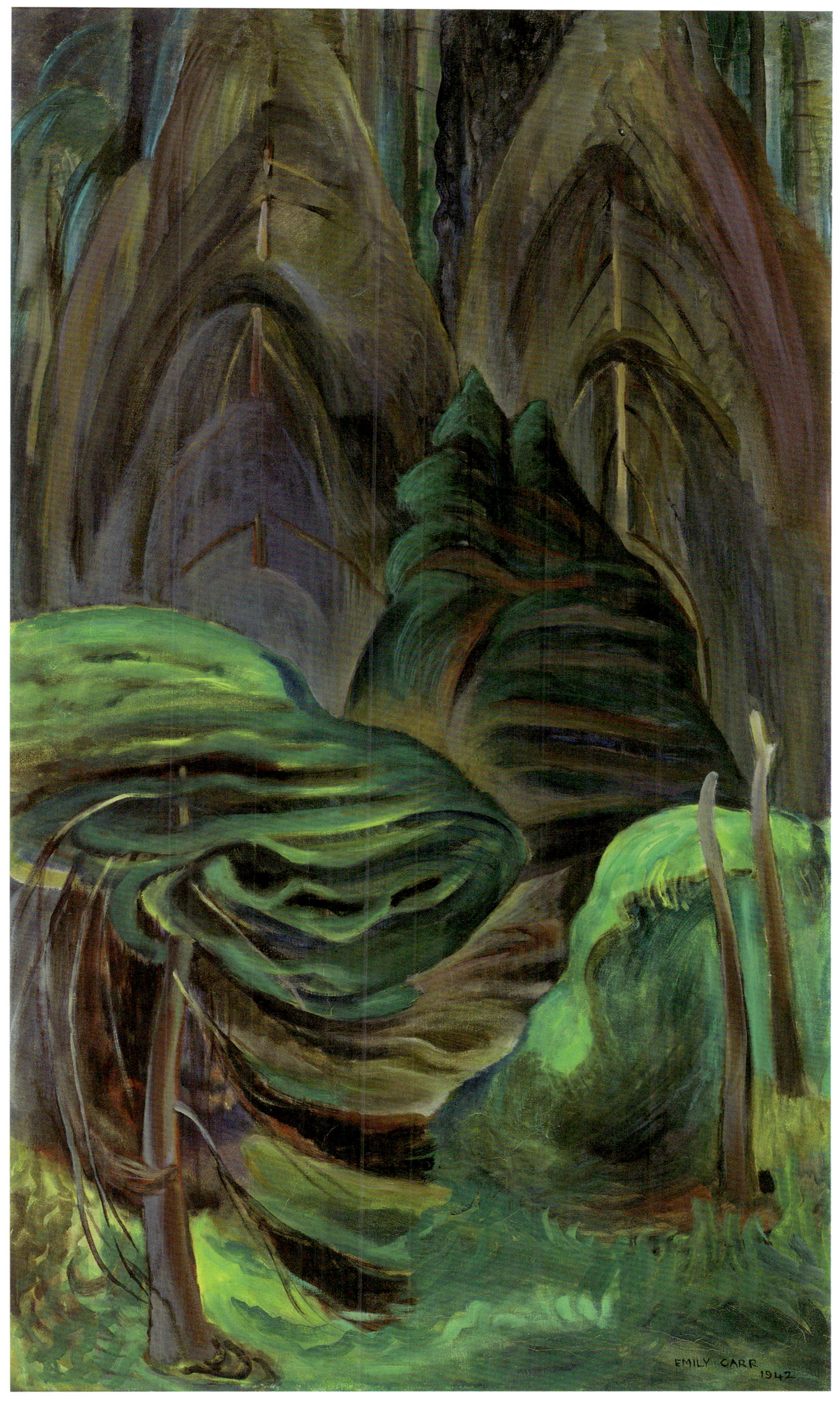
EMILY CARR
1942

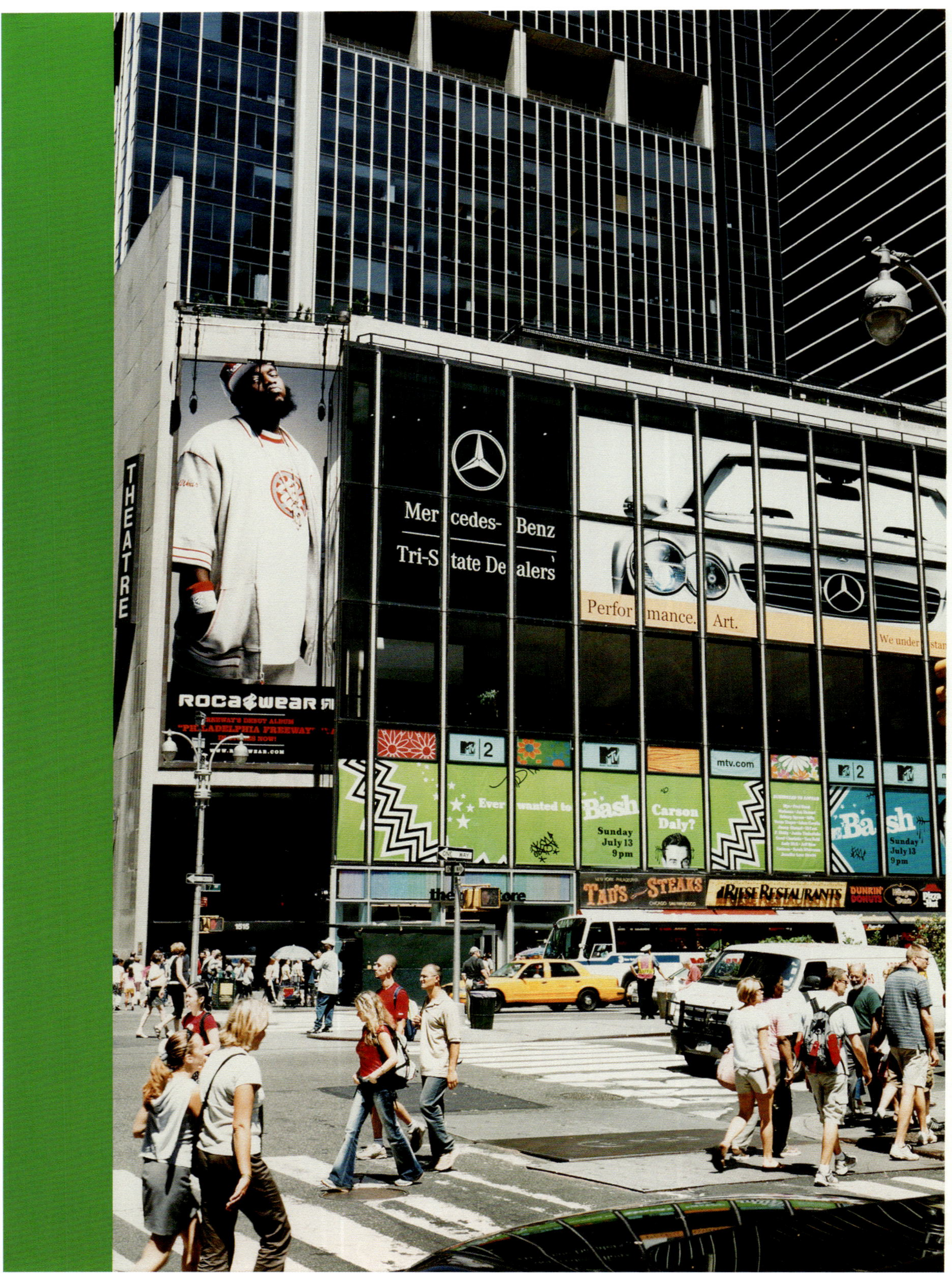

Ian Wallace
Times Square, NYC 2003

Although the Salish artmaking tradition of the Cowichan people in the 1940s was not strong, except in the production of the famous Cowichan Indian sweaters, there was still some carving going on. What impressed me most at the time was an incredible 1950 opera called *Tzinquaw* that I saw performed in the local high school with an all–First Nations cast. The opera opened in Duncan and then toured the province. The masks, costumes, dances and scenery stayed in my mind for years.

The totem poles in Victoria's Thunderbird Park were also a great source of fascination, even more so after I had the opportunity to chat with Mungo Martin, the artist the Government had hired to create replicas for the park.

Lately we have been fortunate to repatriate to B.C. some wonderful nineteenth-century Northwest Coast material, mostly masks, from the United States and Europe. Many of these objects were of ceremonial importance and deserve respect as more than art objects. The important thing is that they have returned to the Northwest Coast and will never again appear on the art market. I am in awe of these sacred objects that silently watch me as I type this message. They are not frozen in time but temporarily resting from their mediation between the world of animals, spirits and human beings, people who in times gone by were so much closer to the natural rhythm of life than most of us today.

This aspect of our collection is not, however, confined to nineteenth-century works. There are so many talented First Nations artists in British Columbia today, and we have been able to acquire some works directly from them. These range from the great names like Bill Reid, Robert Davidson and Jim Hart to a new avant-garde group of artists, including Sonny Assu, who seem interested in working in new media while not ignoring their original identity. We wish that we had room for more contemporary First Nations art of the Northwest Coast, as it is such a burgeoning field with strong collector interest at home and abroad.

EMILY CARR

It is difficult for me to write about Emily Carr because she evokes such intense feelings. When I was young I was firmly of the opinion that I did not like her art—a mindset that originated from my first exposure to her work, sitting with scores of other little boys and girls on portable benches one Saturday morning while Dr. Clifford Carl, director of the Provincial Museum (now the Royal B.C. Museum), projected magic-lantern slides of her pictures through the darkness. Trees in deep greenish-grey tones, dripping forests or the ghosts of old Indians that had become petrified in moss-hung gloom—what were they? I found the images deeply disturbing, the source of uneasy dreams for many years. Thus in the late 1940s, when my father remarked that Emily Carr was a batty old woman who couldn't paint properly—the common opinion in Victoria—I didn't say anything and just thought to myself that whether she was an accomplished artist or not, "Emily Carr was certainly scary."

Fifteen years later, after I had completed a tour of European and New York art museums, I found myself in the Vancouver Art Gallery contemplating Emily Carr's images once again. Something snapped in my mind, and I said to myself, "Oh my

God, for my money this woman is just as good a landscape painter as some of the best artists I have seen on the walls of New York's Museum of Modern Art!" It came to me that what Paul Gauguin had done for the landscape and people of Tahiti, Emily Carr had done for the Northwest Coast.

I love walking through the dark trails of the west coast forest, the sunny arbutus-clad seashores, the stately cedar groves, even recently logged hillsides with their wild underbrush and fireweed. This is my world, and to me Emily Carr is the artist who depicts it best. She captured the spirit of the Aboriginal peoples of the coast a century ago in their communities distinguished by fine cedars temporarily rendered into totem poles, house posts and mortuary poles before nature reclaimed them to add substance to the forest floor.

THE B.C. MODERNISTS

In the decade or so after the Second World War, a number of local artists who rose to prominence were interested in developing ways of artmaking that were new to British Columbia. Notable among them was Jack Shadbolt, whose work showed influences of Mexican and First Nations art as well as of New York Expressionism. B.C. Binning chose a more methodical, semi-abstract way of depicting the landscape. Gordon Smith experimented with various forms of landscape painting until in his seventies he developed an intriguing personal style. Takao Tanabe was another prominent landscapist whose later, grey-clad paintings invoke the ambience of the coast. E.J. Hughes captivated a wide audience with his more realistic style, and by the early 1960s Toni Onley had become known as the master of west coast collages. When I returned to British Columbia in the early 1970s, after an eight-year absence, I found a lot of appeal in the work of these artists and have enjoyed living with their art ever since. Some of these men became close friends.

THE CONTEMPORARY ART SCENE

How can one live in a city that has become world famous for its photo-based art and not collect some of it? At first I found this work intimidating, as I never had much interest in photography, but soon I grew to understand that what was being created in Vancouver, in the sense that it was more intentional, was unlike any photography I had seen before.

Fortunately, in the early 1990s I was still able to buy the work of Ian Wallace (considered the granddaddy of the so-called Vancouver School). It has been more challenging to acquire the work of the many Vancouver artists with dealers abroad. Nevertheless, in recent years I have been fortunate to collect a cross-section of work by artists of international renown, including Stan Douglas, Rodney Graham and Jeff Wall, as well as the work of several younger artists, such as Steven Shearer, whose lamp now burns so brightly on the international stage. Living with contemporary art involves a period of adjustment after which it becomes easier to appreciate what the artist is driving at; although, surprisingly it is sometimes not as profound as one might expect.

I would like to acquire more art by emerging B.C. artists, but sometimes their large installations are not always easy to accommodate in a domestic environment

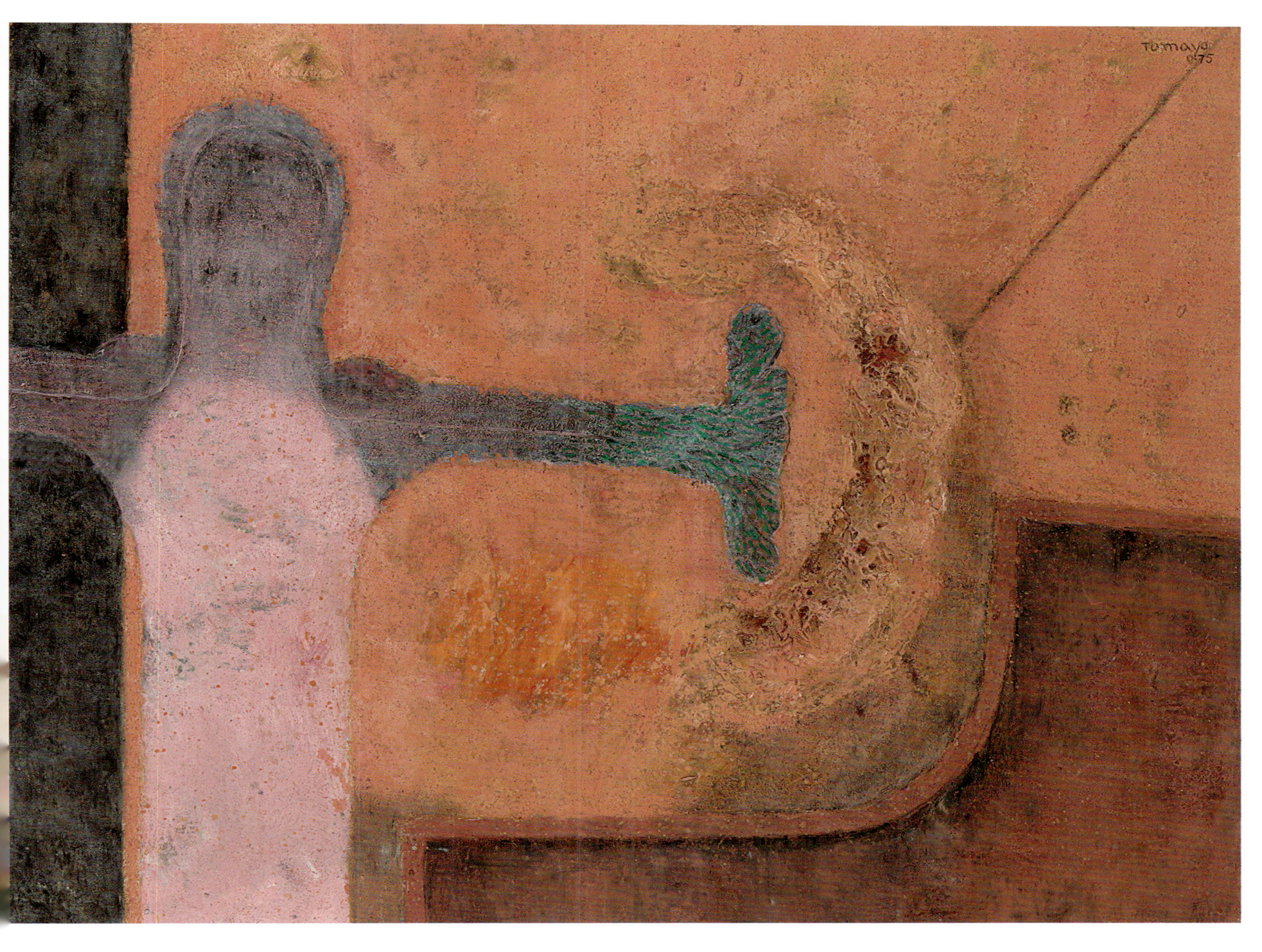

Rufino Tamayo
Hombre contra un muro
[Man against a Wall] 1975

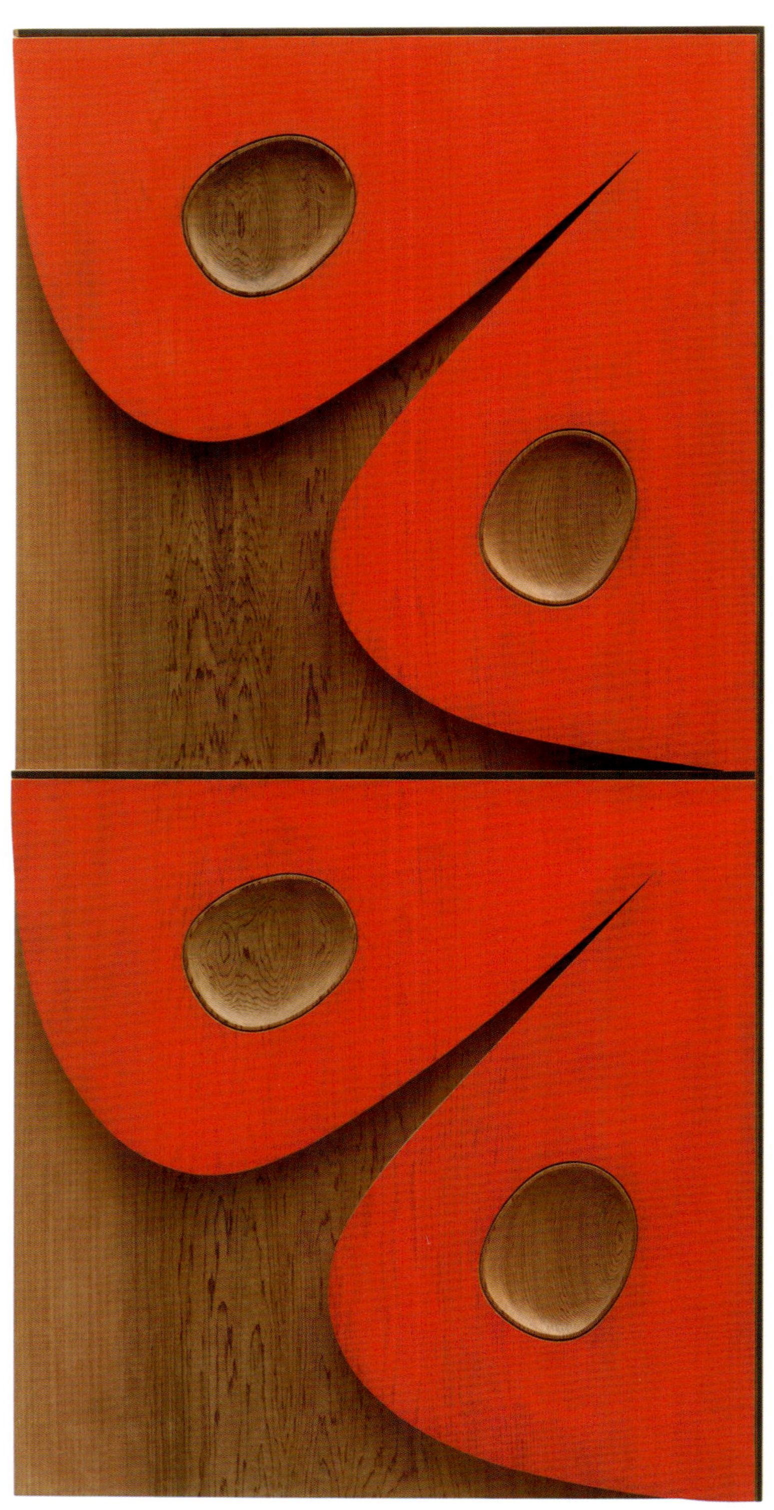
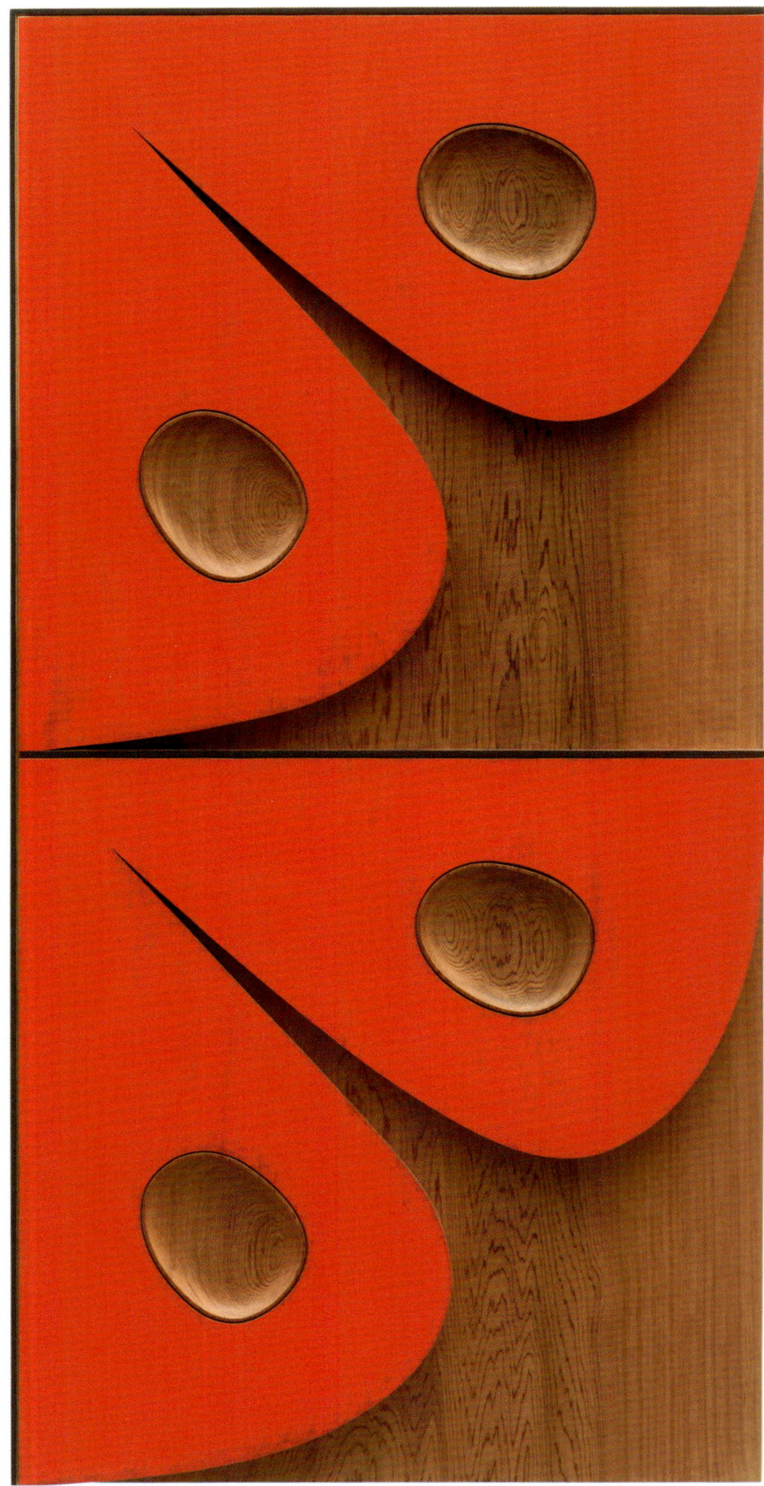

Robert Davidson
Relaxed Symmetry 2003

complete with grandchildren and dogs charging around. Nevertheless, so much of what is being produced in Vancouver today deserves serious attention.

It has been my contention for some years that the art form that is most indigenous to British Columbia is visual art, rather than music, dance or opera. This has been the case for centuries, and I suspect that as the stature of our local artists continues to grow internationally, it will remain so.

MEXICAN MODERNISM

The Mexican Revolution of the 1920s presented artists with an opportunity to create socially relevant murals on a grand scale. In 1921, the most prominent artist of the time, Diego Rivera, had returned to Mexico from France, where his talent had already become well recognized. Rivera, along with David Alfaro Siqueiros and José Clemente Orozco, became known as *Los tres grandes* (the three greats) and attracted great international attention for their revolutionary fervour as well as their art.

As a teenager, I became so interested in the social relevance of Mexican art that I decided to take a Greyhound bus to Mexico City to see the work of the muralists, although the cheap Mexican peso also offered the attraction of a holiday in the sun on a minimal budget. On that visit I never saw the work of Frida Kahlo, as it was some decades before she became an international celebrity, but wandering through the museums I did become enchanted with the work of Rufino Tamayo, who combined the exuberant use of colour and texture with references to his Indian ancestry. Now, over half a century later, it is a privilege to have in our home some works by these giants of the twentieth-century art world.

A FINAL NOTE

Yoshi and I debated for some months about accepting the invitation of the Vancouver Art Gallery to publicly exhibit our art. As much as we were surprised and honoured to be asked, we feared that an exhibition would be interpreted as simply a payoff for someone who has a long record of support for the institution. Our main concern, however, was what the public would think of our extremely personal art collecting.

We have acquired our pictures one at a time, never having any grand plan of building a collection, let alone one that would be publicly exhibited. Our art is something we live with and relate to daily as opposed to being work on a museum wall that we may view occasionally with a fleeting glance. In the end, what won us over to the idea of the exhibition was curator Ian Thom's suggestion that hoarding our art in a home that has never been accessible to the public could be construed as somewhat selfish.

Of course, we need to express our appreciation to the team at the Vancouver Art Gallery, captained by curators Ian Thom and Grant Arnold, who worked so hard to assemble this exhibition from the various locations in which the art normally resides.

So that is how these works arrived at the Vancouver Art Gallery. If some of this art is not for you, that's fine. Art appreciation is a subjective matter, and we each bring our own experience, knowledge and taste to the party.

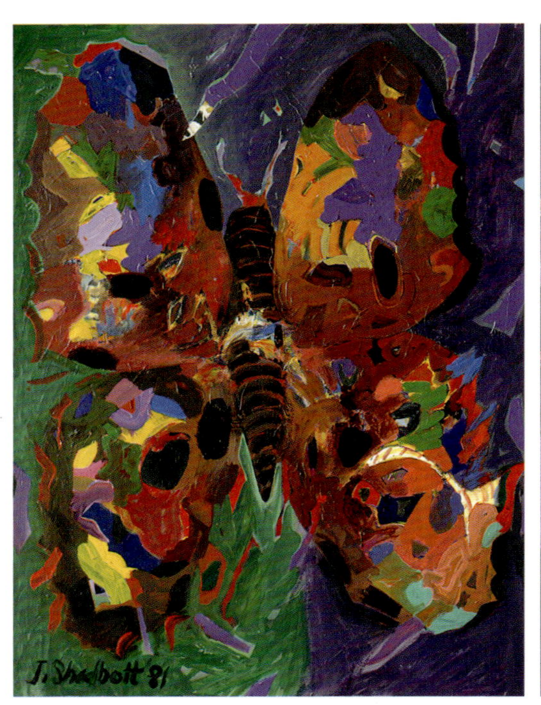
J. Shadbolt '81

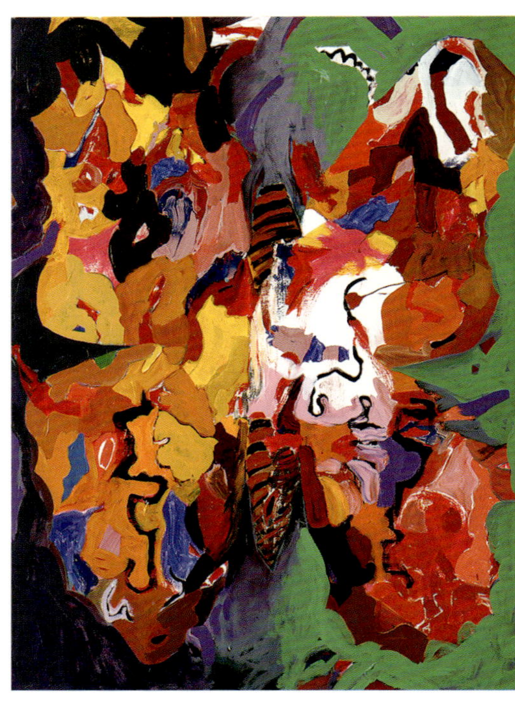

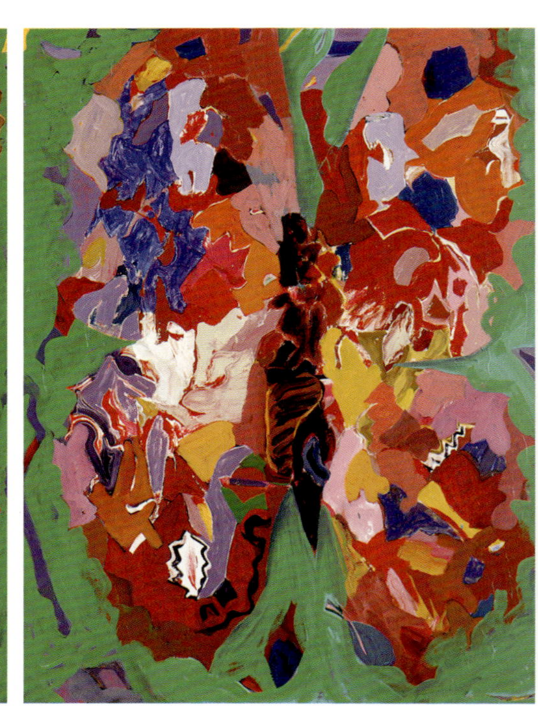

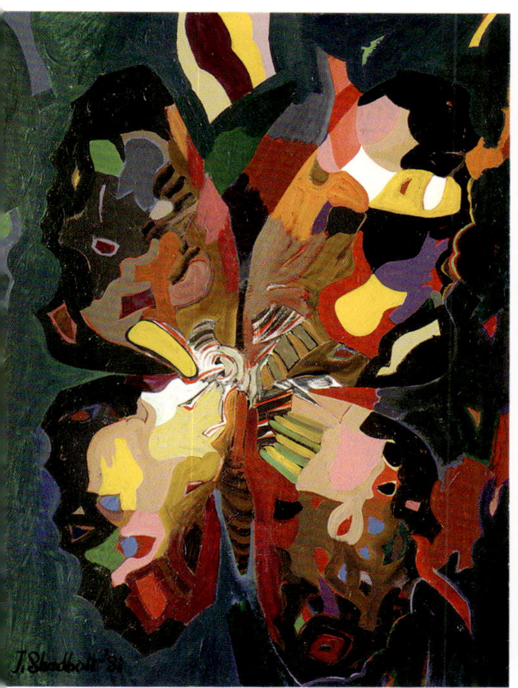

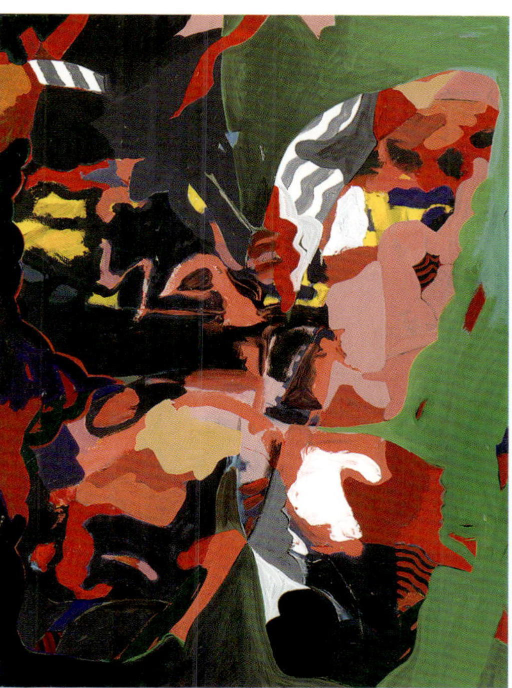

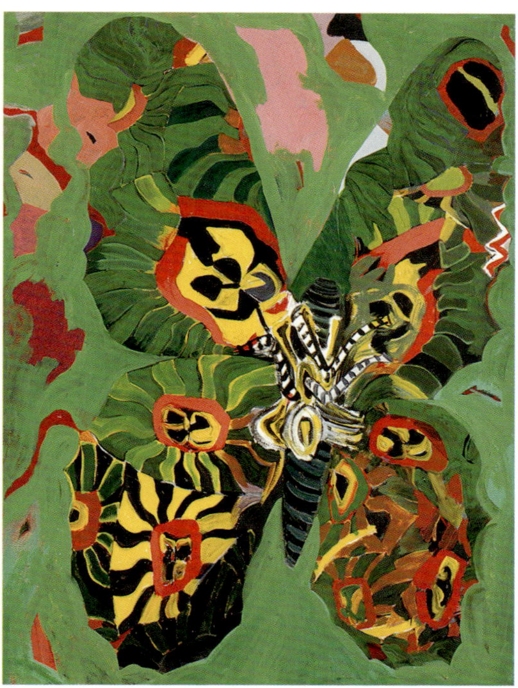

Jack Leonard Shadbolt
Butterfly Transformation
Theme **1981** 1981

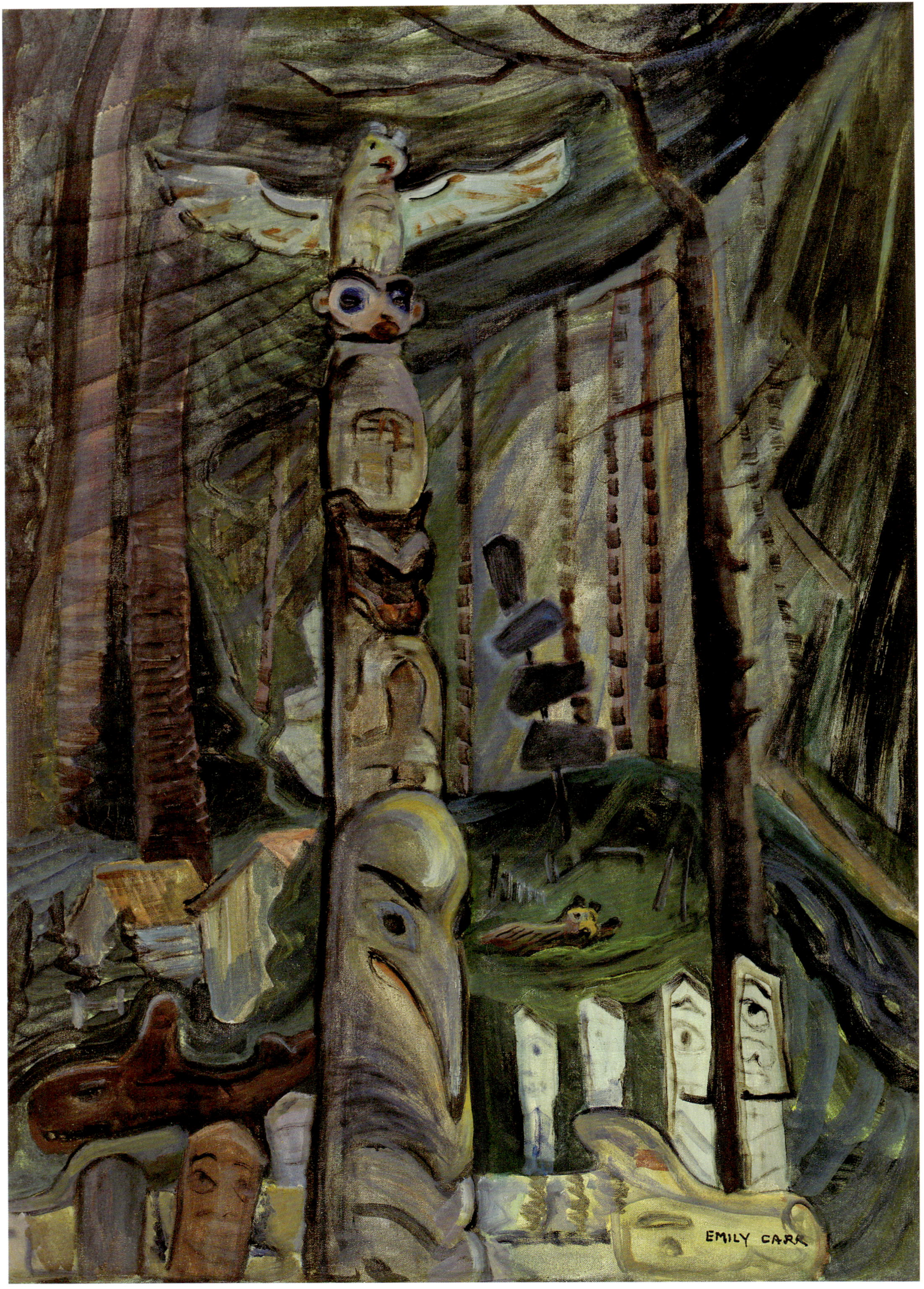
EMILY CARR

QUIET
EMILY CARR AND BRITISH COLUMBIA LANDSCAPE PAINTING

IAN THOM

WHILE THE LANDSCAPE of this province has been a central subject for many of our artists, no one is more intimately linked to it than Emily Carr. Over time her aesthetic ideas have proven so powerful that anyone who now considers the landscape of B.C. cannot do so without reflecting upon her work in some way. For many people, her art defines what British Columbia looks like.

Born in Victoria in 1871, the year British Columbia entered Confederation, Carr was an unlikely figure to bring a radically new approach to landscape painting in the province. The youngest of a family of five girls (a brother died in childhood), Carr received little encouragement to pursue art during her early years. Her first real artistic training, when she was almost twenty, was in San Francisco, which was not a bastion of Modernist ideas in 1890. She was still making small, relatively traditional watercolours and drawings on her trip to Ucluelet in 1898, where she made some of her earliest images with First Nations subject matter. Carr's later training in England (1899–1903), which was disrupted by her illness at the time, was equally conservative. It was only following a trip to Alaska with her sister in 1907 that Carr determined that her subject matter should be, in addition to the landscape, the totems of the First Nations peoples. Realizing that these strong works needed a more forceful approach to artmaking she sought further training in France, where she believed she would encounter "modern art." This trip in 1910–11 was the turning point in her artistic development.

Carr's journey to a position of importance in the history of Canadian art was not an easy or a direct one, and the Audain collection is remarkable for documenting each of the steps that she took along the way. Her time in France is well represented by *House with Slanted Roof—Brittany,* 1911 (page 34). Other works, such as *Gitwangak,* 1912; *Memkish,* 1912 (page 14); *Skidegate,* 1912; *War Canoes, Alert Bay,* 1912 (page 35) and later works such as *Arbutus Tree/Untitled Portrait,* c. 1912–20 (page 3) and *Oak Wood,* 1913–27, clearly show the results of her pivotal studies there. Before Emily Carr no one had depicted the landscape of this province in such a radical fashion.

The important works that Carr did when she returned from France manifested her deep love of British Columbia and memorialized the First Nations totems that she

facing
Emily Carr
Alert Bay Burial Ground 1937–39

had seen in Skidegate and Alert Bay. She feared the totemic subjects of her paintings were destined to disappear. This work gave her entry to the larger Canadian art world when she participated in the exhibition *West Coast Art: Native and Modern*, held in Ottawa in 1927. Although Carr had mixed feelings about the experience, the show undoubtedly revivified her career and brought her into the larger narrative of Canadian art. Later, at the urging of her colleague and friend Lawren Harris, she turned her attention toward the landscape; the paintings of her last decade of work are among the most powerful evocations of nature in Canadian art. These later career works, characterized by a freer handling of paint, are represented by wonderful oils on paper such as *Gaiety*, 1935–37 and *At Beacon Hill Park*, c. 1935 (page 36–37). *Summer, Mount Douglas Park* (page 154–55) and *Quiet* (page 21), done in the final year of her active painting career, 1942, show the visual resolution of all her ideas.

Ironically, although Carr has a dominant place in the history of landscape painting in this province, artists who have followed her have tended to define themselves in visual contrast to Carr rather than emulating her distinctive approach. For example, Frederick Horsman Varley opened up new approaches to the B.C. landscape when he came to the province in 1926 to teach at the Vancouver School of Decorative & Applied Arts (now Emily Carr University of Art and Design). He encouraged not only his students but also his fellow teachers William Percival (W.P.) Weston and James Williamson Galloway (Jock) Macdonald to work directly in the coastal landscape that he himself found so revelatory a subject. His enormous skills as a colourist are evident in paintings such as *Dusk—Tantalus Range*, c. 1929 (page 160). Varley's vivid panels, painted directly from the motif, have a spiritual richness that, while different from that of Carr's work, is equal to it.

Influenced by Varley and other members of the Group of Seven, W.P. Weston's initial timid approach to the landscape evolved into dramatic and bold compositions. These images, such as *Jotunheim*, 1923 (page 40), have an adamantine quality that suggests the primal strength of the landscape, as it vividly captures the evanescent qualities of west coast light.

Jock Macdonald might not have become a painter had he not come to British Columbia in 1926 to teach design at the Vancouver School of Decorative & Applied Arts. He was originally a textile designer, but after Varley encouraged him to paint outdoors in the landscape, Macdonald became a very keen hiker and produced an important series of paintings that show the rugged beauty of the province, including a number of works in what is now Garibaldi Provincial Park. One of the most striking of these paintings is *The Black Tusk, Garibaldi Park, B.C.*, 1932 (page 39), which depicts the massive form of the Black Tusk, the park's distinctive volcanic rock pinnacle, with an almost visceral strength. The work is also marked by the strong sense of design that animates his later abstract images.

A dramatically different approach to the landscape of the province is seen in the work of Edward John (E.J.) Hughes. Contrary to Carr and Varley, who, for the most part chose to paint landscapes without any human presence, Hughes, who painted the landscape of B.C. beginning in the 1930s, sought to depict a maritime world of humans in harmony with nature. He was a careful and meticulous observer of

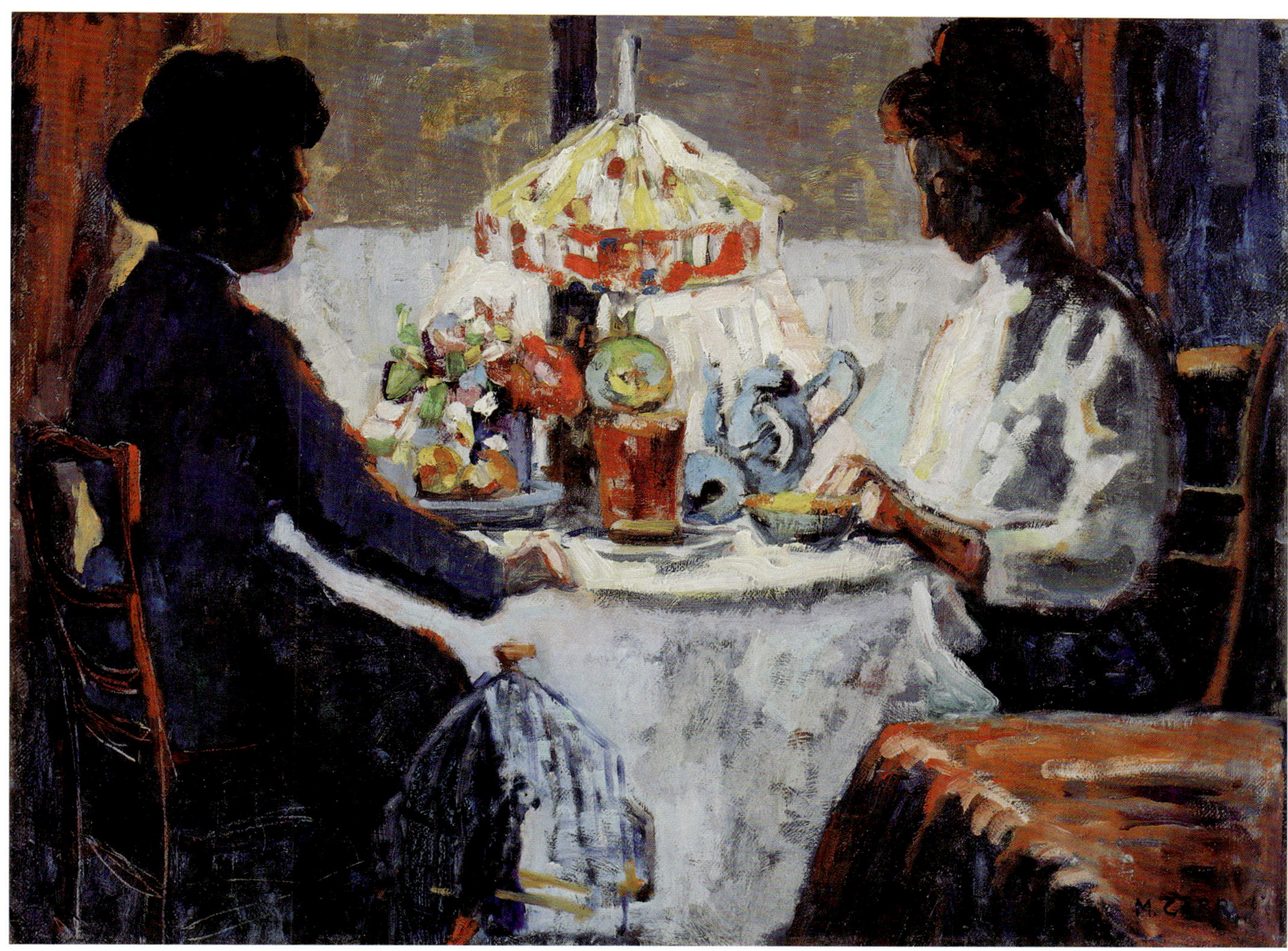

the natural world, and his paintings have, at times, an almost unsettlingly clarity. Works such as *Departure from Nanaimo*, 1964 and *Echo Bay*, 1953 (page 6) bespeak his wonder at the natural world and our place within it.

Other contemporary painters, such as Takao Tanabe and Gordon Smith, have approached the landscape in ways that are cognizant of earlier history but distinctly their own. Tanabe's limpid, atmospheric coastal landscapes such as *Strait of Georgia 1/90: Raza Pass*, 1990 (page 42) are at the same time dramatic and highly effective. In his art, Smith's relationship with the natural world is deep but moves between realism and abstraction. Recent works based on photographs have a complexity and power that transcend the descriptive; they function equally well as pattern and form. *Winterscape*, 1991 (page 43) is a good example of a work in which Smith's impulse toward abstraction is balanced by his painterly allegiance to the natural world.

Touching as it does on the highlights of this artistic history, with a particularly strong representation of Emily Carr's work, this selection of artworks offers rich insights into the story of landscape painting in British Columbia.

Emily Carr
Emily and Lizzie c. 1913

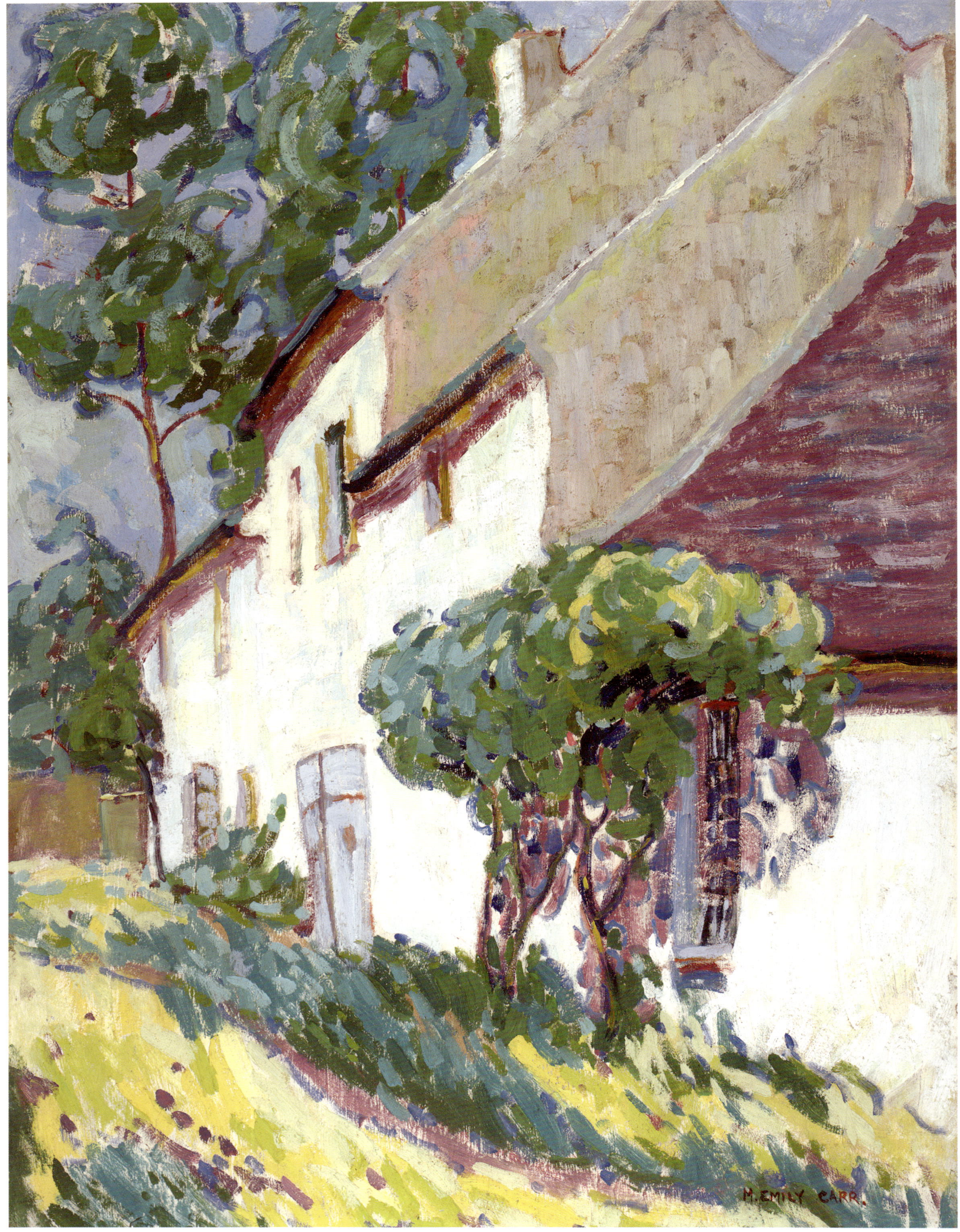
M. EMILY CARR.

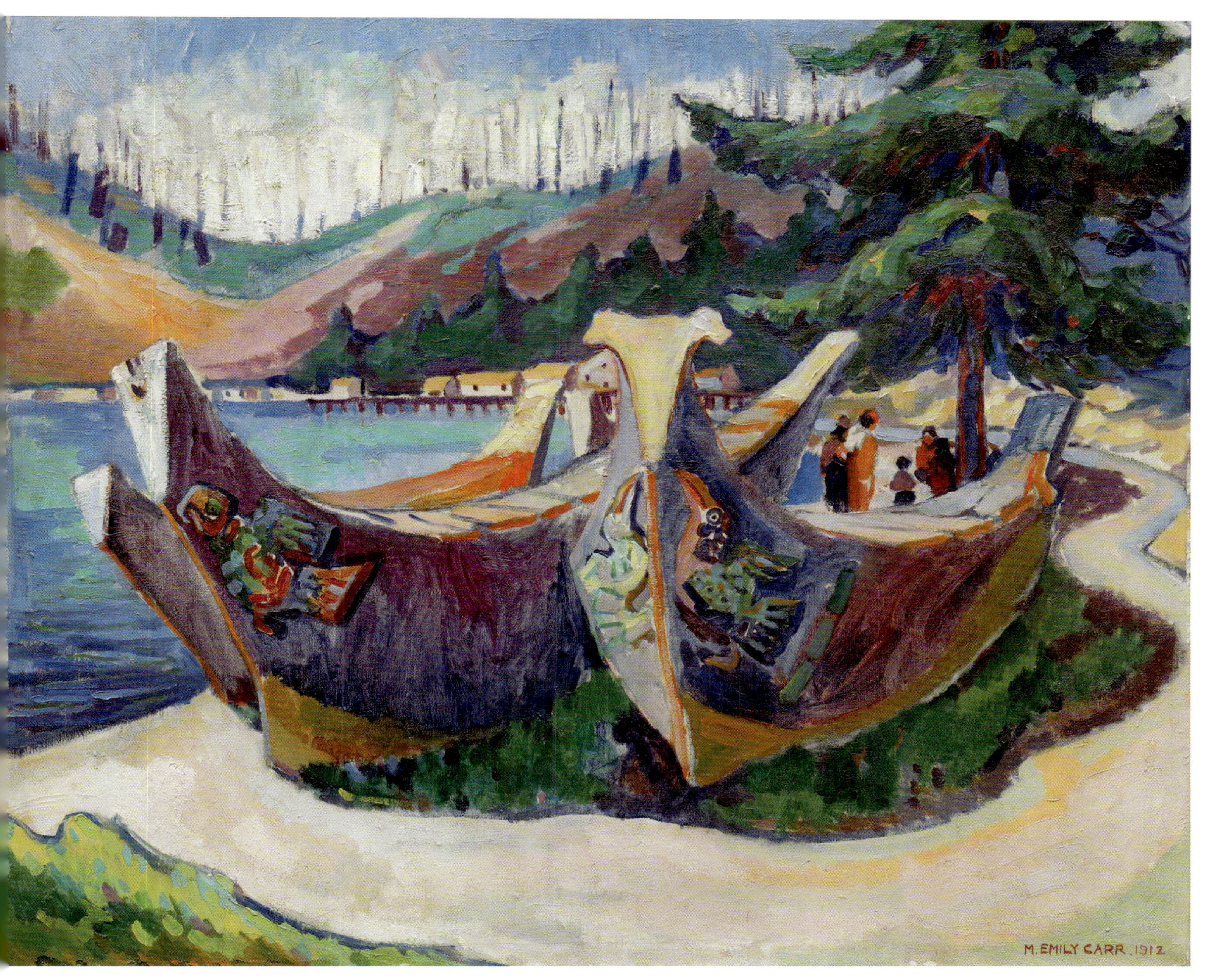

facing
Emily Carr
House with Slanted Roof—Brittany 1911

above
Emily Carr
War Canoes Alert Bay 1912

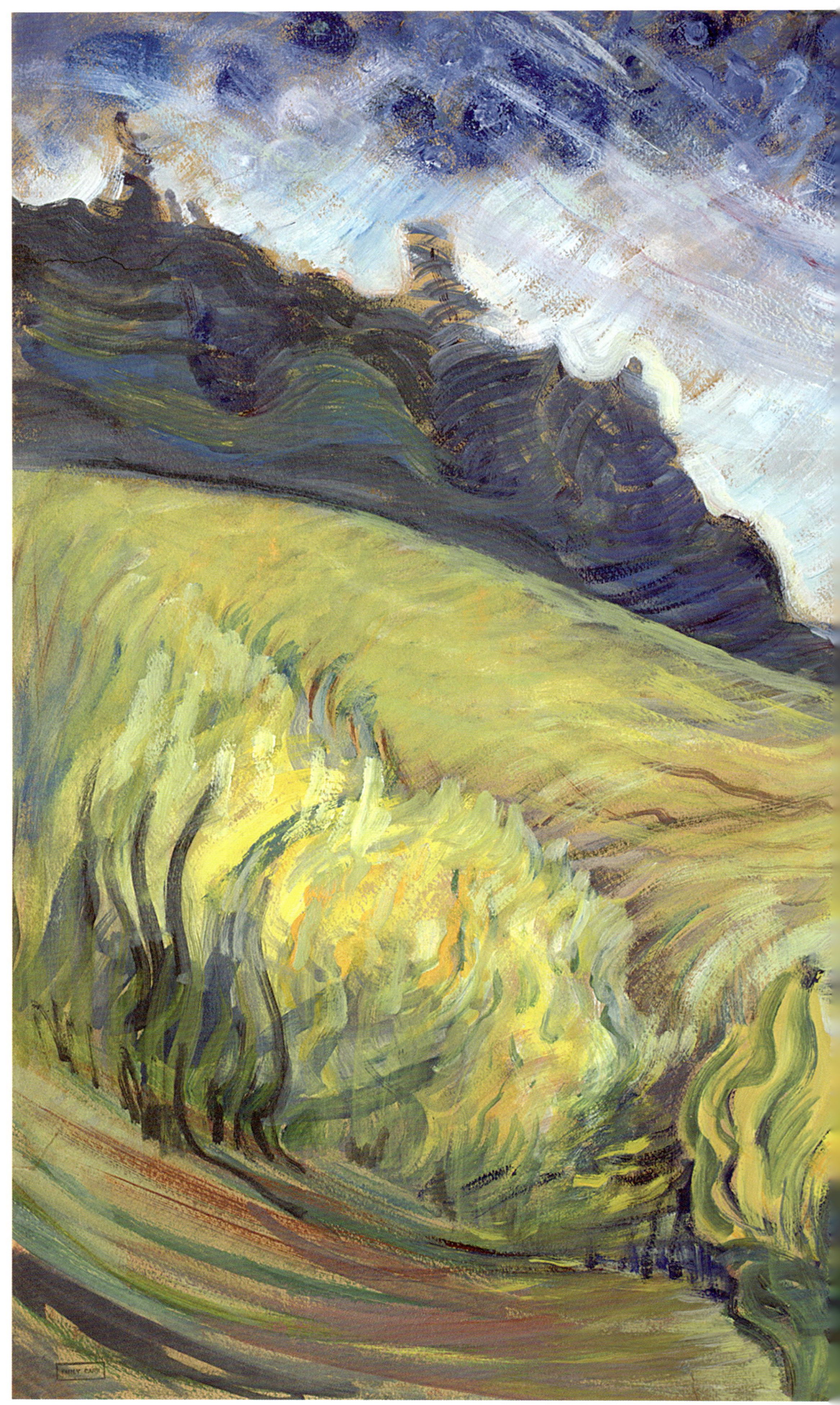

Emily Carr
At Beacon Hill Park
c. 1935

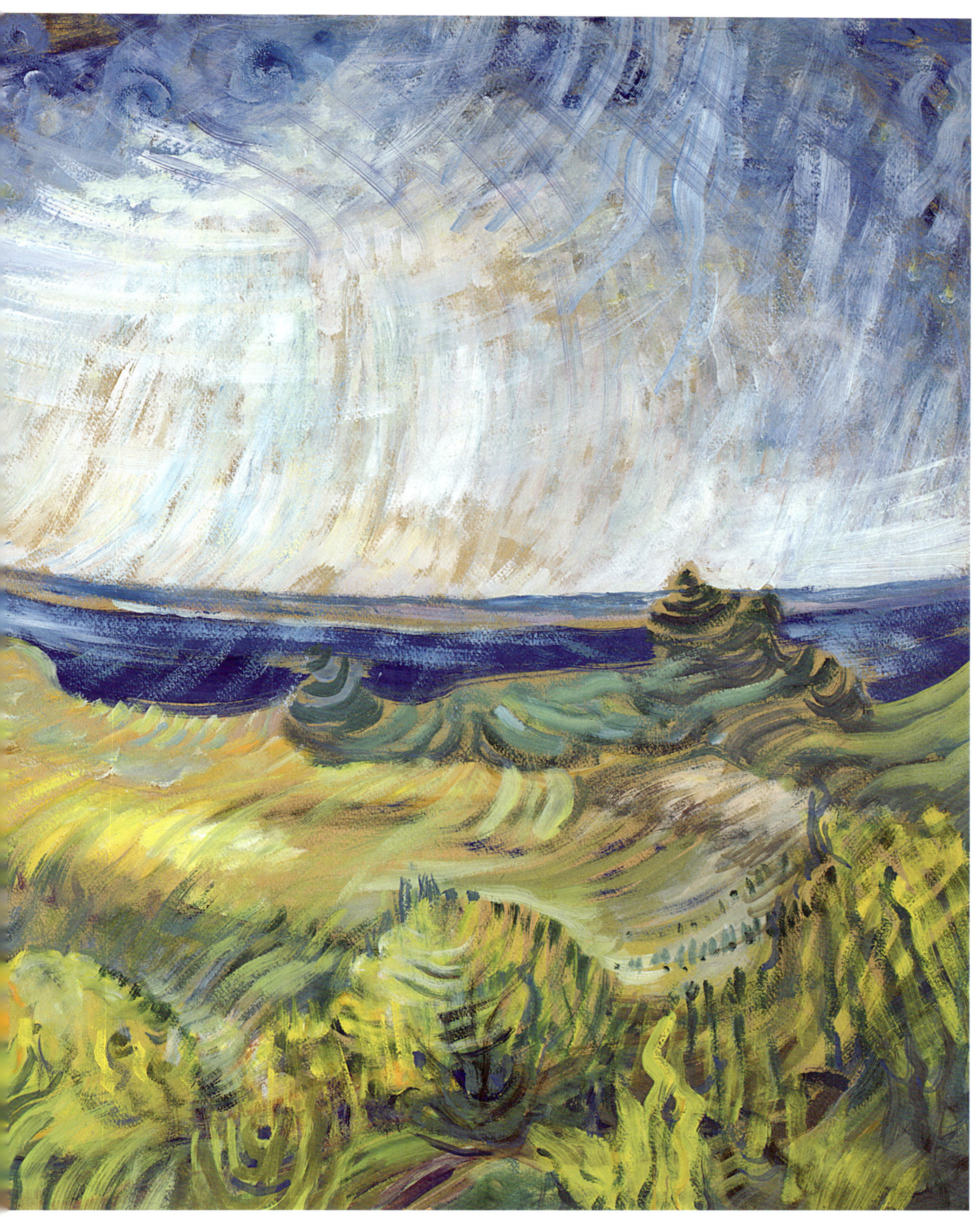

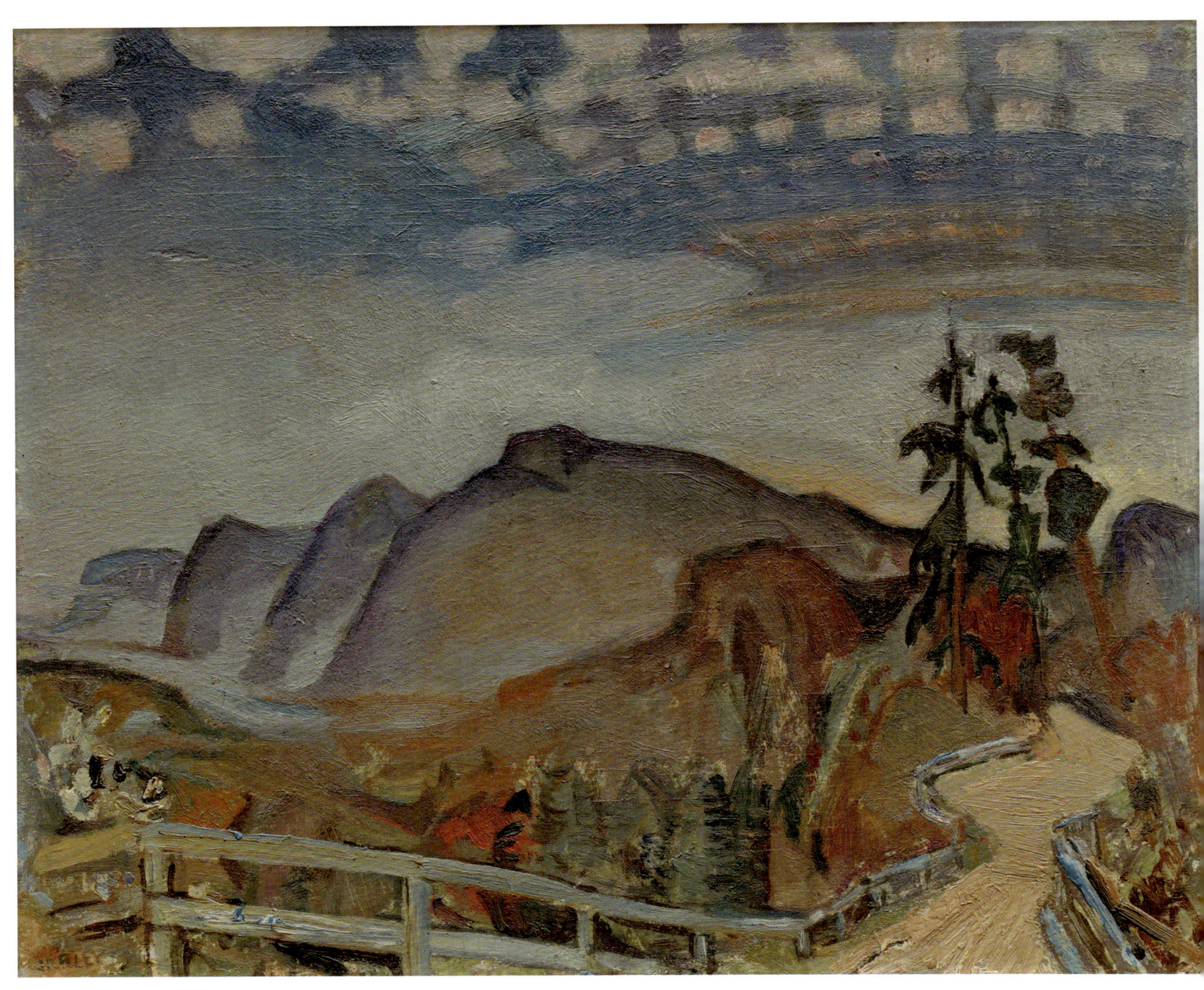

Frederick Horsman Varley
Bridge over Lynn Creek c. 1933

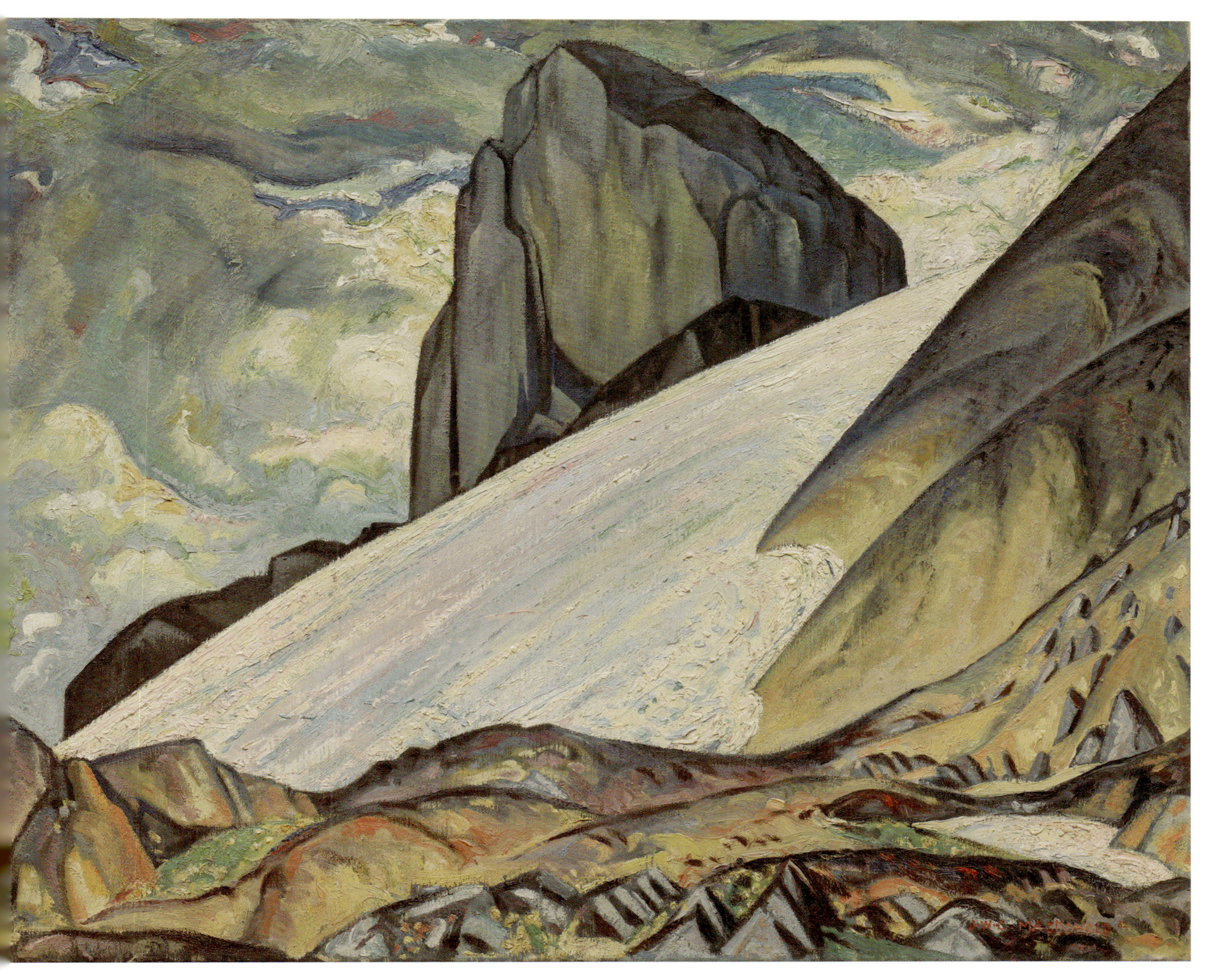

James Williamson Galloway (Jock) Macdonald
The Black Tusk, Garibaldi Park, B.C. 1932

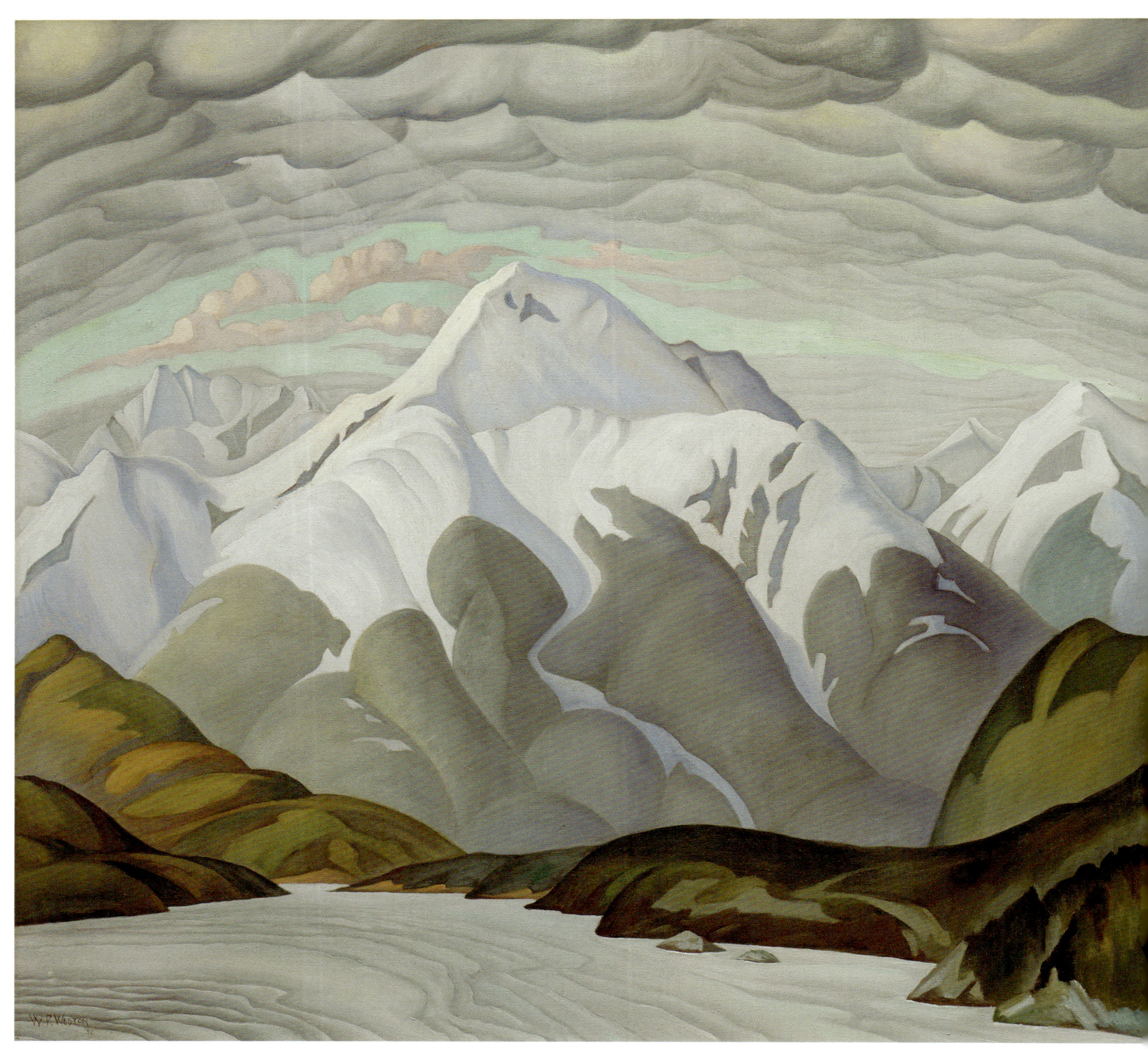

William Percival Weston
Jotunheim 1932

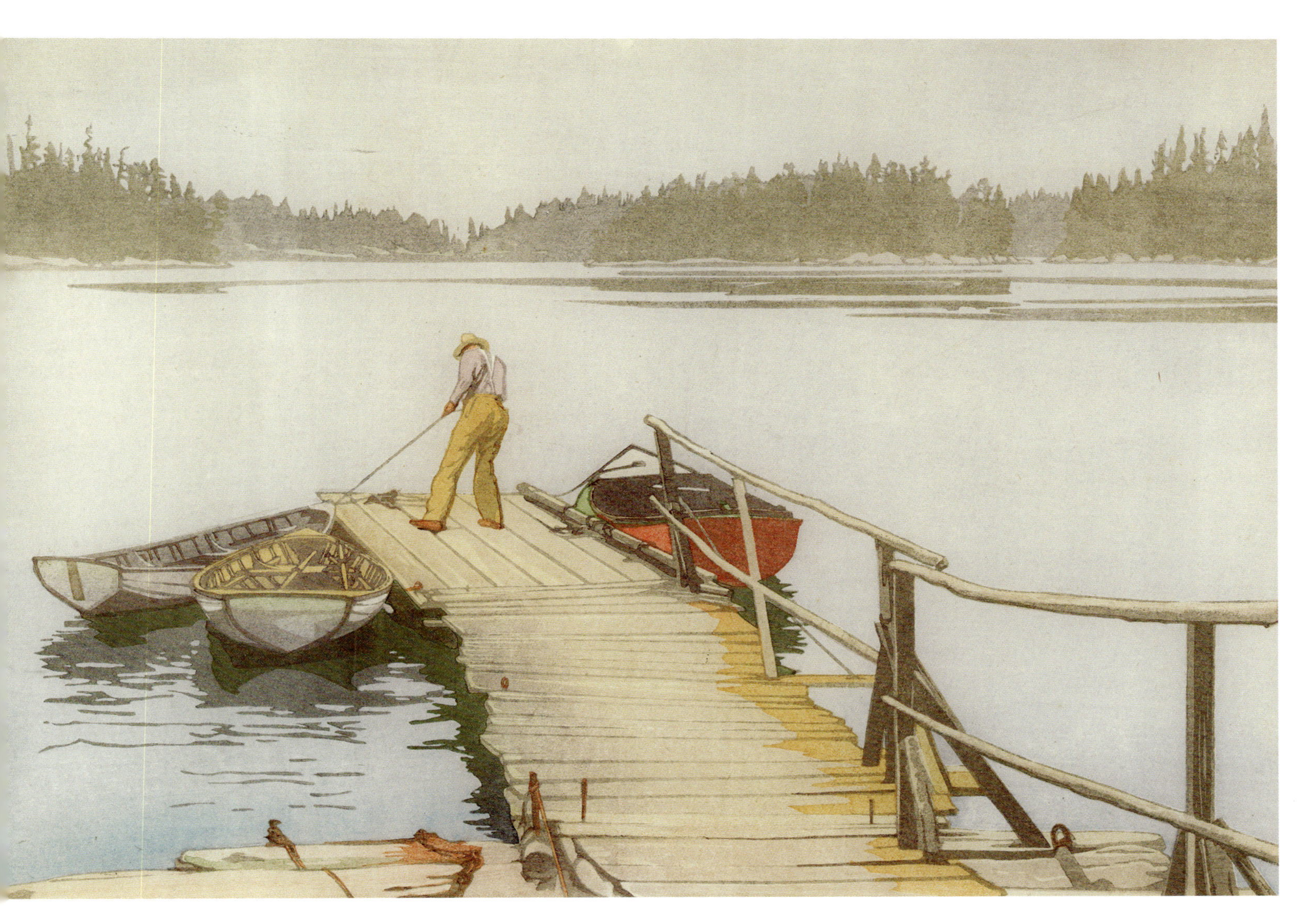

Walter Joseph Phillips
Sharp's Dock,
Pender Harbour 1952

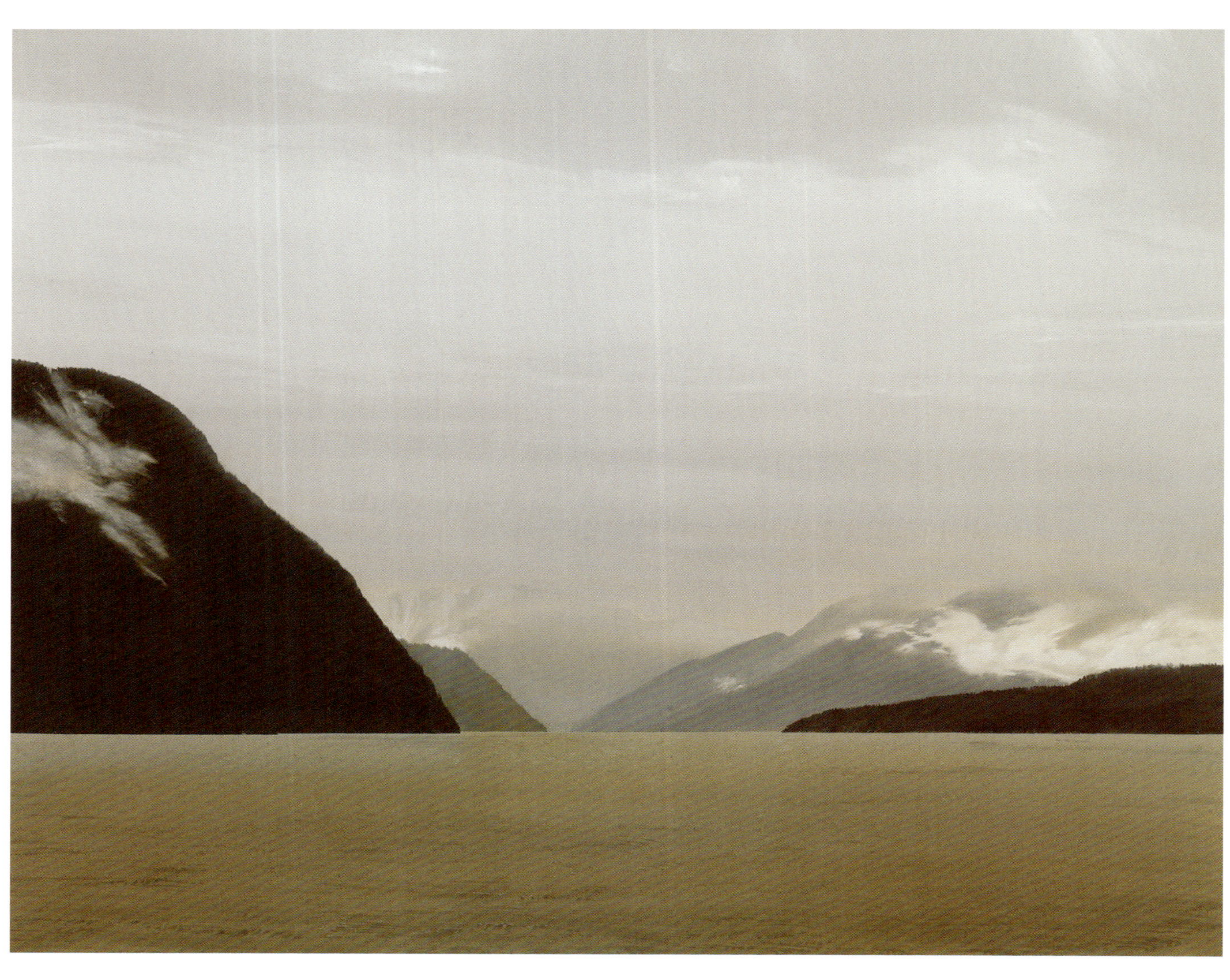

Takao Tanabe
Strait of Georgia 1/90:
Raza Pass 1990

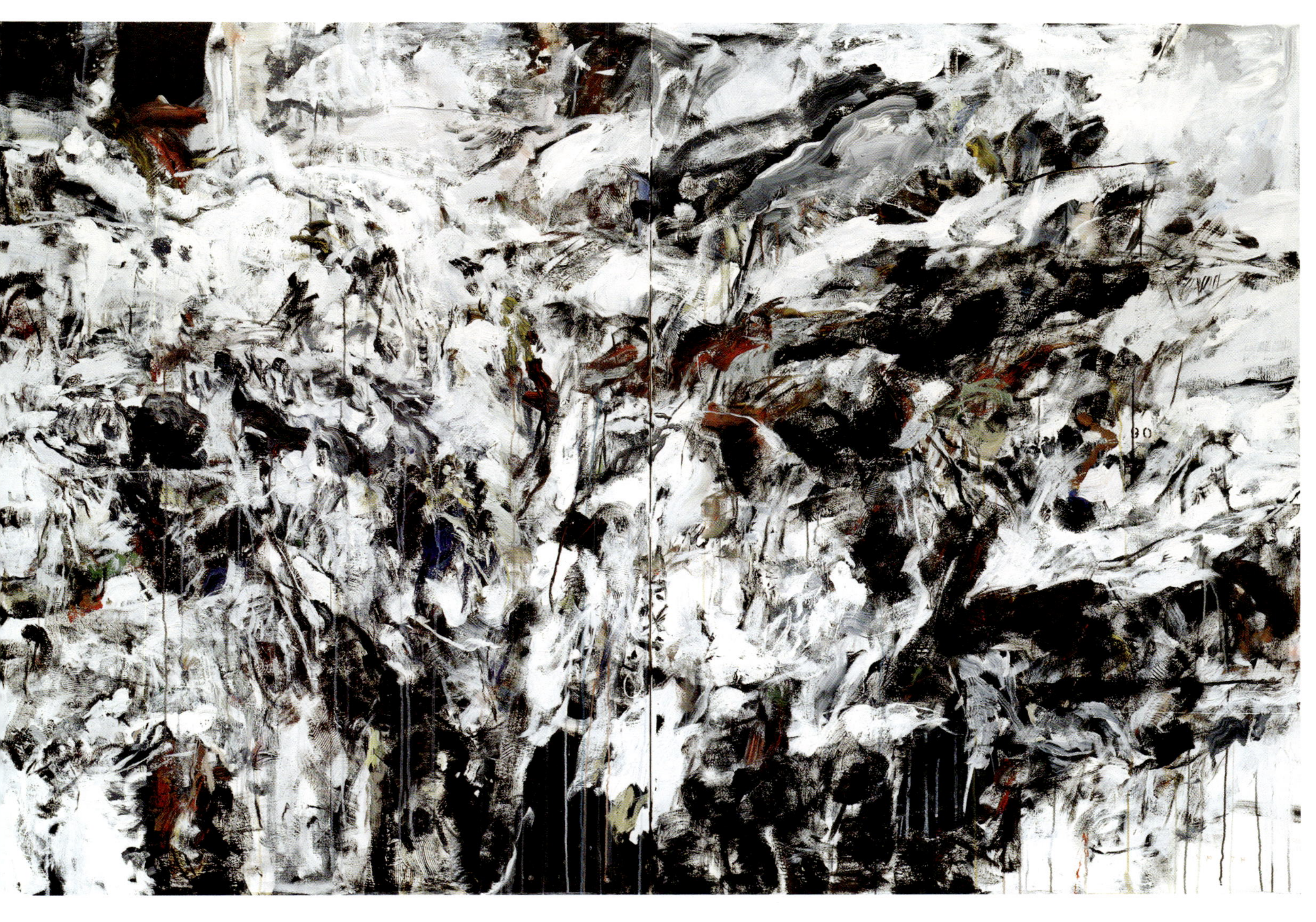

Gordon Appelbe Smith
Winterscape 1991

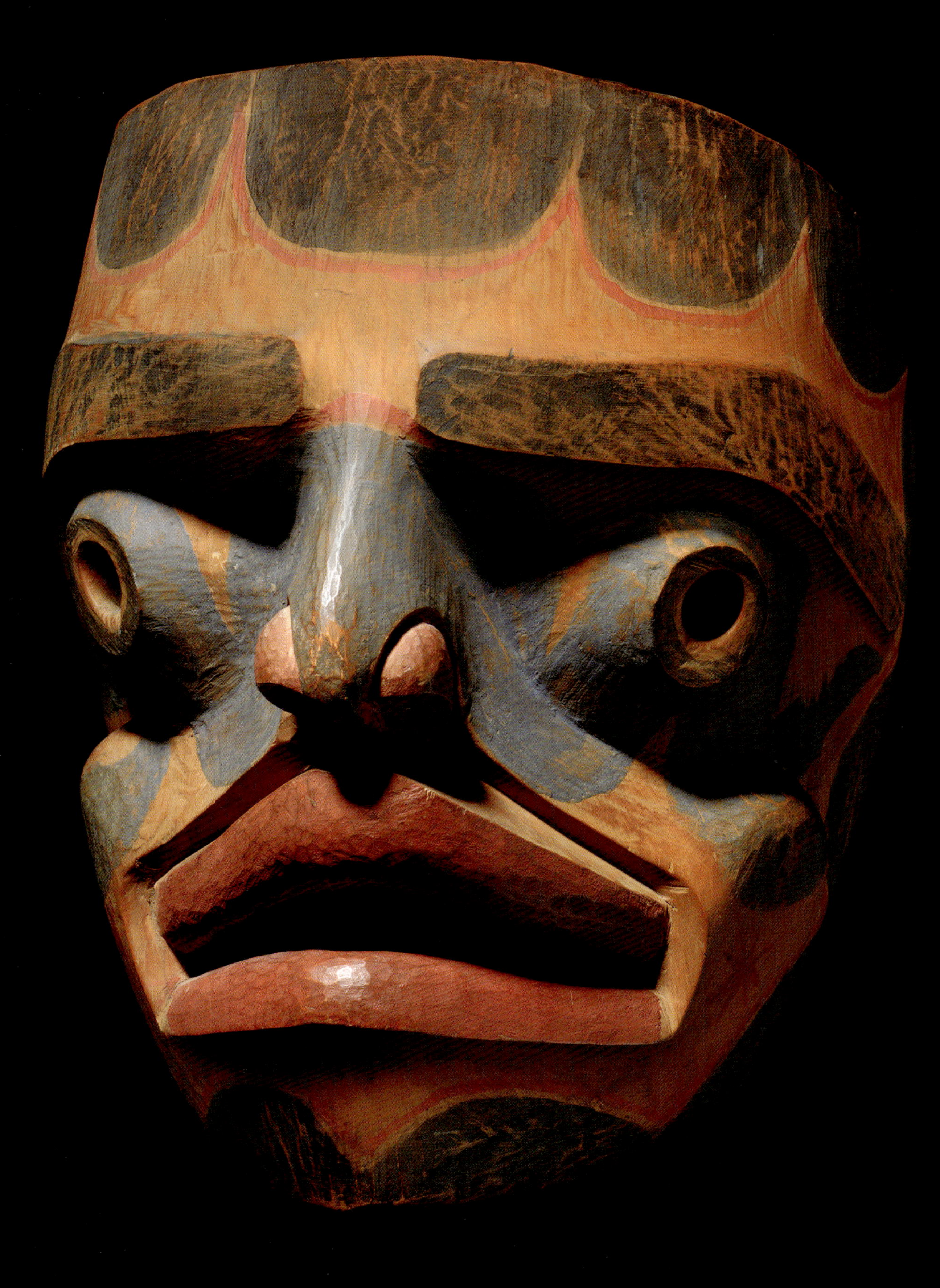

CONNECT THE LINES, FOLLOW THE LINKS

COASTAL FIRST NATIONS ART

CHARLOTTE TOWNSEND-GAULT

ART CAN BE used by artists and audiences alike to tell, to restore or to disguise a history. And artworks can become the icons made to carry history's weight, as has happened with the work of Tom Thomson and Emily Carr, Inuit art in general and Bill Reid's *Jade Canoe.* Haida artist Robert Davidson is often quoted because his words give some coherence, give a through line, to the often inchoate—because it is often devastating—history of First Nations people in British Columbia:

"We have many threads connecting us to the past. My grandparents' generation was one of those threads, and when these threads come together, they form a thick rope. It is that thick rope that connects us to our culture, the values which we are claiming."[1] ROBERT DAVIDSON in a speech delivered 7 July 1991, Old Massett, Haida Gwaii

The attenuated but unbroken thread is the metaphoric timeline for Northwest Coast art, a reminder of its continuity. The Audains' art collection, which reaches across two hundred years, includes pieces that have been important markers along this timeline. It provides a glimpse into what was happening here before the arrival of Juan Pérez, James Cook and George Vancouver, and what has happened since. It touches on encounters and exchanges, on efforts to record and to remember.

The objects and images in this collection were devised in very different places, for different people and purposes; even though the exact provenance of many of these works remains unknowable, their diversity should never be forgotten. Considering them only chronologically is limiting, as such linear thinking can lead to simplistic binaries—traditional/assimilated or traditional/contemporary—and, in the process, to a static definition of what is designated as "tradition." Equally hazardous is enshrining what is persistent along this timeline, which can lead to the trap of authenticity: "too authentic," means "stuck in the past"; "not authentic enough" means "too messed up in the present." It may be that bringing disparate pieces together creates a distracting disorder, even discord. Spectacular juxtapositions can make it difficult to comprehend the objects, which are more than mere objects themselves, and yet a collection that brings together, in the same space, work from distinct historical moments is able to give linear thinking a new twist—a spatial one.

1. Ian Thom, Aldona Jonaitis, Marianne Jones, *Robert Davidson: Eagle of the Dawn* (Seattle and Vancouver: University of Washington Press and Douglas & McIntyre), 1993, 19.

facing
Nuxalk Artist
Earthquake Mask c. 1880

In this collection, the lucid geometry that distinguishes Nuu-chah-nulth carving and painting is well represented in an early mask with a subtle patina of time that must be a connoisseur's delight (Nuu-chah-nulth Artist, *Articulated Mask*, c. 1840, page 50), whereas even to the uninitiated the small, balanced Coast Salish bone figures transmit the spiritual potency ascribed to them (Salish Artist, *Figure*, late 19th century, page 48). The complex intensity of a lined Tlingit mask with articulated red eyelids was immediately evident to Jackson Pollock. His appreciation suggests that this very mask was one of the objects that made the bridge between indigenous art and Modernism so influential (Tlingit Artist, *Owl Mask*, 1840–60s, page 59). Equally remarkable, with their Modernist discrete and decontextualized surfaces, are the refined façades of Tsimshian bentwood boxes that instantly fill and hold the viewer's field of vision. The chest pictured here was once in the Dundas collection of treasures that was repatriated to Canada from Scotland, and both the object and its trajectory tell a story of loss and restitution (Tsimshian Artist, *Chest*, 19th century, page 60). Here too is a fine copper, its fame extended beyond the immediate Seaweed family via a famous photograph of Willie Seaweed holding it. The camera and the photos become part of the timeline as a witness to the status of the copper (Unknown First Nations Artist, *Copper (belonging to Willie Seaweed)*, 18th century, page 65). The Kwakwa̱ka̱'wakw have always excelled at the dramatic articulation of status; examples in the collection include *Sun Mask* by Charlie James, late 19th century–early 20th century (page 63) and Beau Dick's looming *Tsonokwa Mask*, 2007 (page 76).

The Audain collection is an assemblage of images and objects that sets up some compelling connections in space, relationships that are contingent on who is following which historical links. For example, one of the great puzzles of the Northwest Coast is the ubiquitous graphic line that was termed "formline" by those looking and thinking through the lens of Modernist formalism. Along with other formal elements such as the ovoid and the U-form, the formline has become established as a defining aspect of Northwest Coast Native art. Is that accurate, however? Has the right characteristic been identified? Newer work shown here says yes. Form can hold its own. Line is its own idea, which offers a direction alongside, even in lieu of, cultural references or cultural histories. Its impact is spatial. The formline contains, separates and conjoins. Always active, even when creating symmetry, it emphasizes the eyes and a dense conglomeration of beings, looping and tense. It designates the relationships between creatures, beings, both human and supernatural—the whole cosmological pantheon—before it outlines the components.

Arguably, when the formline is used to disassemble it becomes a compelling metaphor for the stranglehold of the past on the present. Since the 1970s Robert Davidson has been taking the lines to what he punningly calls an "abstract edge," giving them a workout in terms that owe something to Abstract Expressionism's concerns with figure and ground and framing edge but also to the push and pull of Haida low-relief carving, to his ancestor Charles Edenshaw's taut and disciplined painting (*Painted Spruce Root Hat*, late 19th century, page 57) and to an anonymous Haida artist's cedar-bark and spruce-root weaving. The proven elasticity of the line is used by Sonny Assu

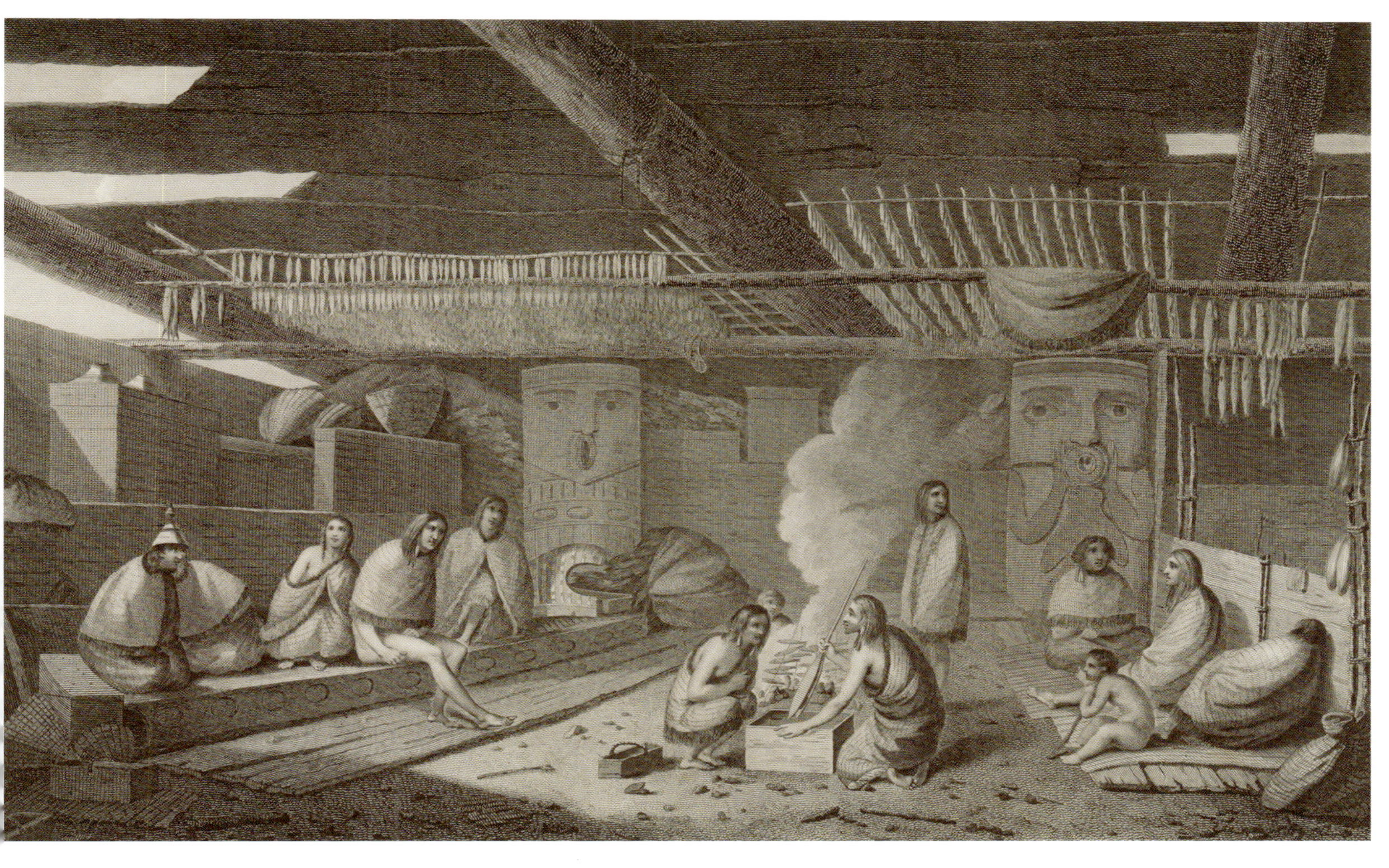

John Webber
The Inside of a House in
Nootka Sound 1784

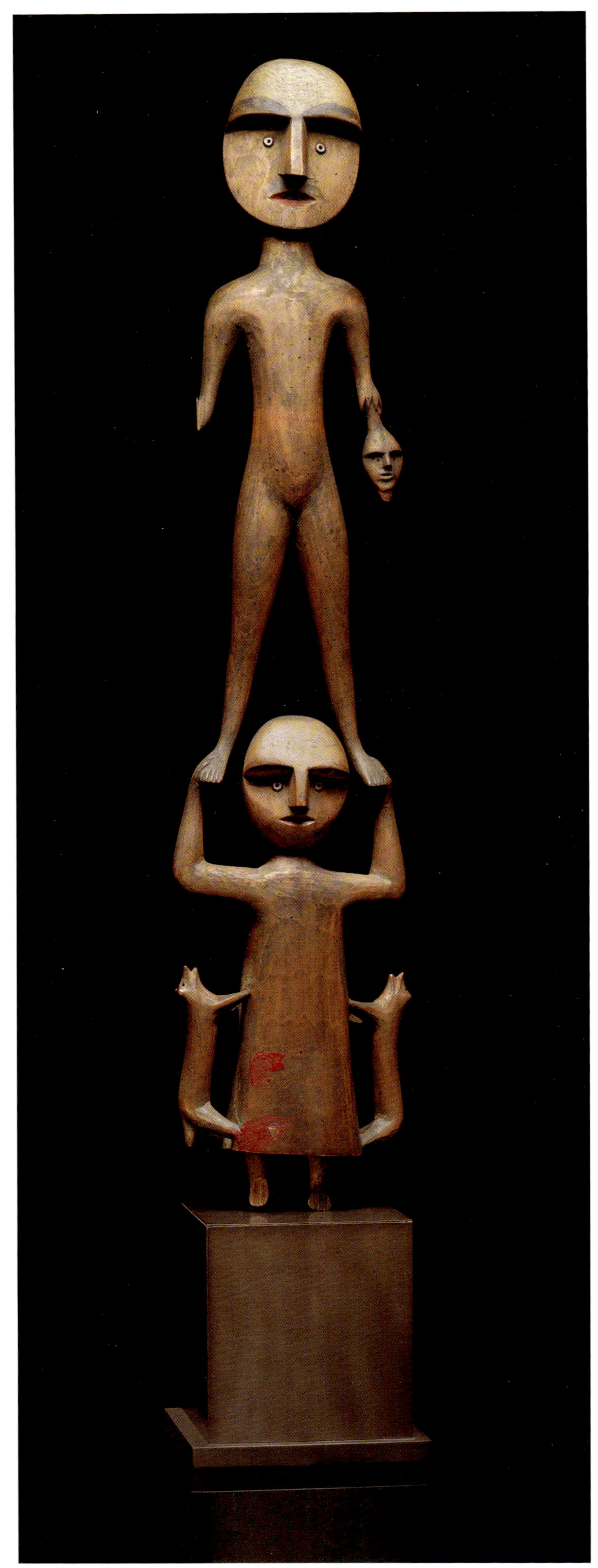

Salish Artist
Figure late 19th century–
early 20th century

to tie up, and silence, a pile of drums (*Silenced #2*, 2010). He is activating the painted line in this and his other drum works in order to deactivate something else. Assu's formline ties the drums together and deadens the life in them.

In a related manoeuvre, Michael Nicoll Yahgulanaas has twisted the formlines and ovoids off the totem poles, and all the other places where they organize and disorganize space, and run them across the printed page (*Fishing*, 2008, page 140). His book *Red*, 2010, comes with the injunction to take two copies apart and, following the lines, see how the story can be re-assembled and read from left to right or out from the centre. Compare this with the central assaults of the Tsimshian box fronts in the collection. The symmetrical, compressed/intermeshed and flattened eyes, ears, paws and claws—not quite flat, not quite locked in—jump together in spatial symbiosis when the whole story can be seen spread out and Yahgulanaas's deft linking of formline to timeline can be grasped. Or compare it with Jim Hart's devotion to feats of memory and historical imagination in work that maintains the massed intricacies well known from nineteenth-century Haida poles (*Model Pole*, 2006–09, page 80). Follow the links between them—grounding, paying homage, re-evaluating, deconstructing. The formline leaps between Tsimshian and Haida and then out to Brian Jungen, who in *Variant 1*, 2002 (page 85), engages with the Northwest Coast in a different register. The line is recompressed in Jungen's massed symmetry of interlocked, anything-but-static, running shoes.

Containment is one of the formline's principal actions. Marianne Nicolson is interested in recovering the epistemological significance for the Dzawada'enuxw of box and house forms as containers. Her paintings are inquiries into visual and spatial relationships between line elements and their possible linguistic equivalents in Kwakwala. Someone in the past once painted tunic designs on woven cedar bark. Someone else made a model canoe and painted it with exemplary linked ovoids. They may have done so to leave records, object lessons about ways of life that were under assault. Decades separate them from Nicolson's paintings that now revivify the tunics, but as lines in space one set picks up where the other left off (*Tunic for a Noblewoman*, pages 78–79).

Contemporary Native work tends to be positioned and judged on the way it follows the links across time; however, when looking at these works it becomes evident that those links are both supple and controlled. Must today's artists be judged by the standards of the past, or always in light of traditions both mourned and desired? What were these standards and traditions exactly? Do they imply an idea of traditional purity corrupted over time, hybridized and then revivified? The contradictions inherent in Northwest Coast Native art are both suggested and overturned by the works here.

Lawrence Paul Yuxweluptun's large canvases, for instance, are alive with ovoids and formlines compacted and attenuated into figures, trees, rivers and mountains. Even when freighted with the heaviness of history and a polluted present, the connections dance. This collection includes his largest painting, *Burying Another Face of Racism on First Nations Soil*, 1997, which could be a history lesson, if the timeline were ever to lead to such a scenario.

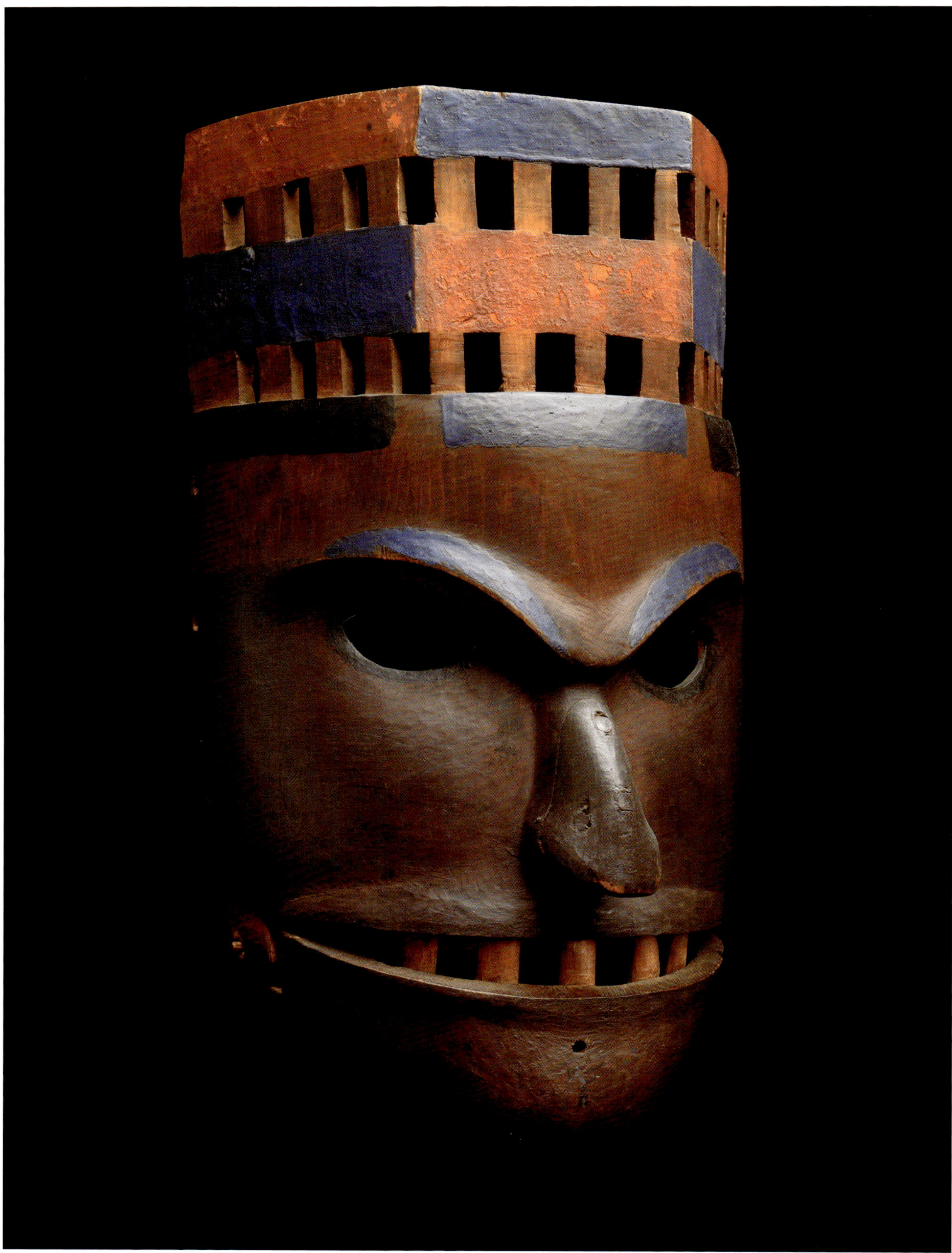

above
Nuu-chah-nulth Artist
Articulated Mask c. 1840

facing
Heiltsuk Artist
Ancestor Mask c. 1850

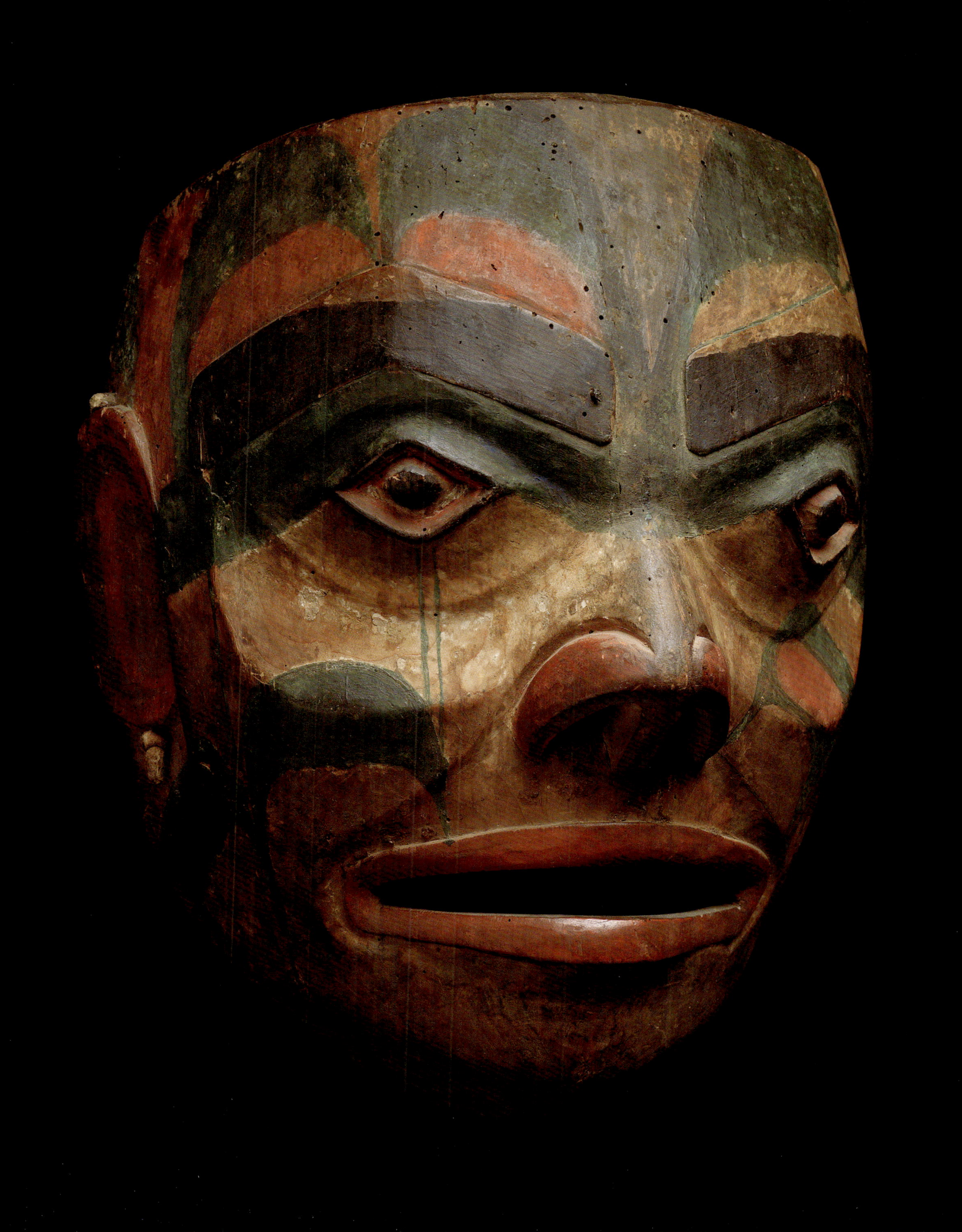

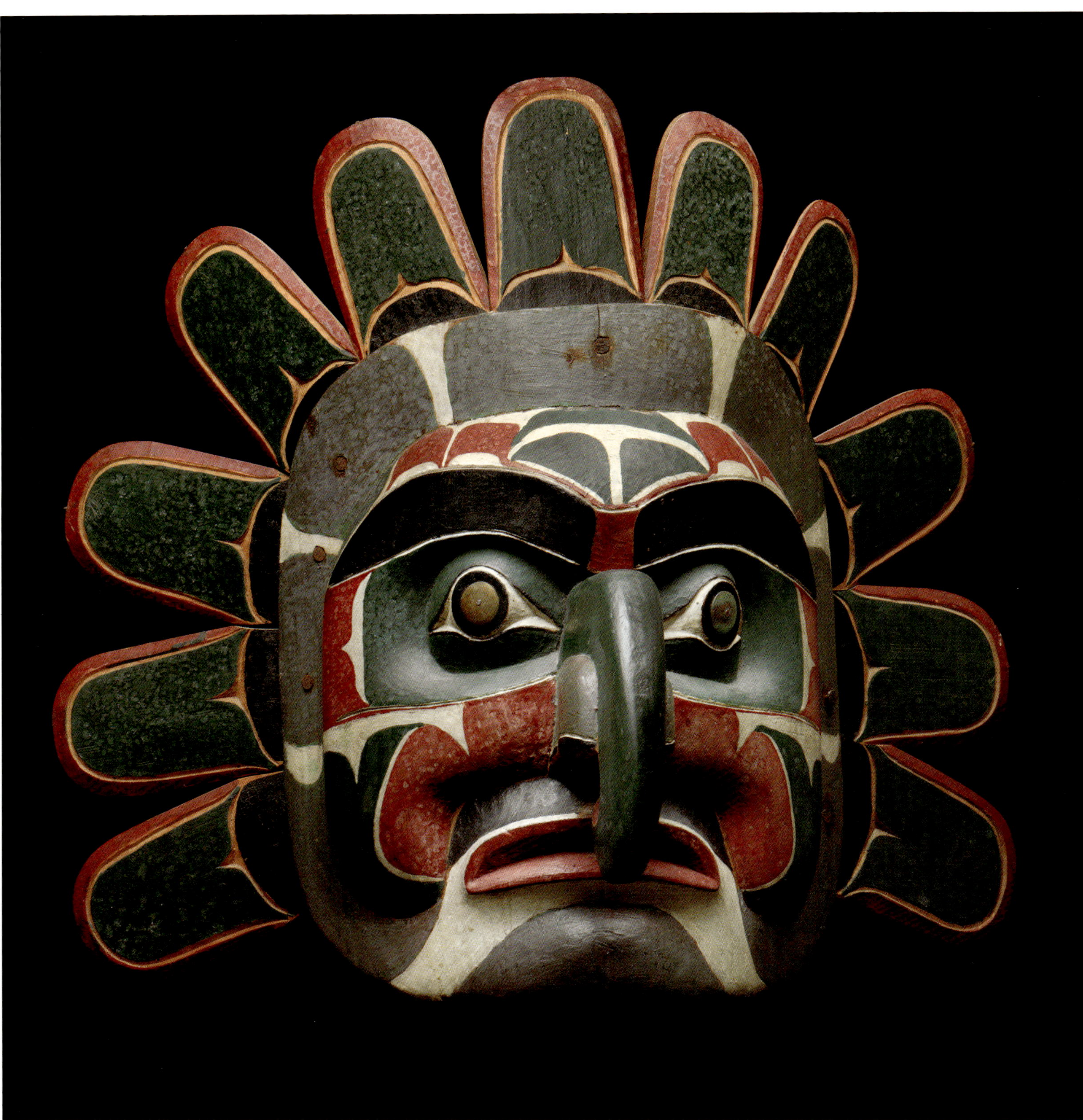

Kwakwaka'wakw Artist
Sun Mask 19th century

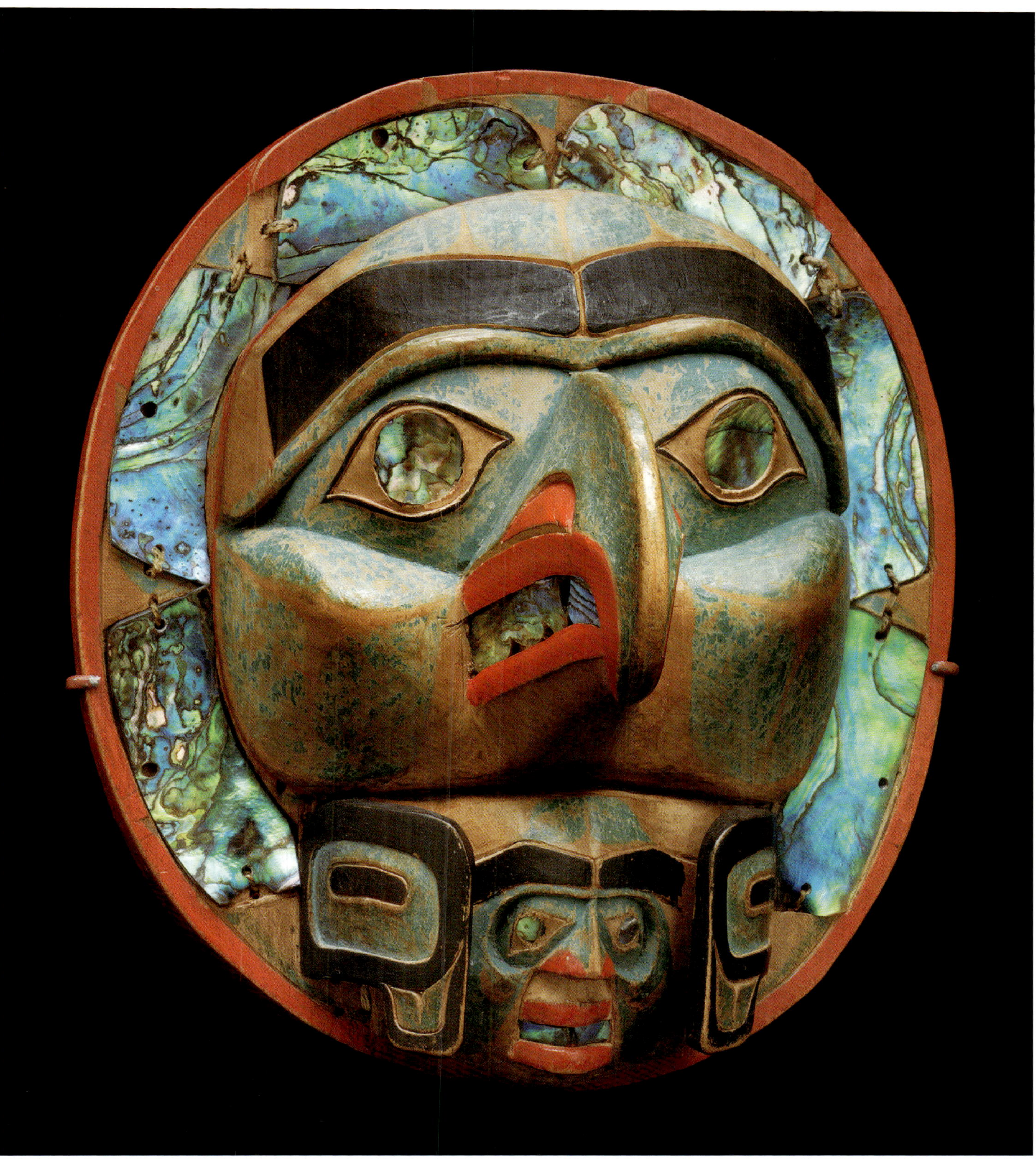

Heiltsuk Artist
Frontlet c. 1860–80

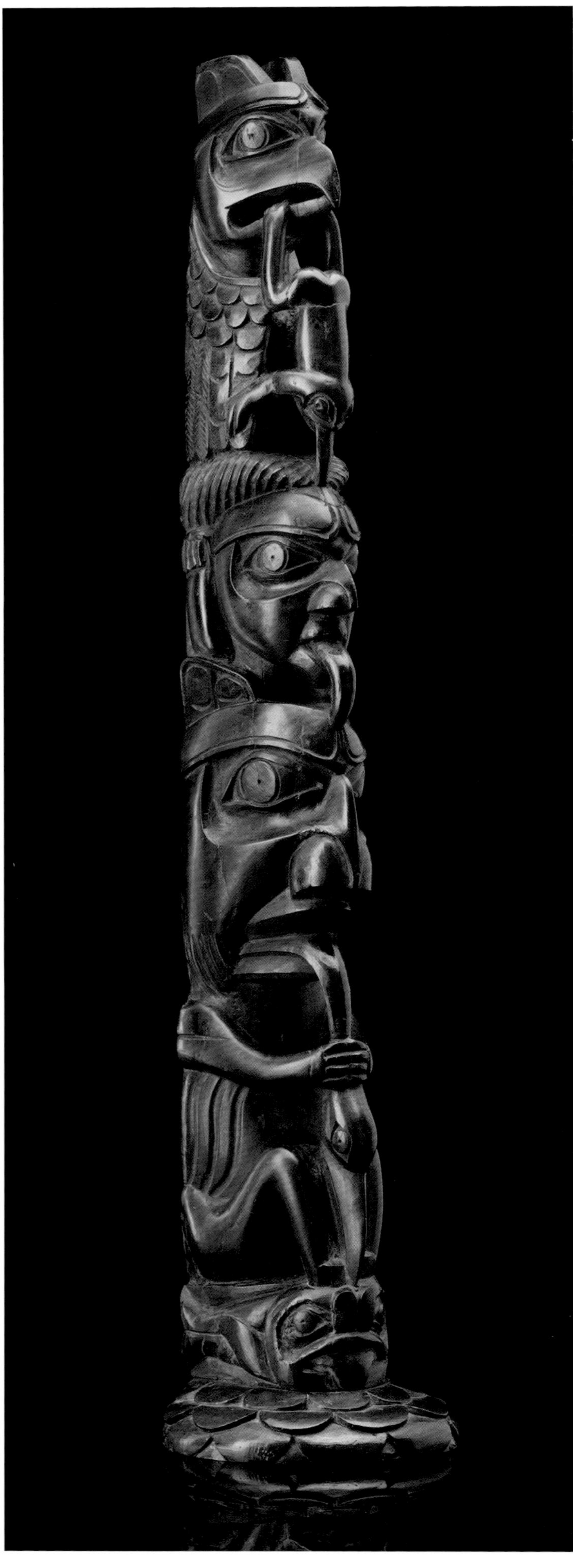

right

Haida Artist

Model Totem Pole 1860s

facing

Nisga'a Artist

Portrait Mask c. 1880

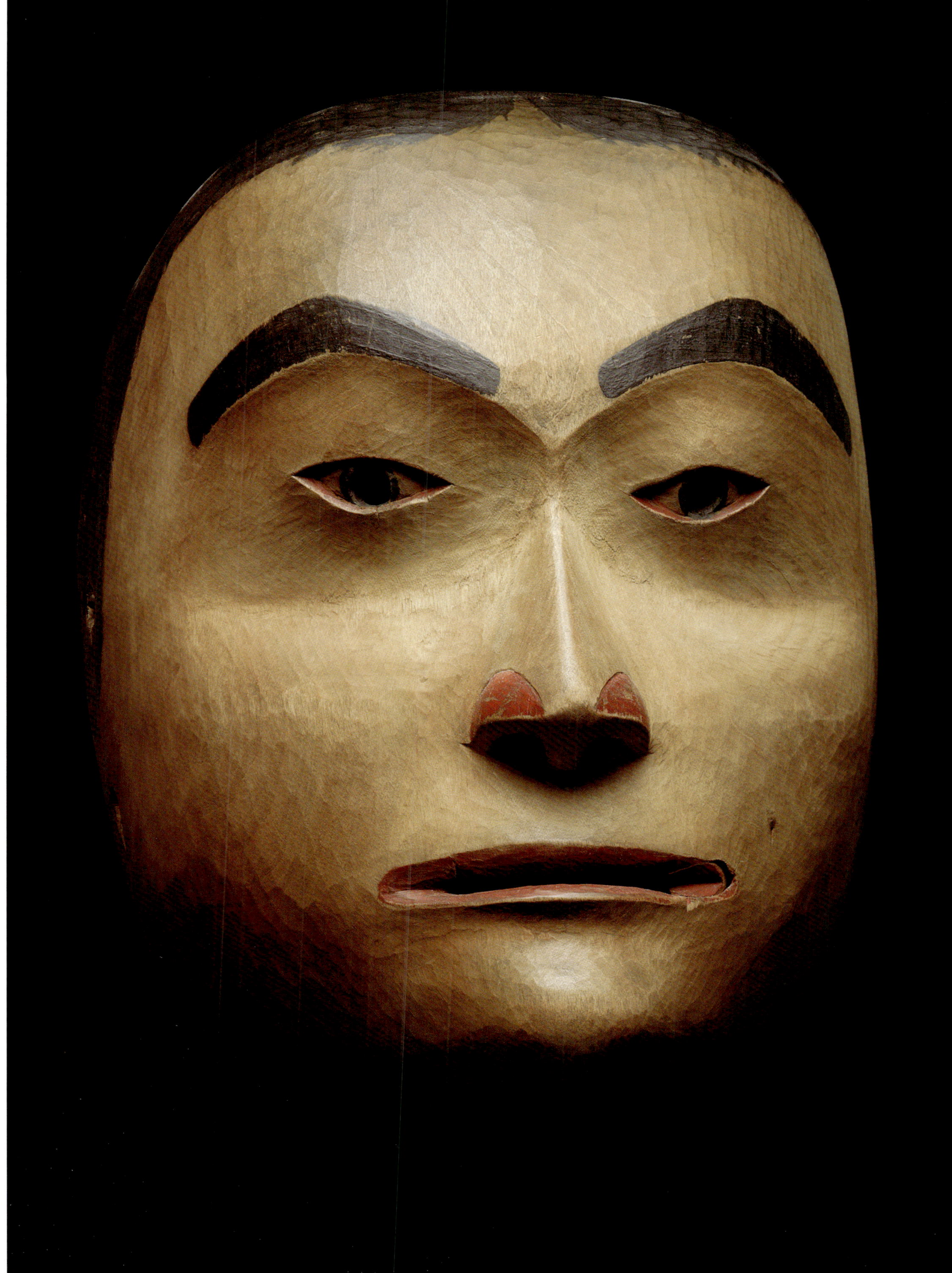

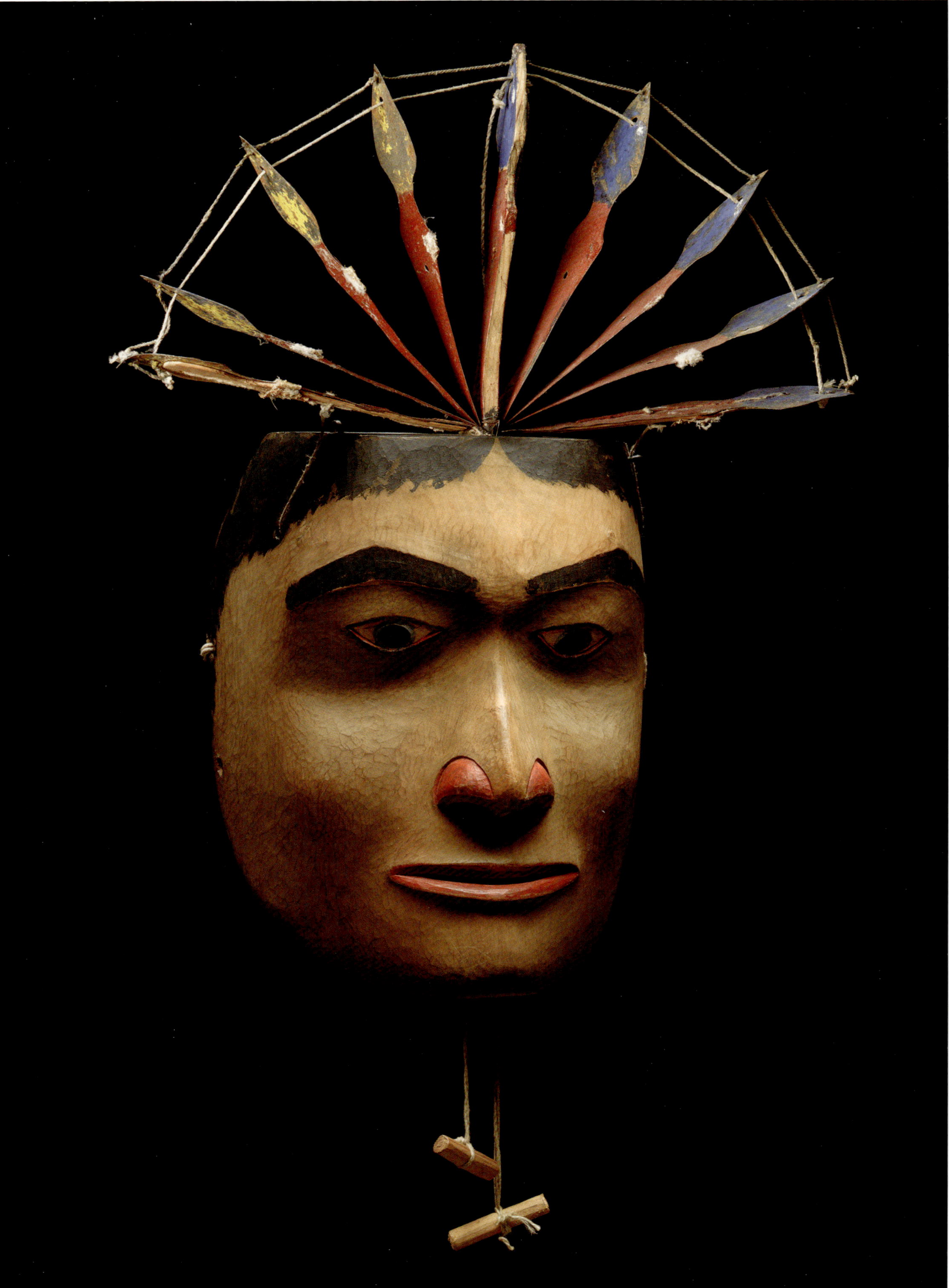

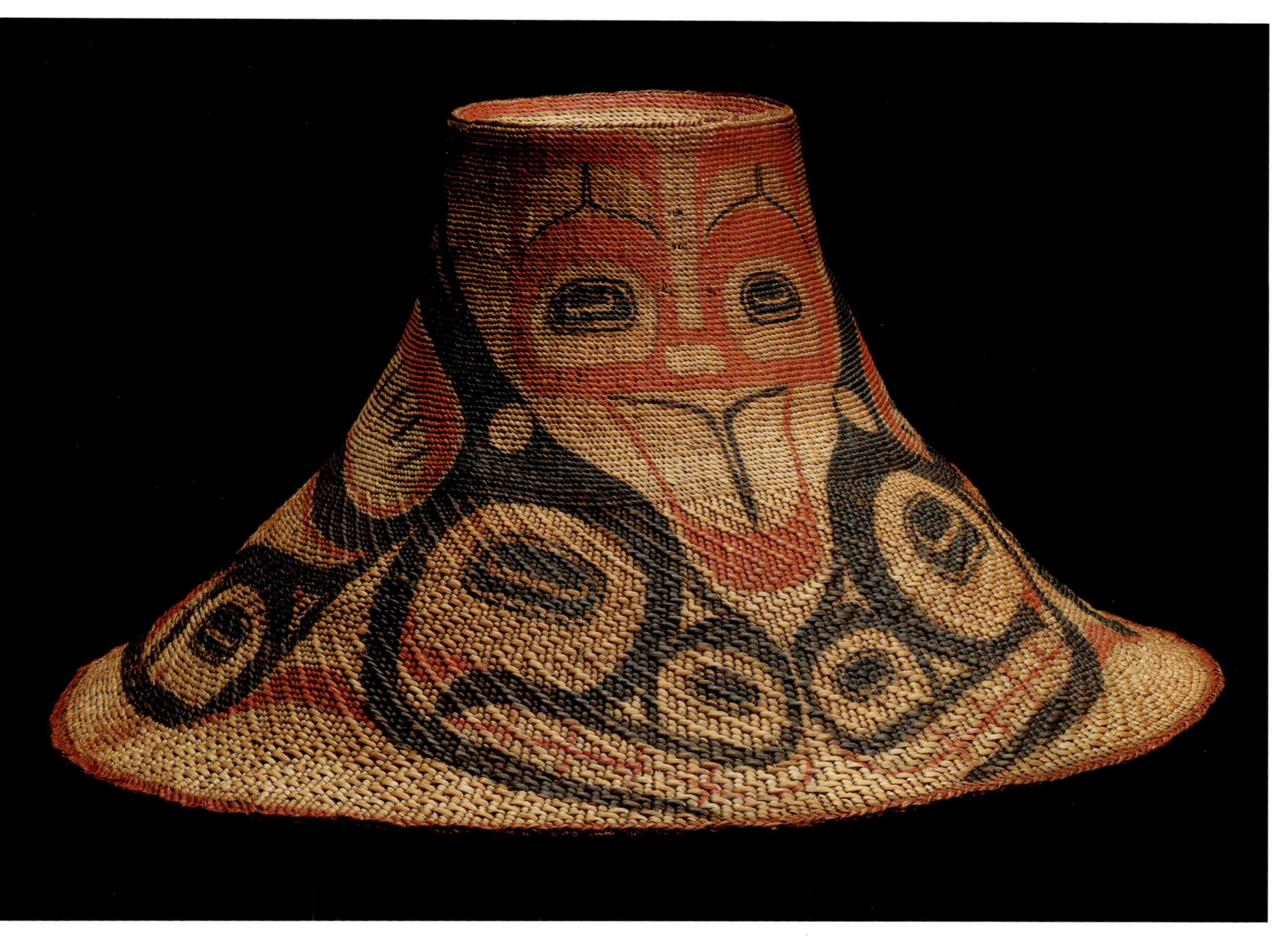

facing
Gitk'san Artist
Portrait Mask
c. 1800

above
Charles Edenshaw (Tahagen)
Painted Spruce Root Hat
late 19th century

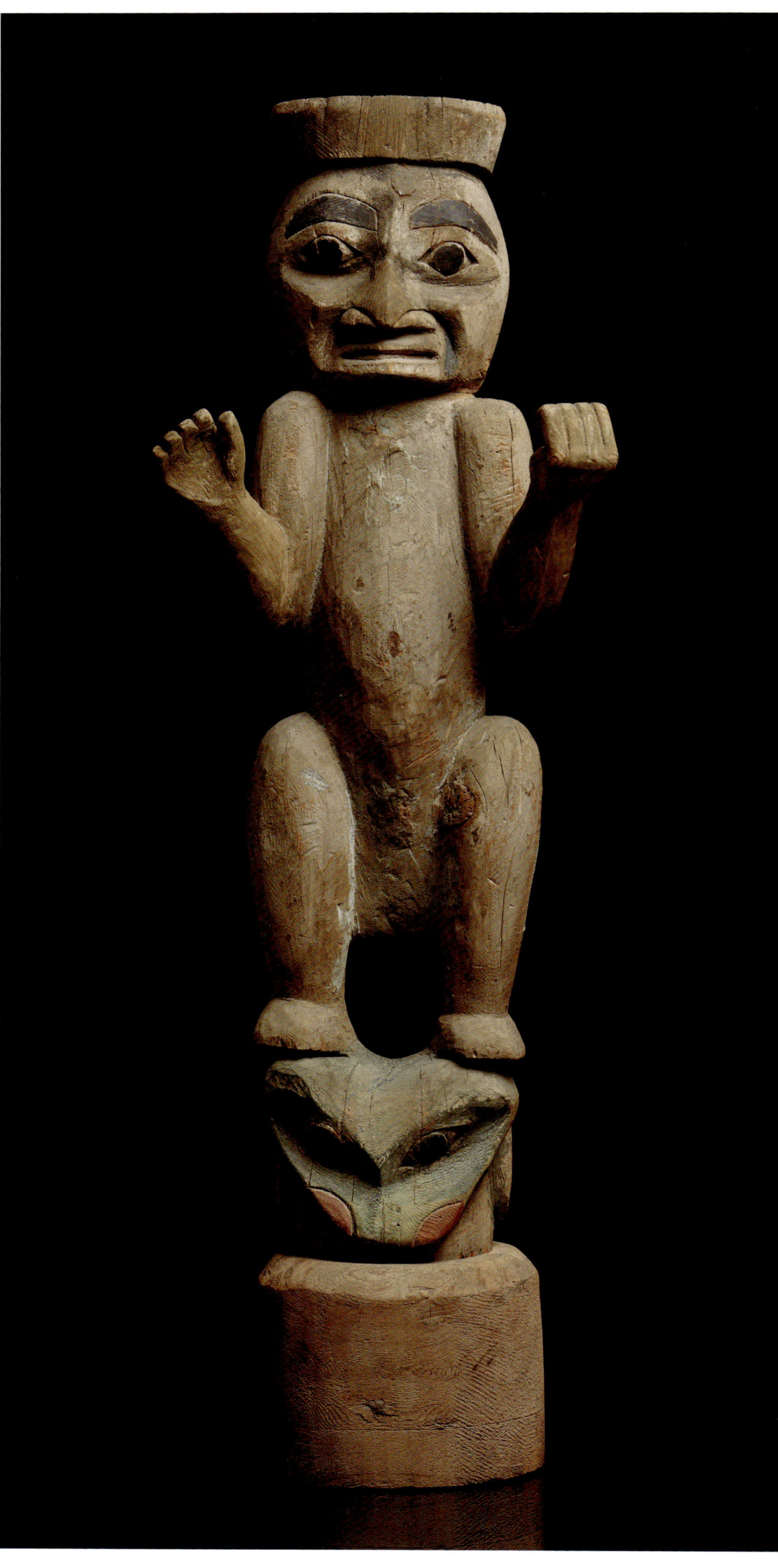

right

Gitk'san Artist

Guardian Figure c. 1900

facing

Tlingit Artist

Owl Mask 1840–60s

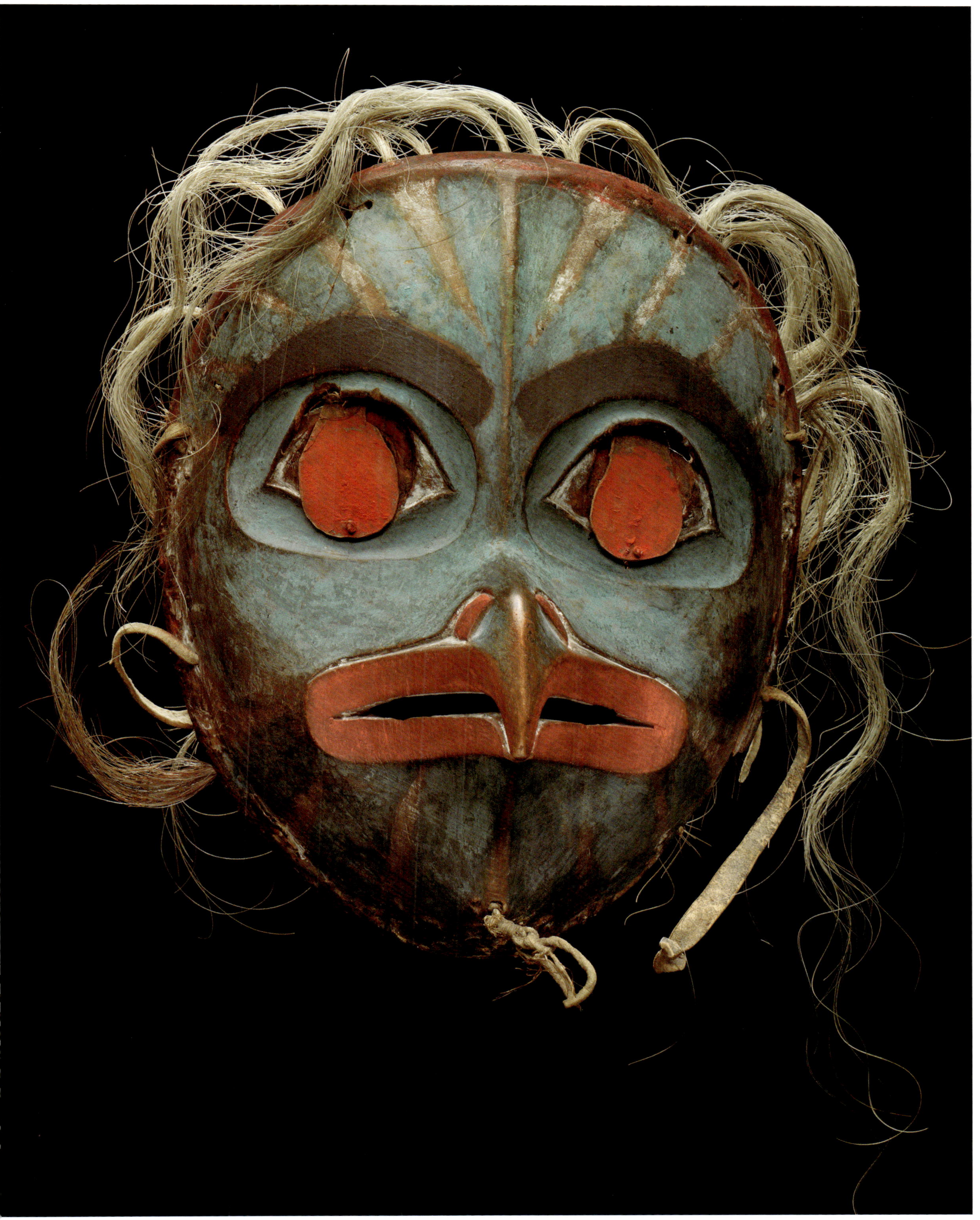

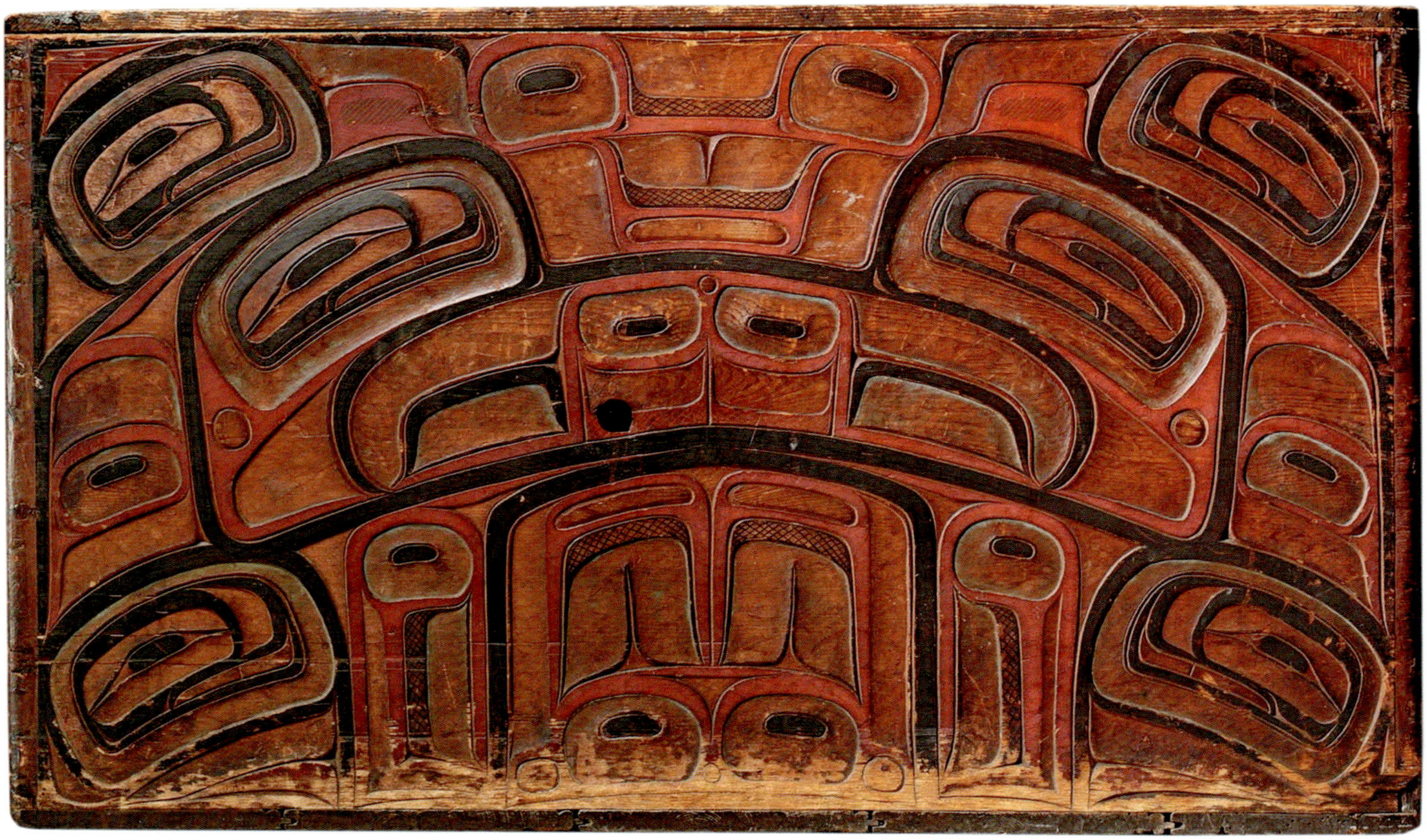

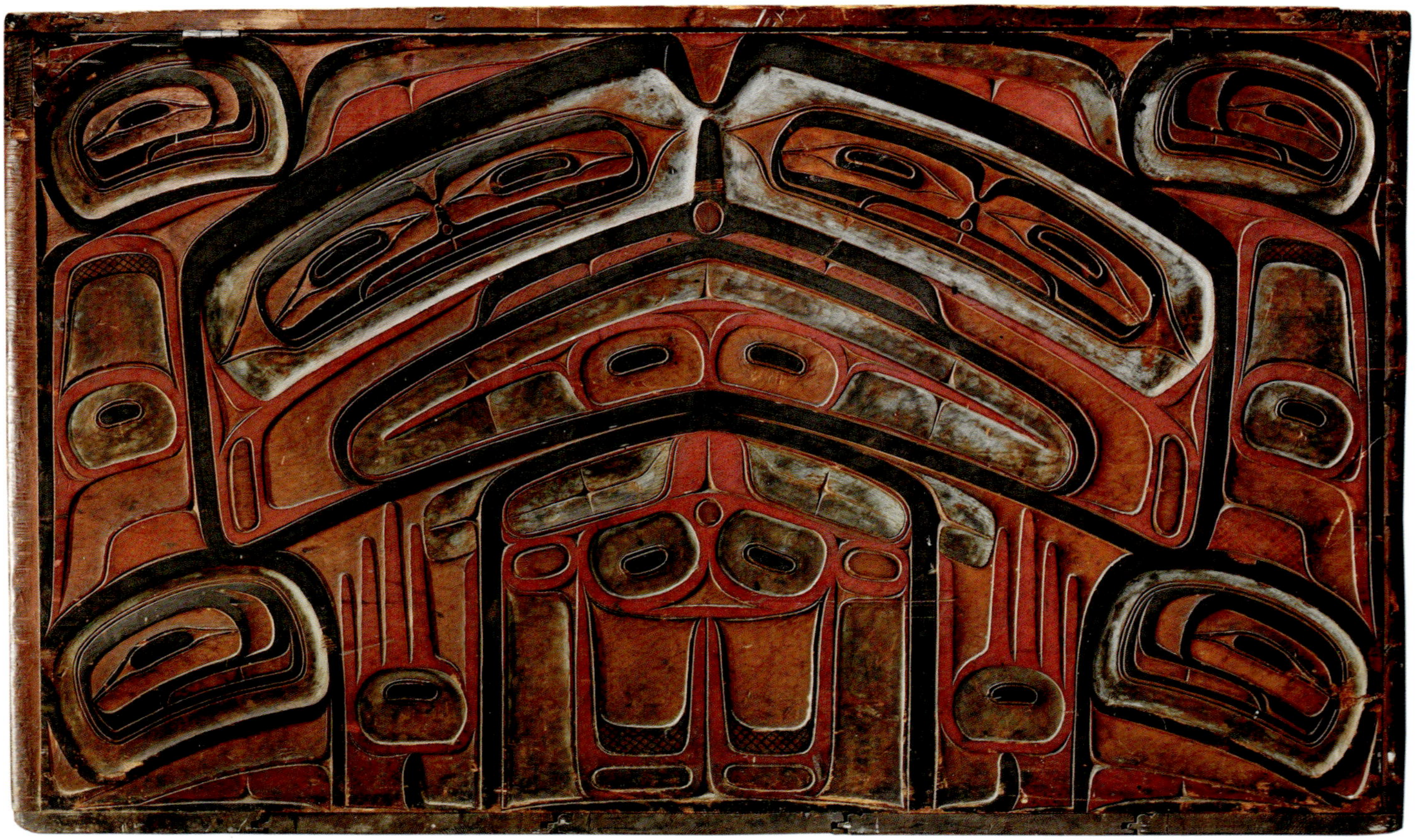

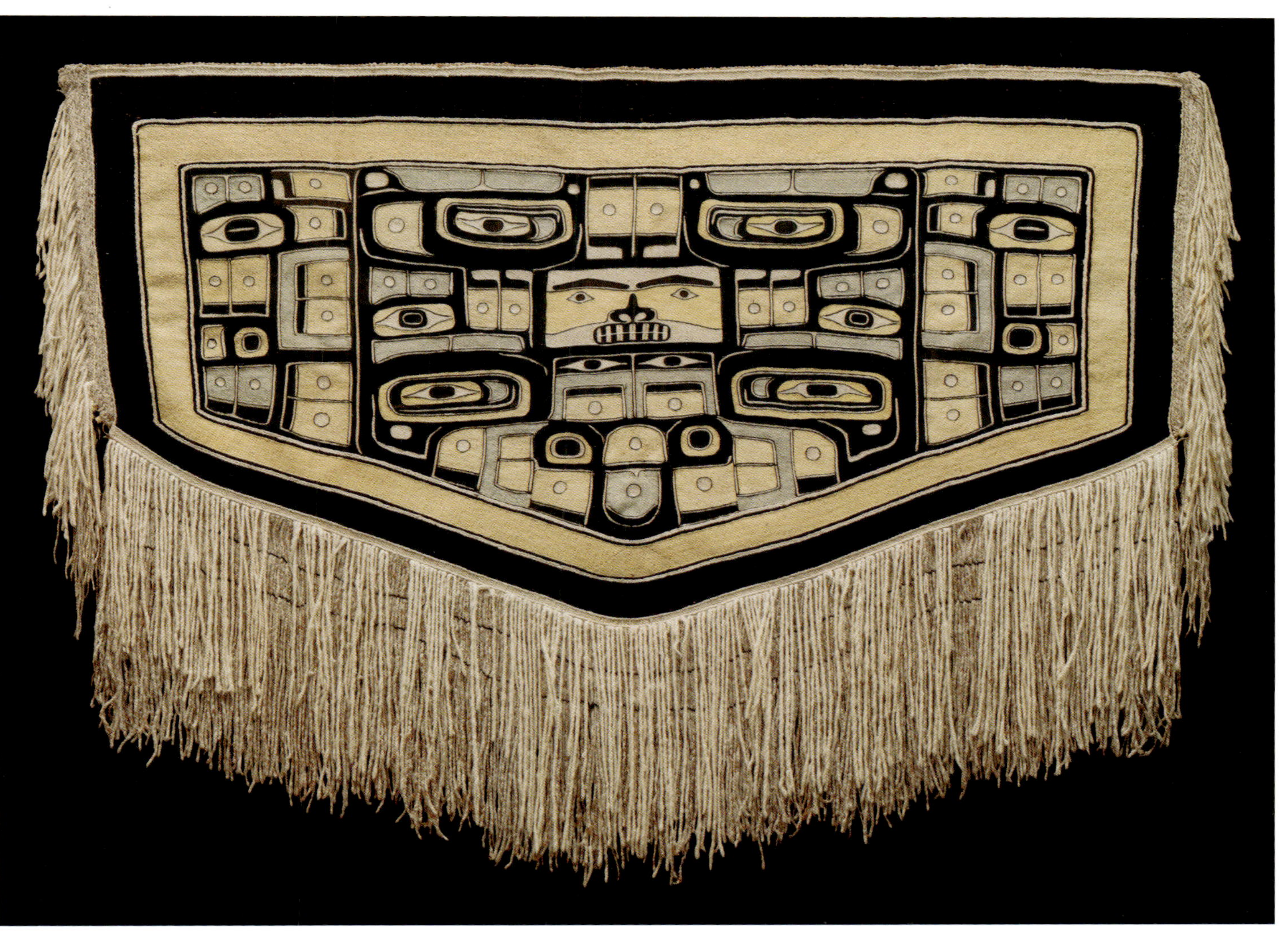

facing
Tsimshian Artist
Chest 19th century

above
Tlingit Artist
Chilkat Blanket c. 1870s

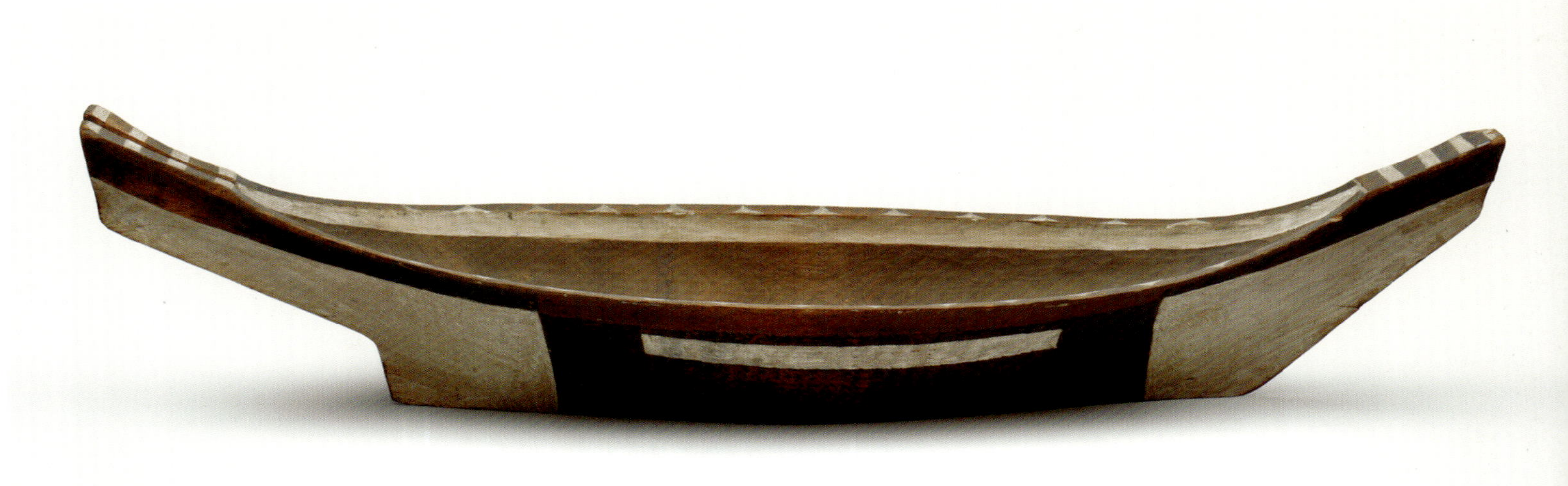

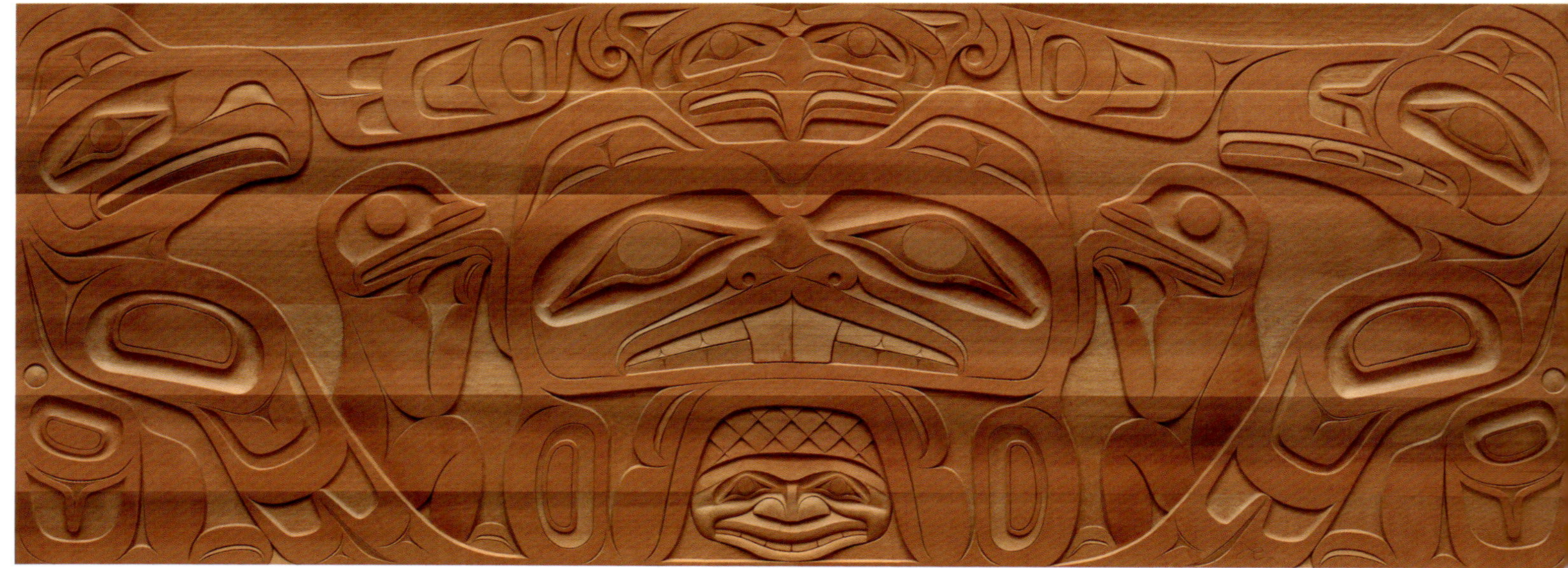

above, top

Unknown First Nations Artist (Haida?)

Canoe Form Bowl c. 1880

above, bottom

Larry Rosso

Beaver with Two Frogs Eagle, Raven and Thunderbird 1997

facing

Charlie James

Sun Mask late 19th–early 20th century

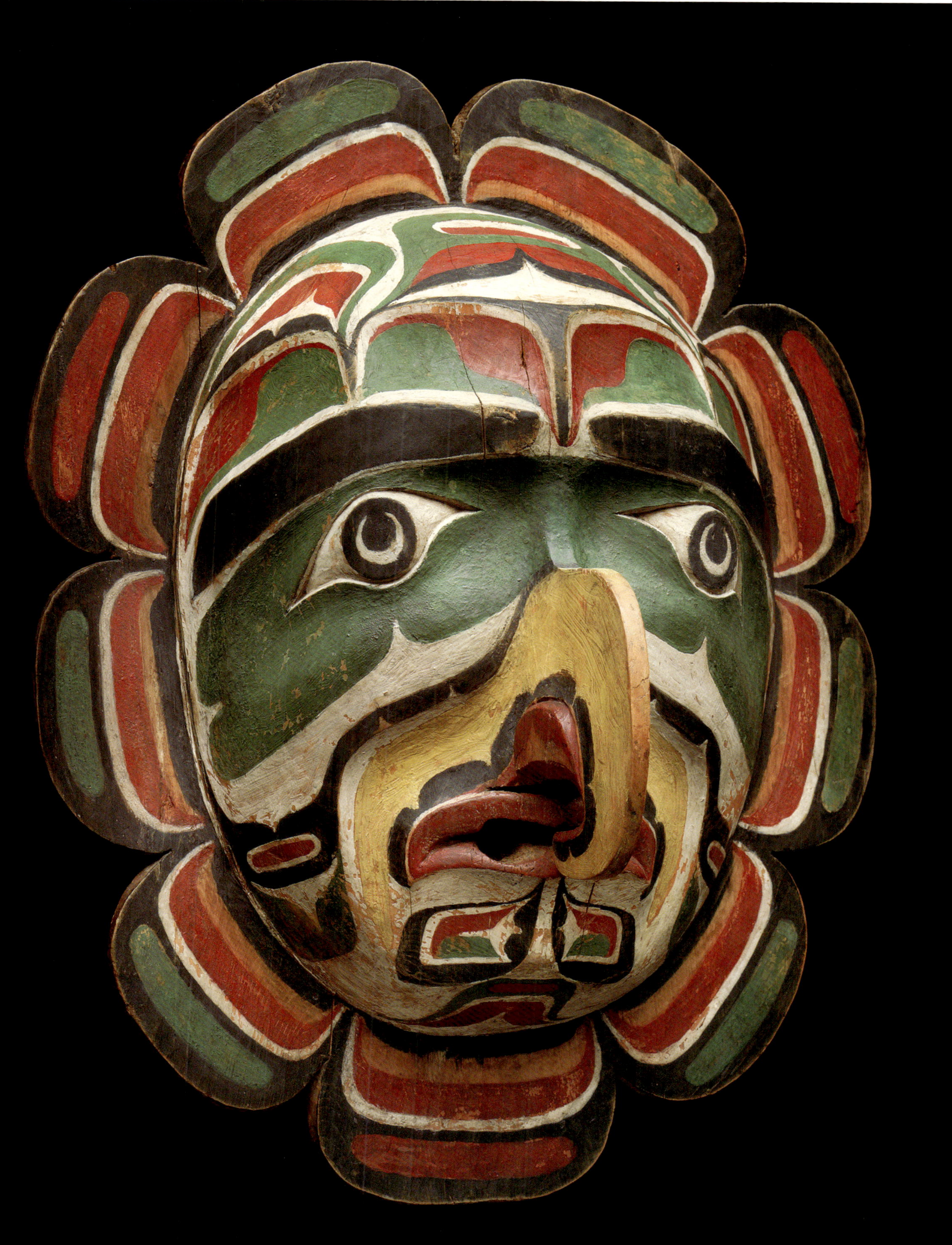

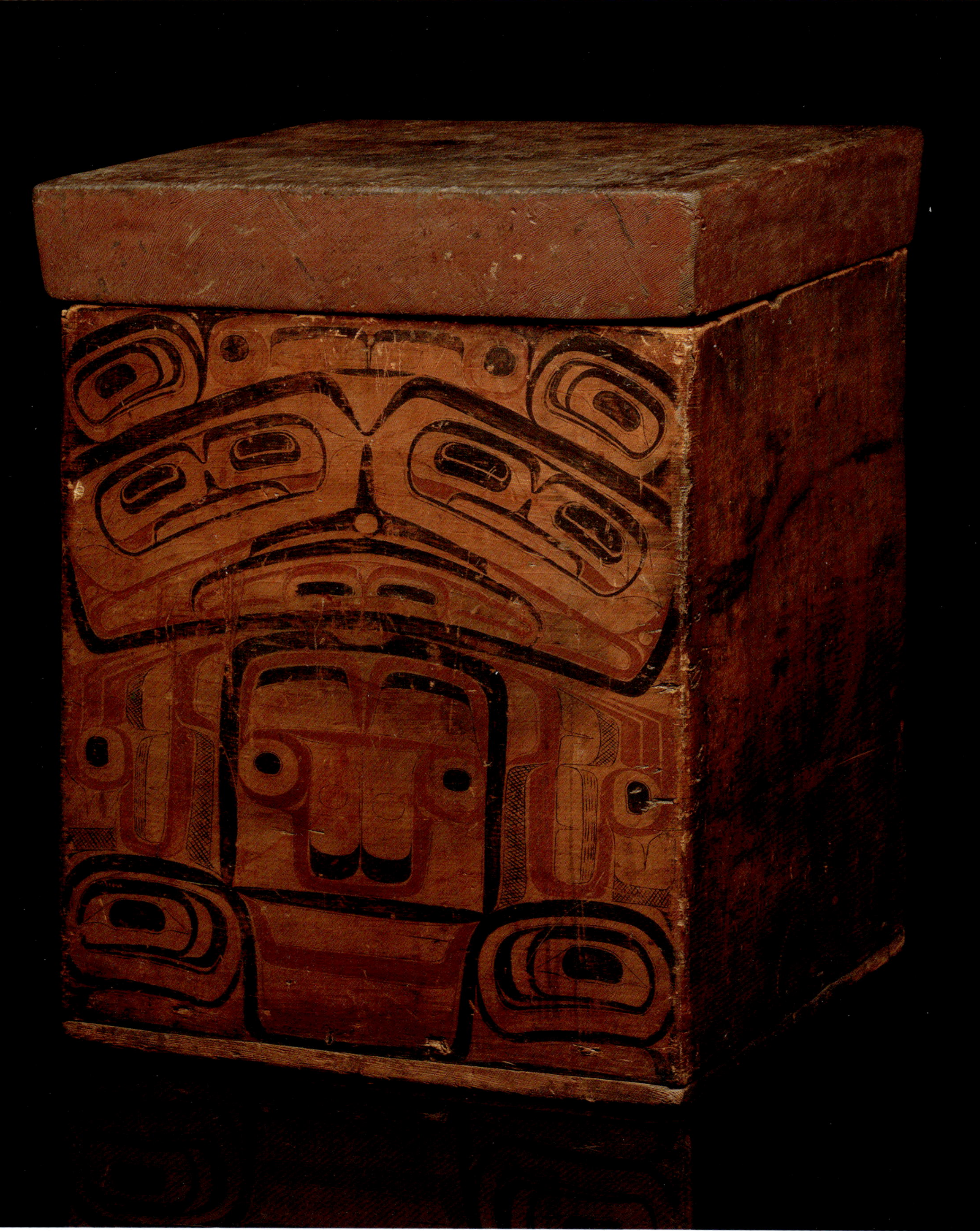

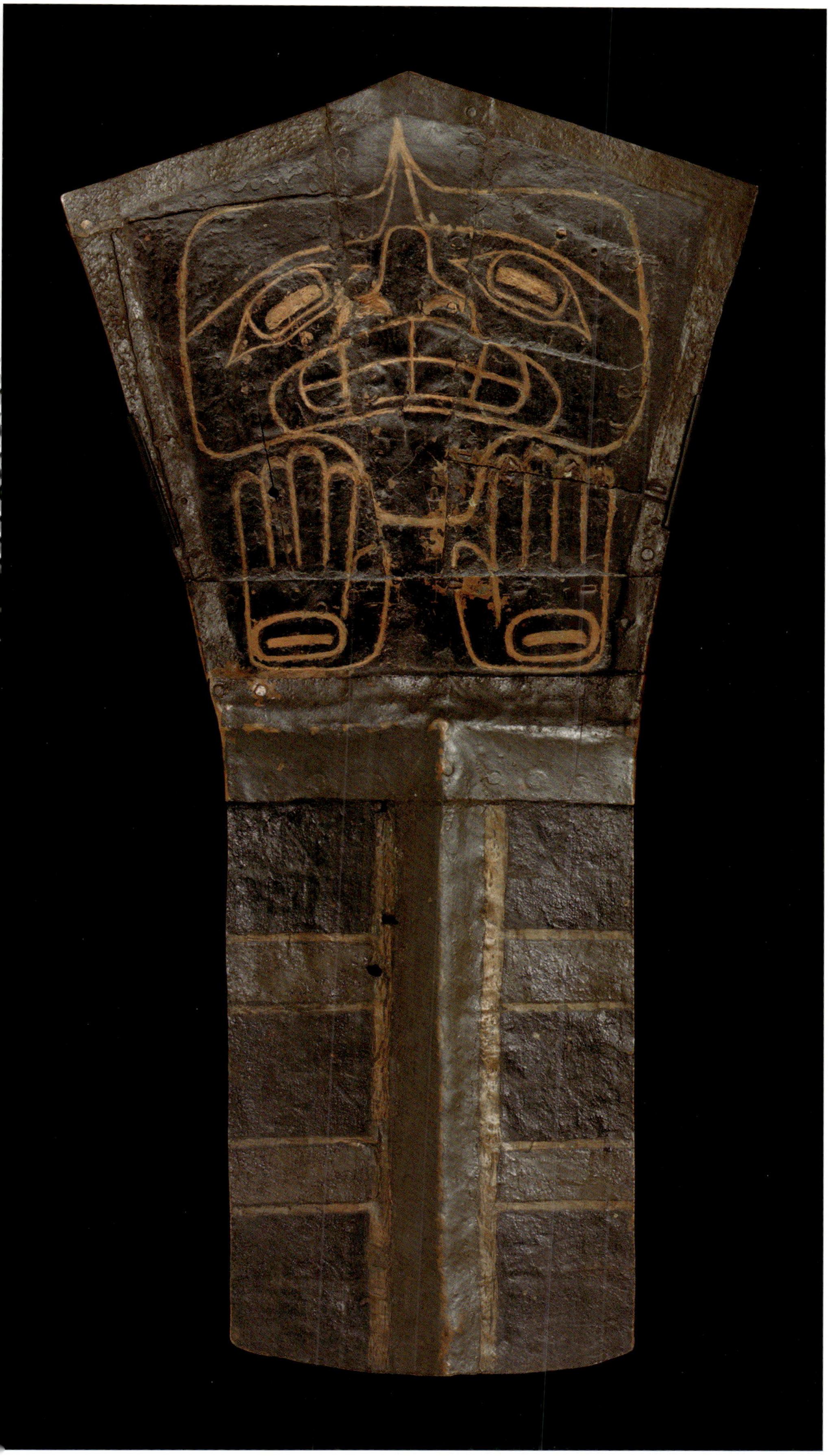

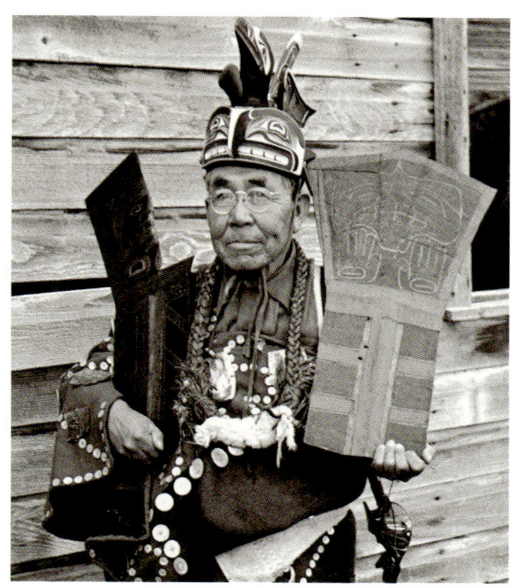

facing

Unknown First Nations Artist
Bent Wood Box and Lid
19th century

left

Unknown First Nations Artist
Copper (belonging to Willie Seaweed) 18th century

above

Ba'a's [Blunden Harbour], Chief Willie Seaweed holding two coppers May 1955

Photo: Wilson Duff. Courtesy of Royal BC Museum · PN 02300-B

right

Richard Hunt

Totem Pole 2003

facing

Art Thompson

Killer Whale Moon Mask

c. 1997

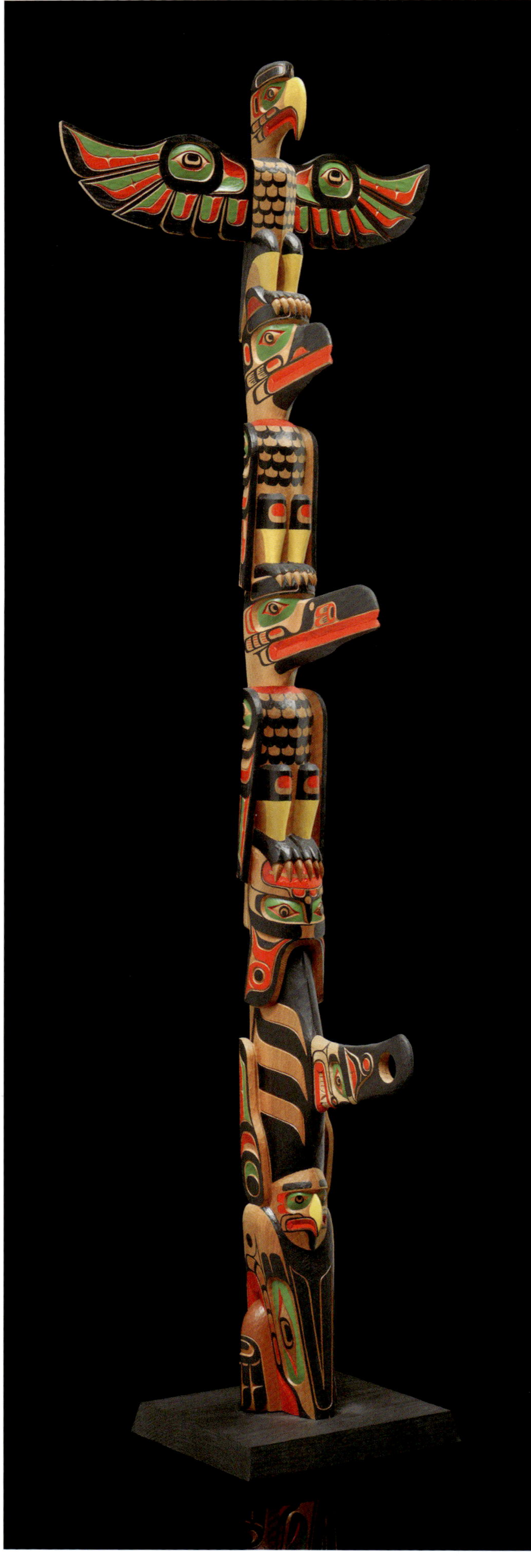

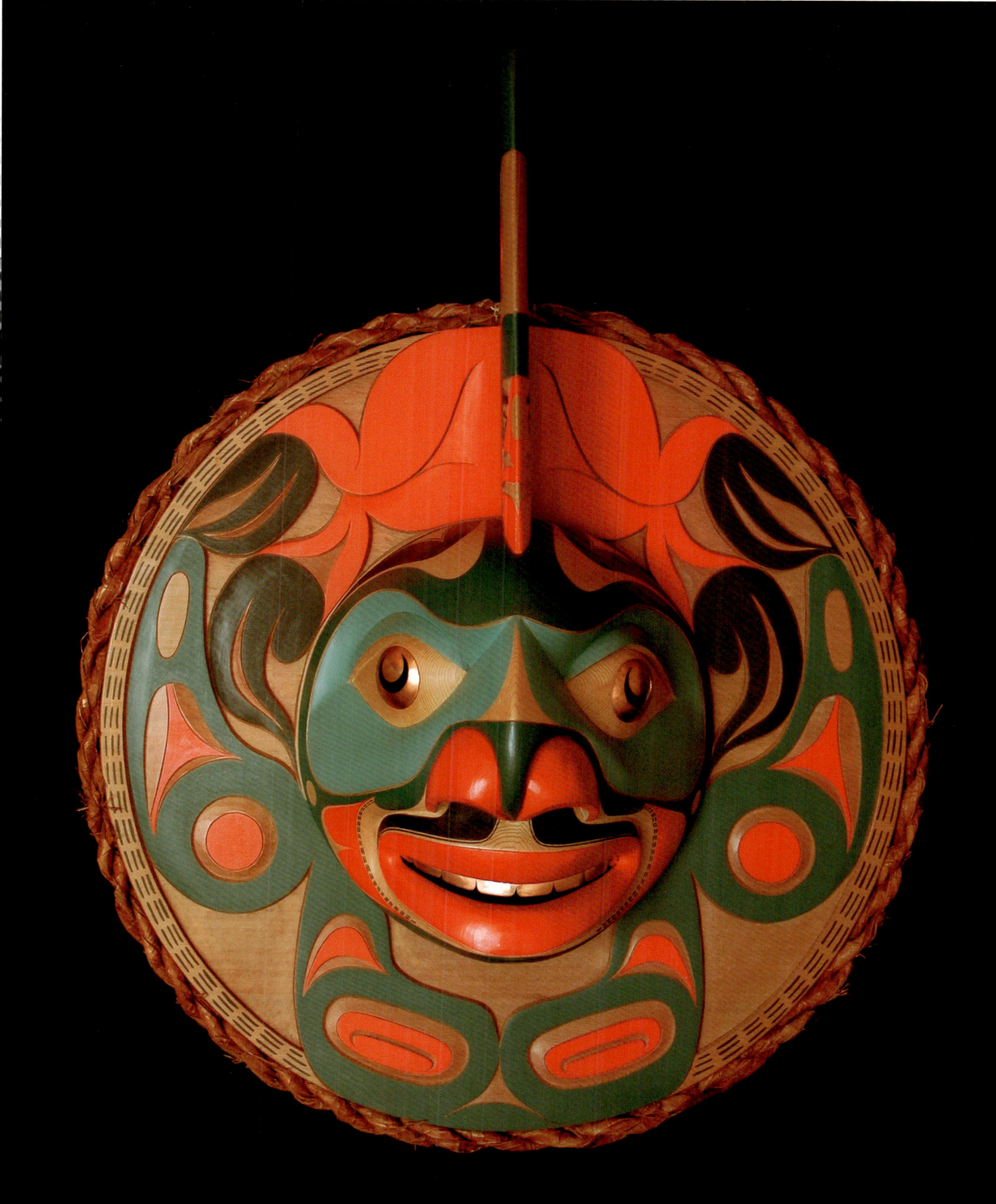

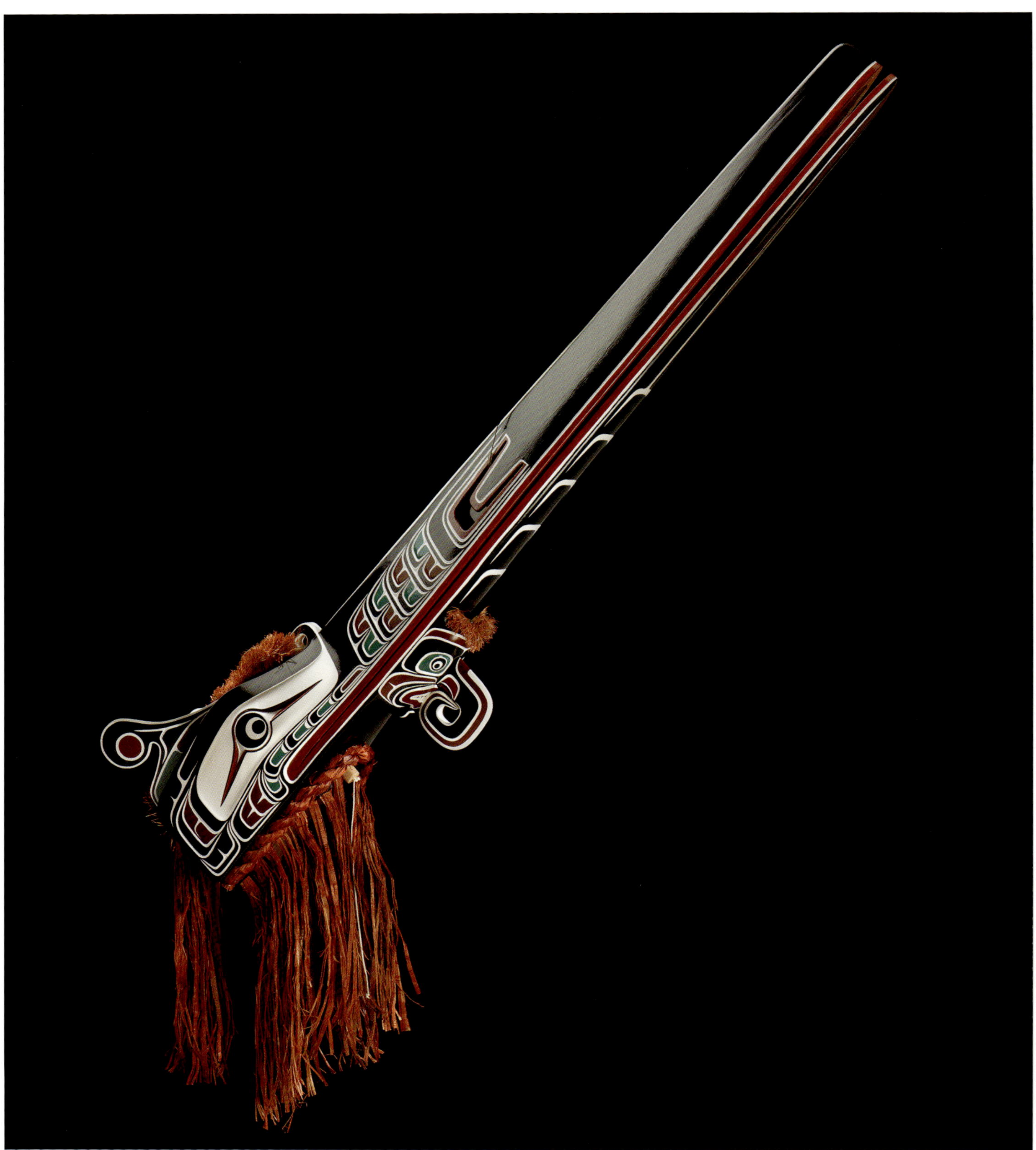

above

Henry Speck, Jr.

Hok Hok Headdress 2004

facing

Tony Hunt, Jr.

Tsonokwa Mask 2006

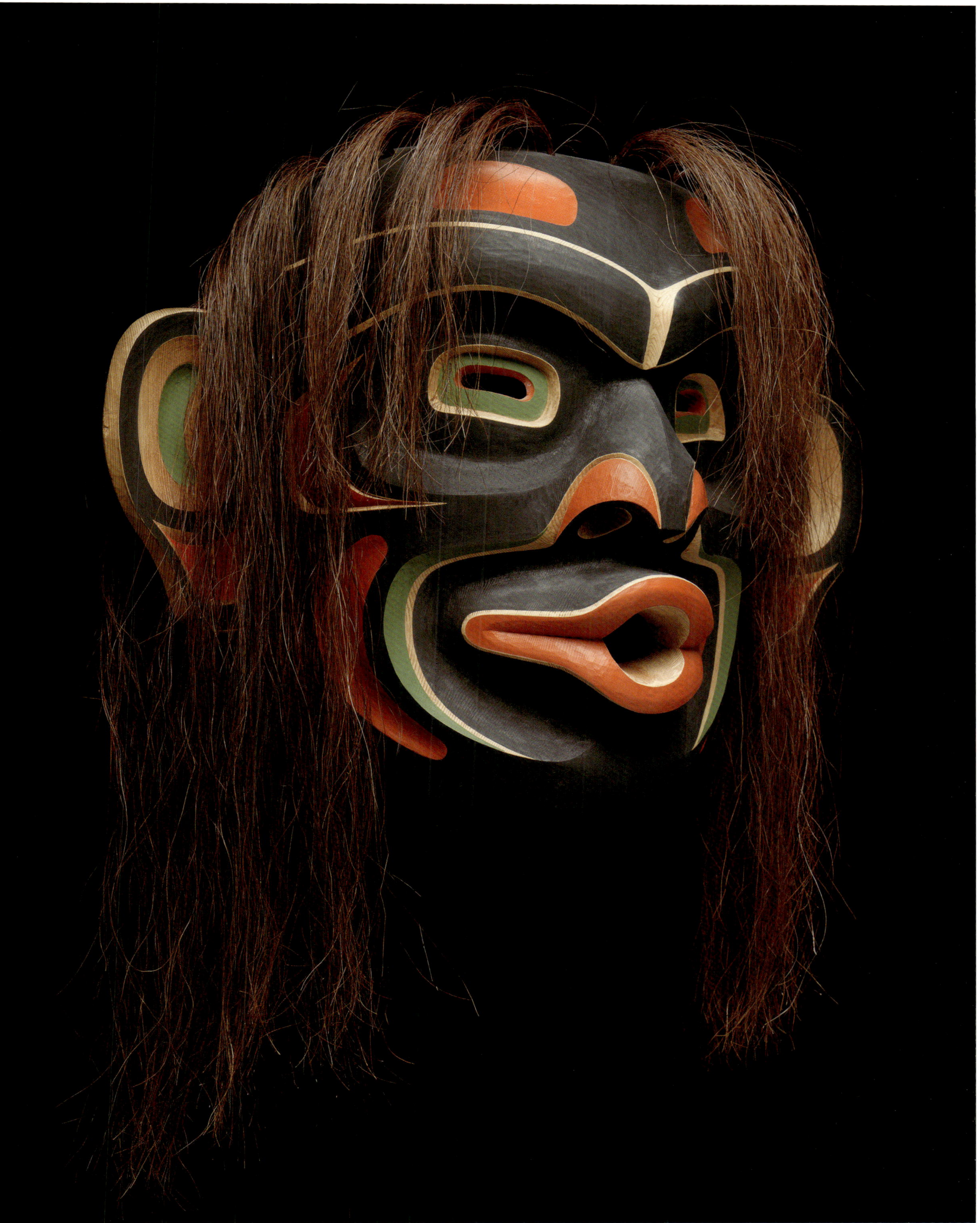

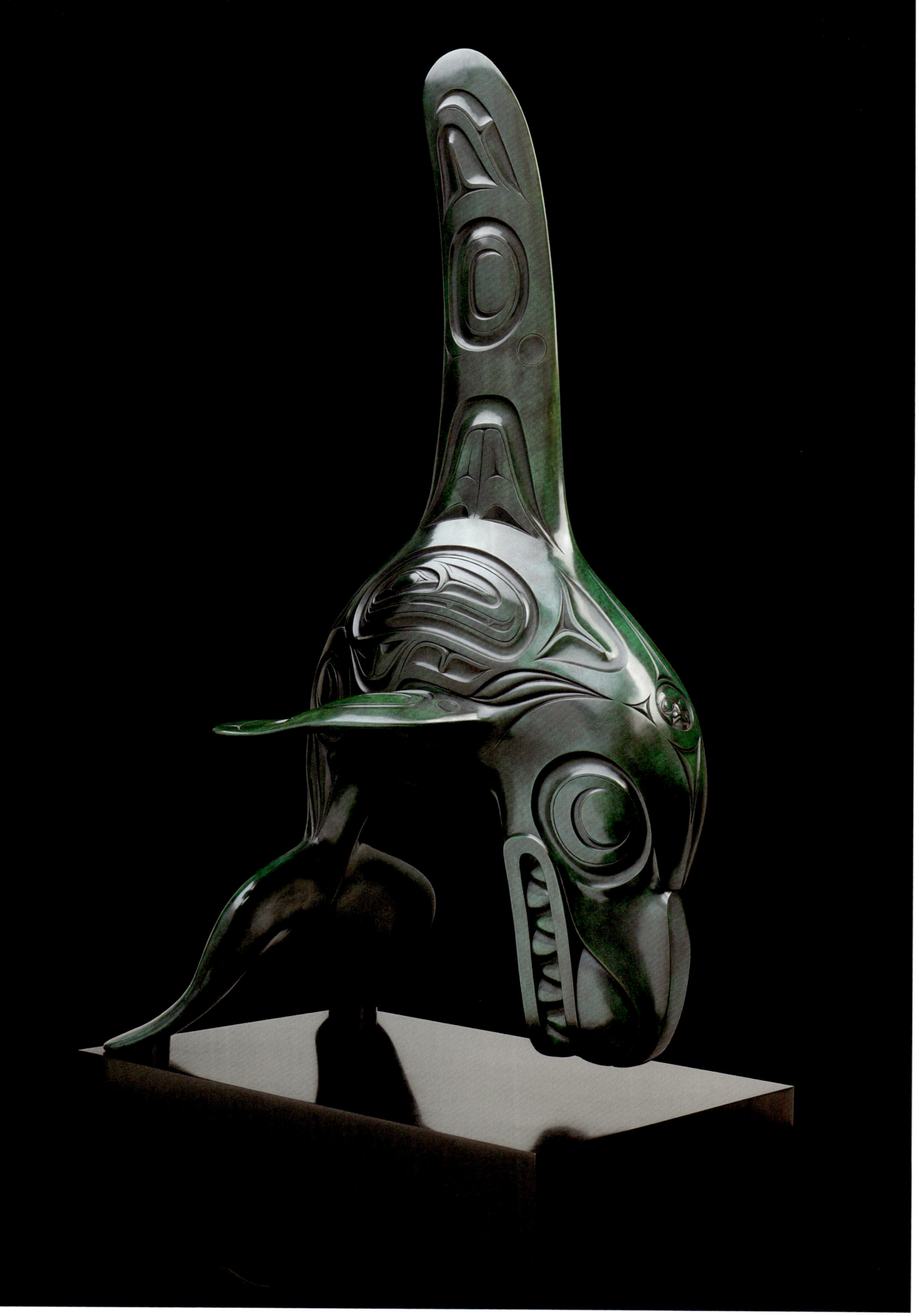

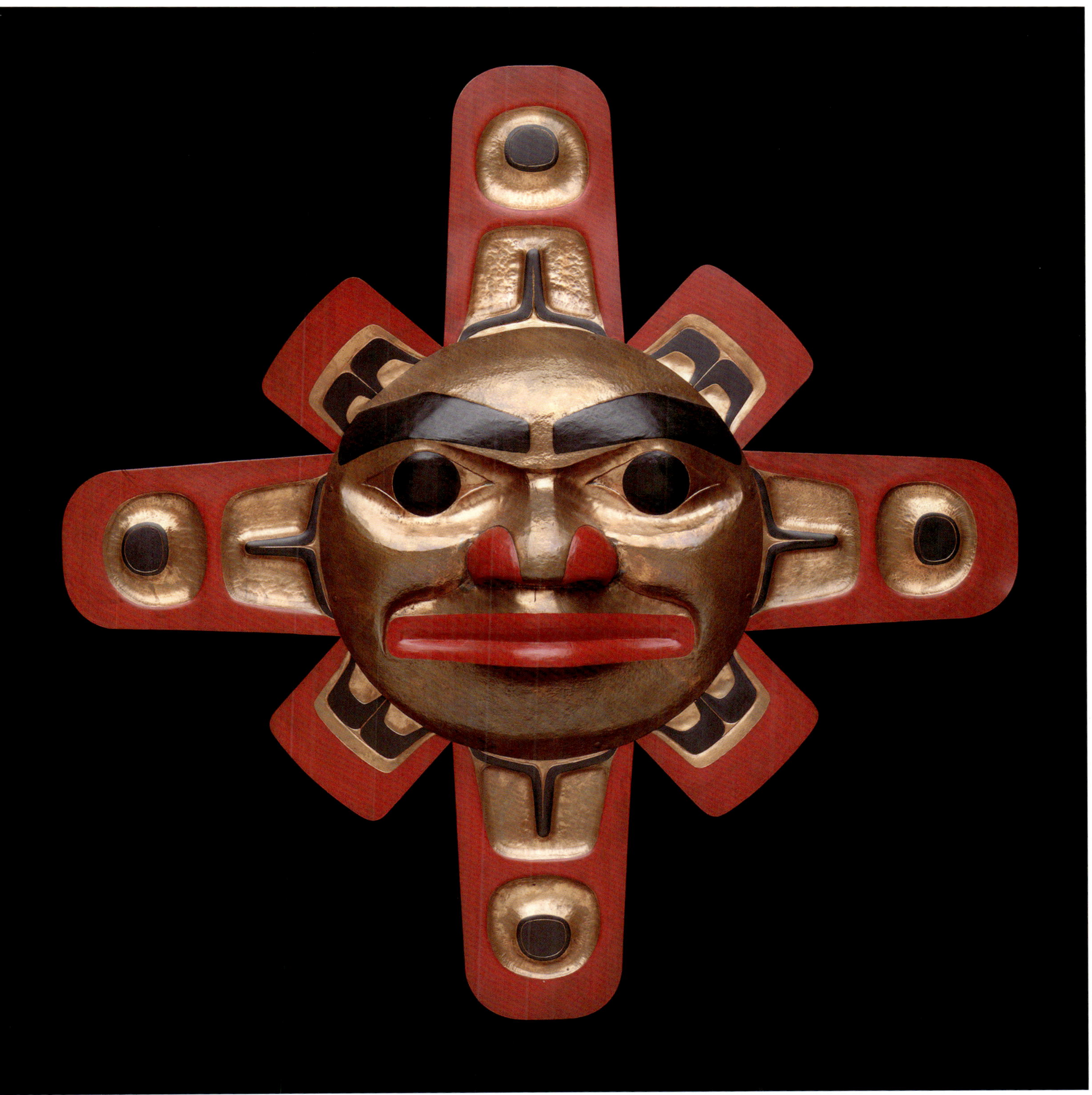

facing
Bill Reid
Killer Whale 1984

above
Philip Janze
Sun Mask 1986

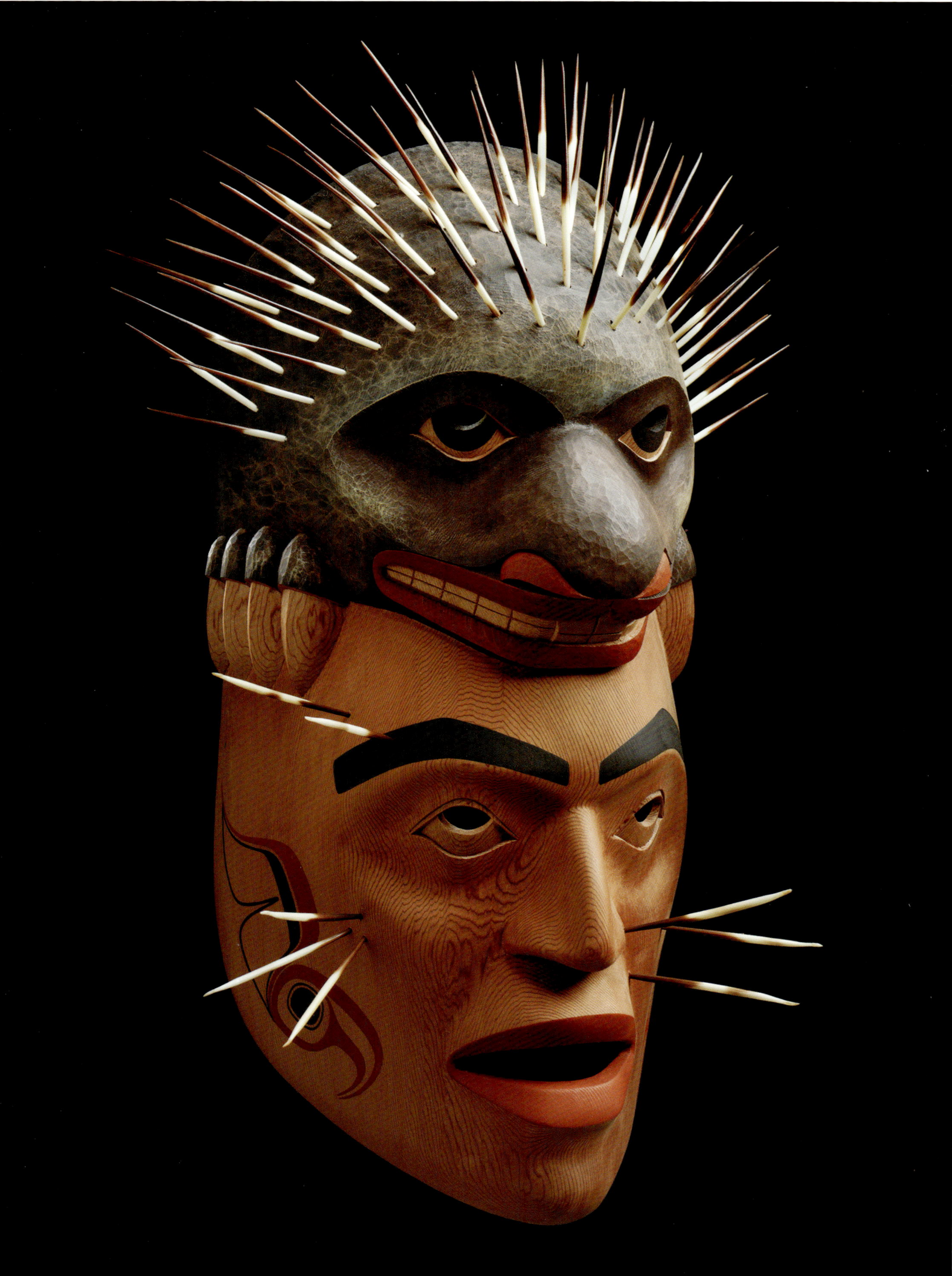

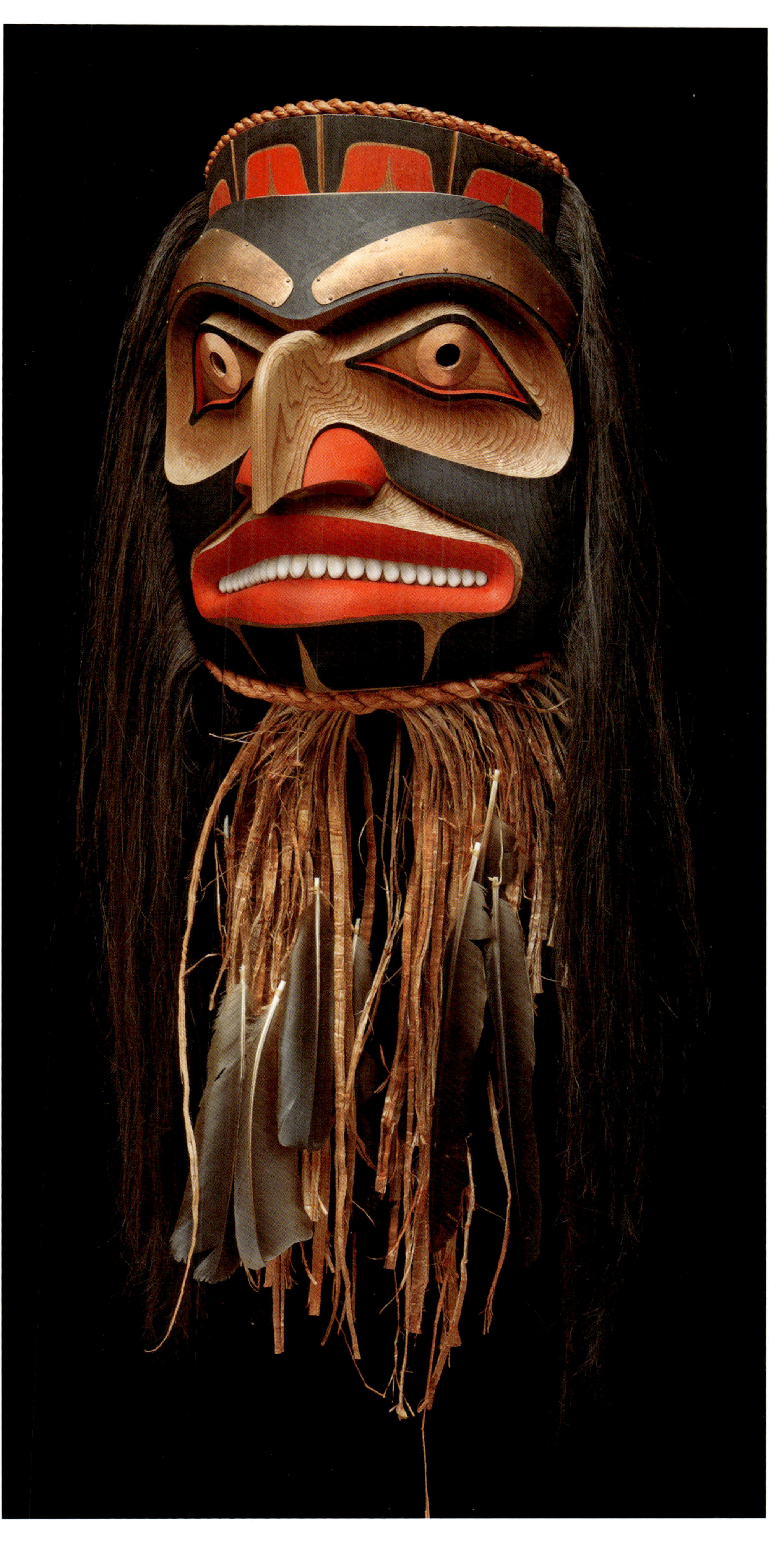

facing

Philip Gray

Porcupine Hunter Mask 2010

left

Robert Davidson

Raven's Tail Mask 1992

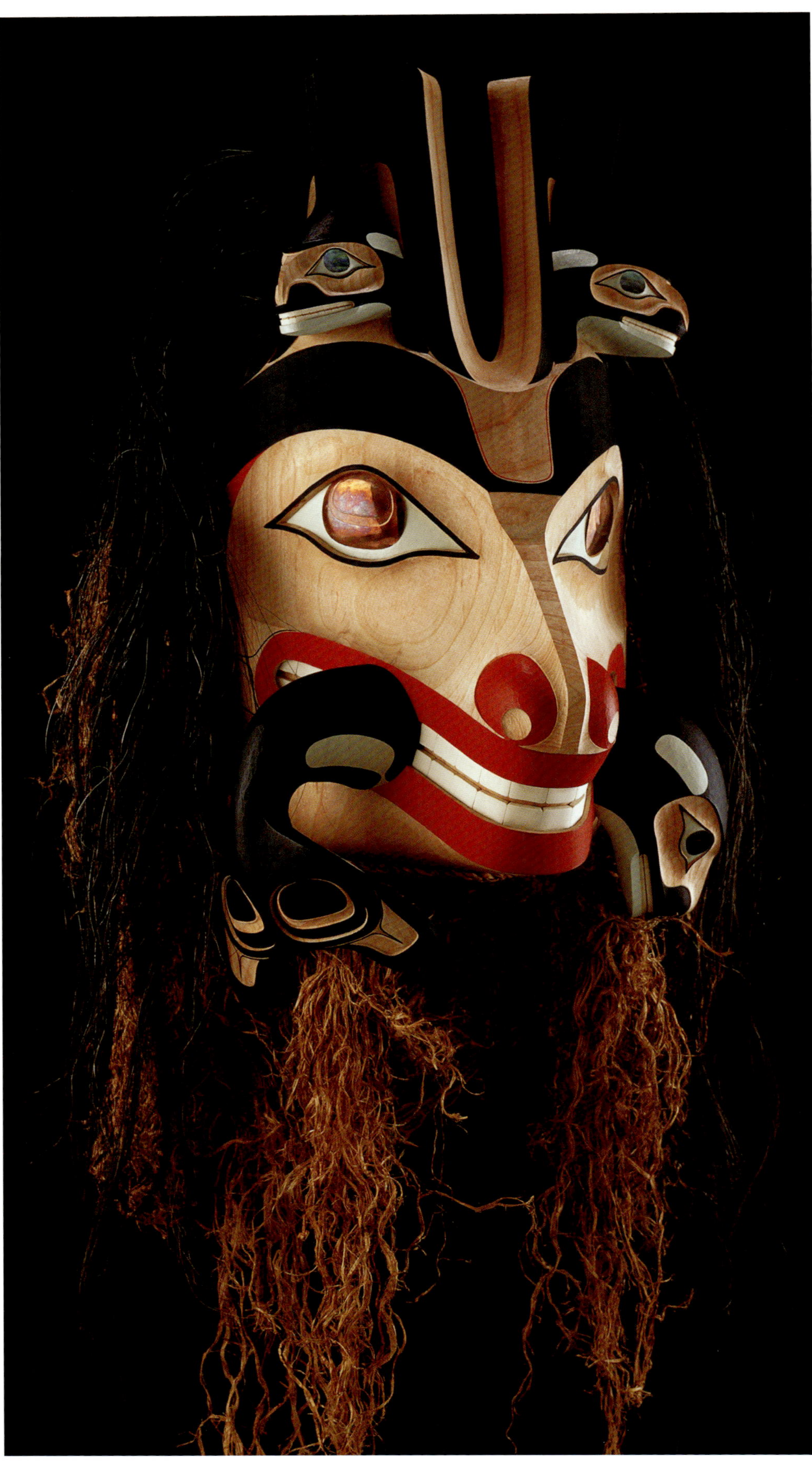

right
Jay Simeon
Seawolf and Killer Whale Mask 2008

facing
Dean Hunt
PK'vs: Wild Man of the Woods 2009

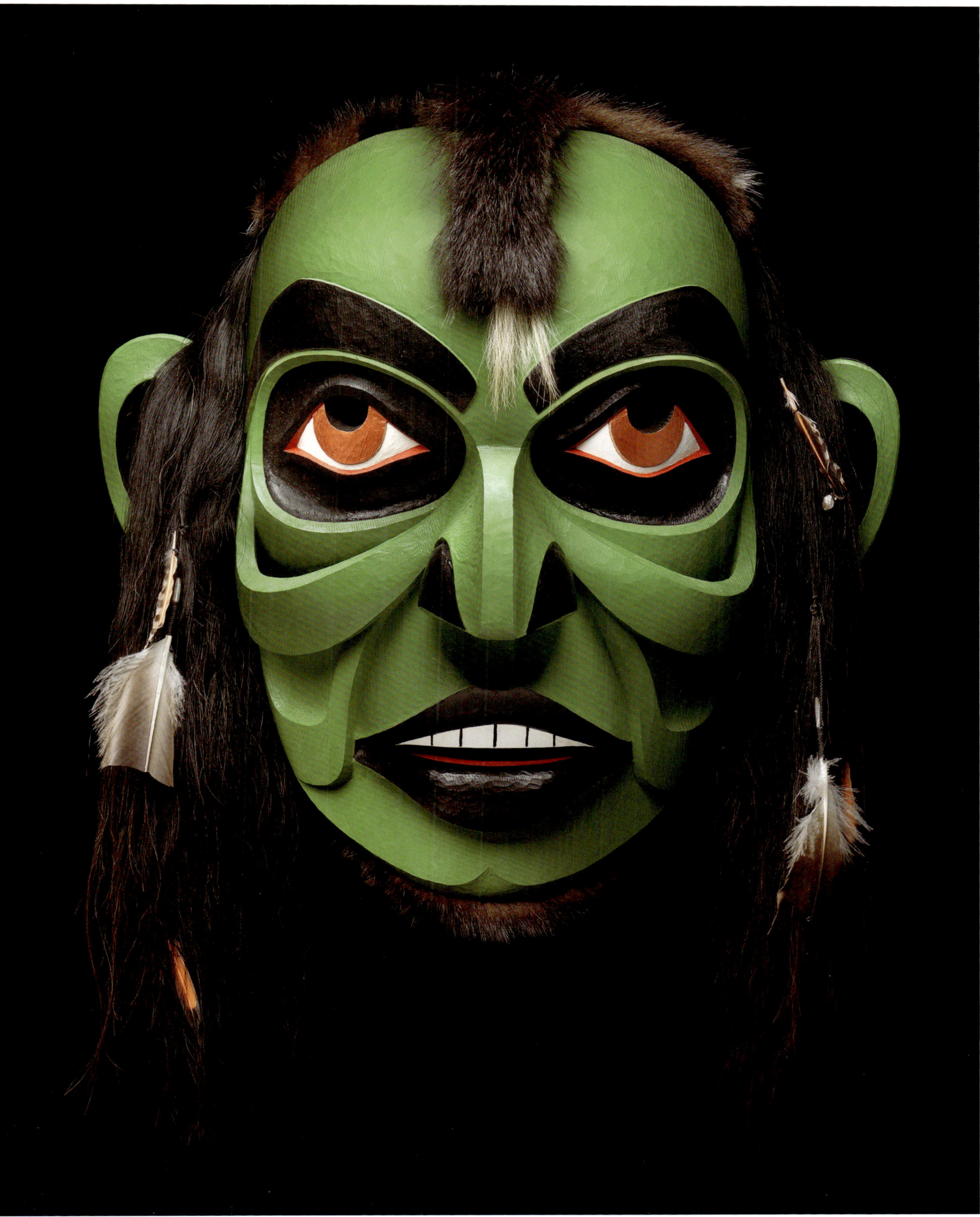

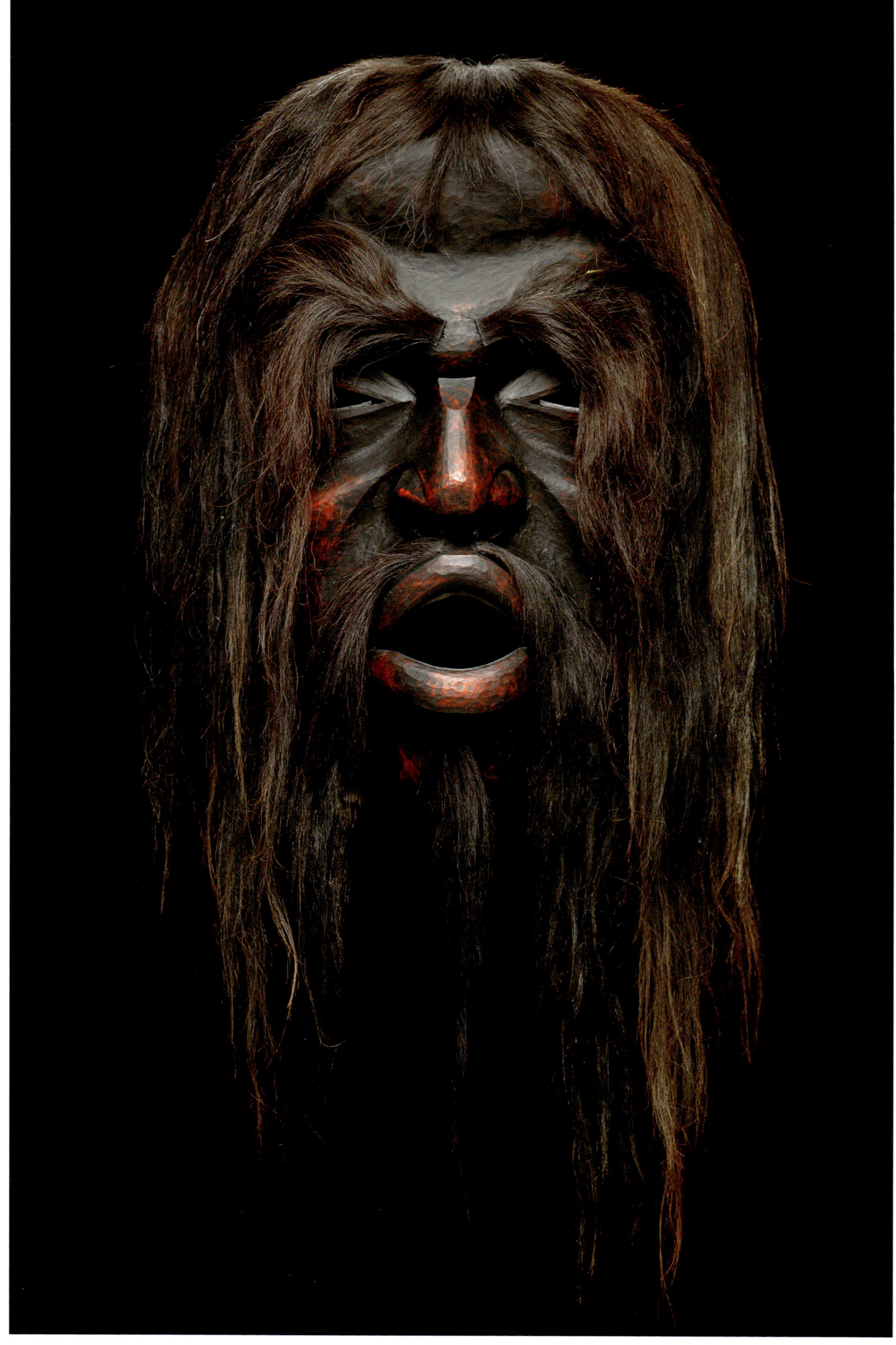

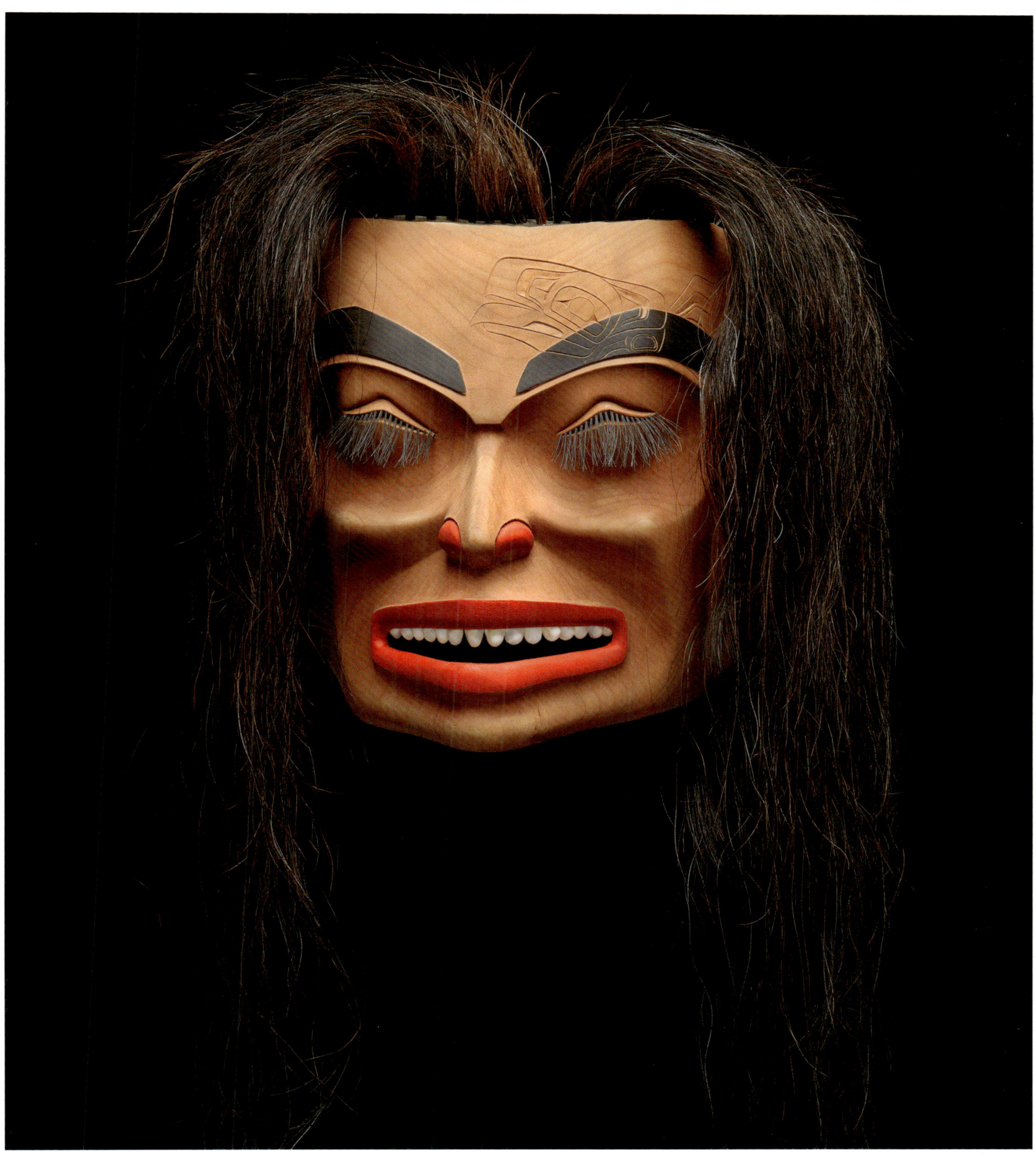

facing
Beau Dick
Tsonokwa Mask 2007

above
Norman Tait
Mischievous Man Mask 2008

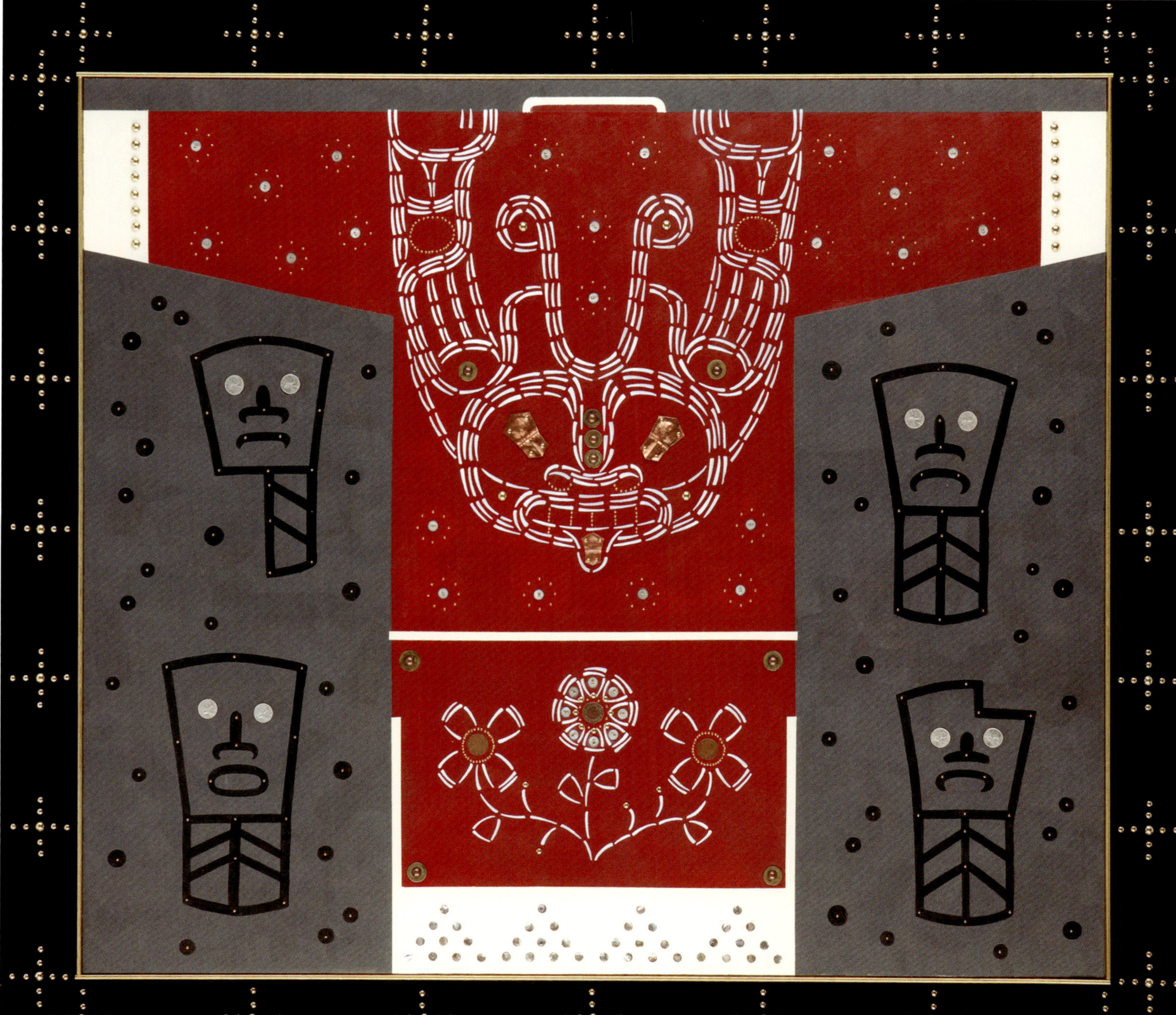

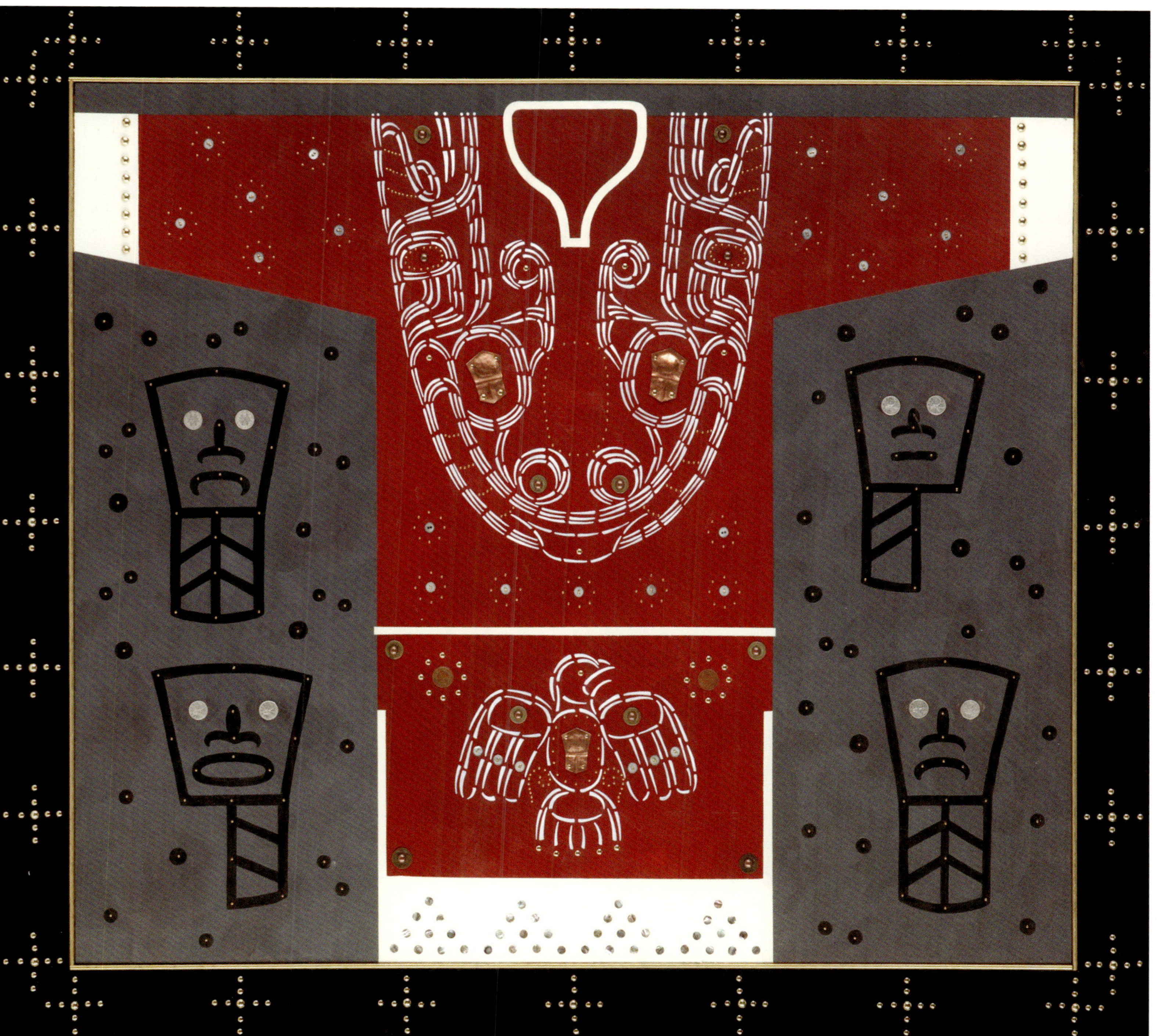

Marianne Nicolson
Tunic for a Noblewoman:
In Memory of
Wadzidalaga 2009

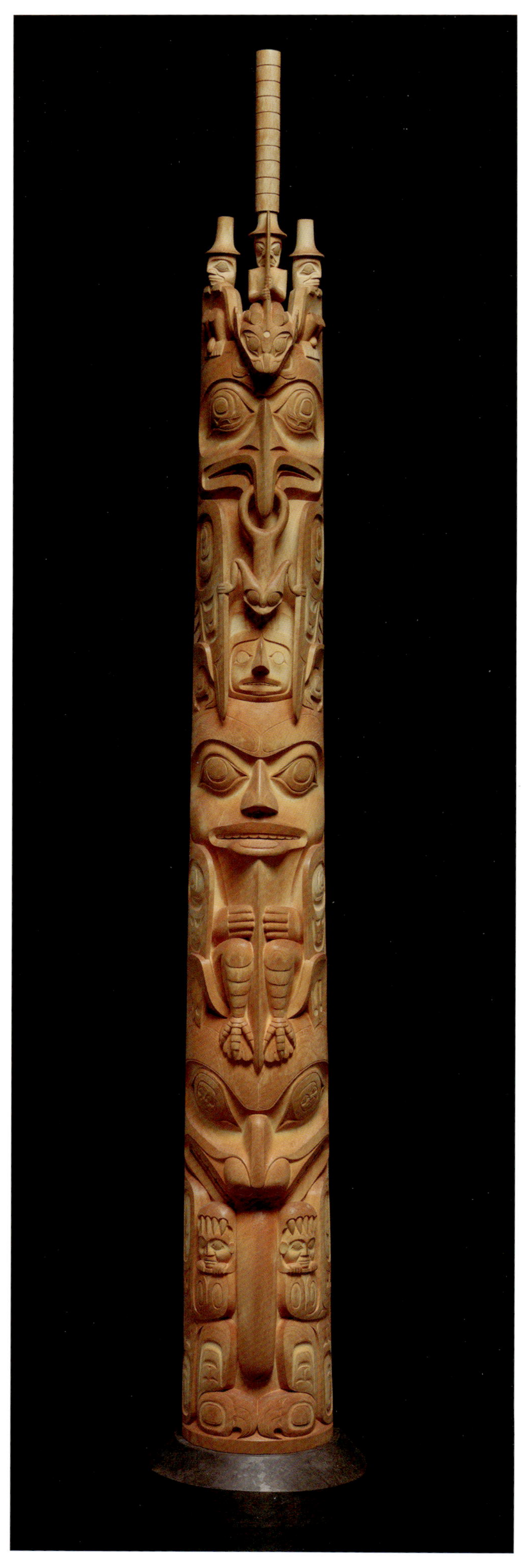

Jim Hart
Model Pole 2006–09

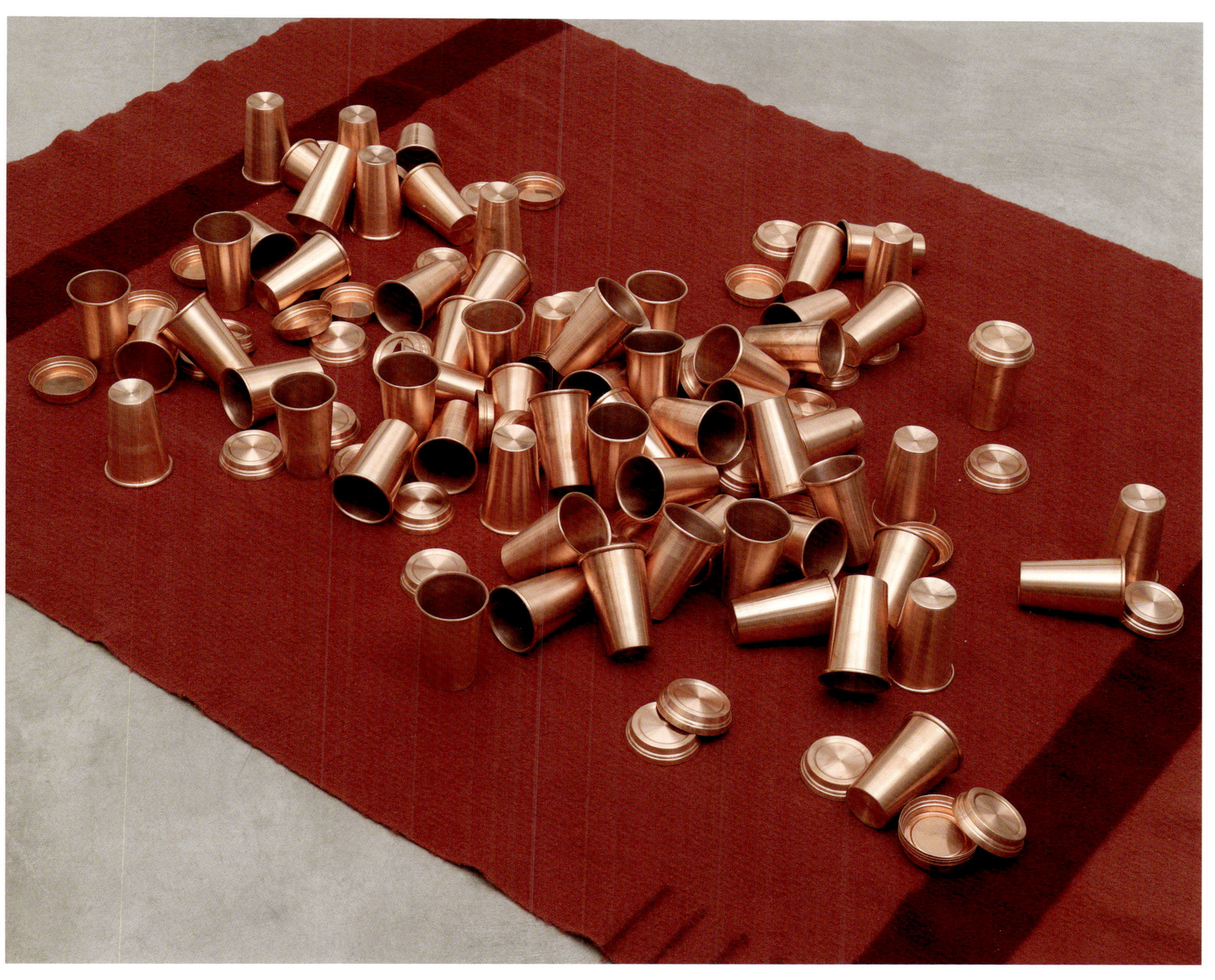

Sonny Assu
1884–1951 2009

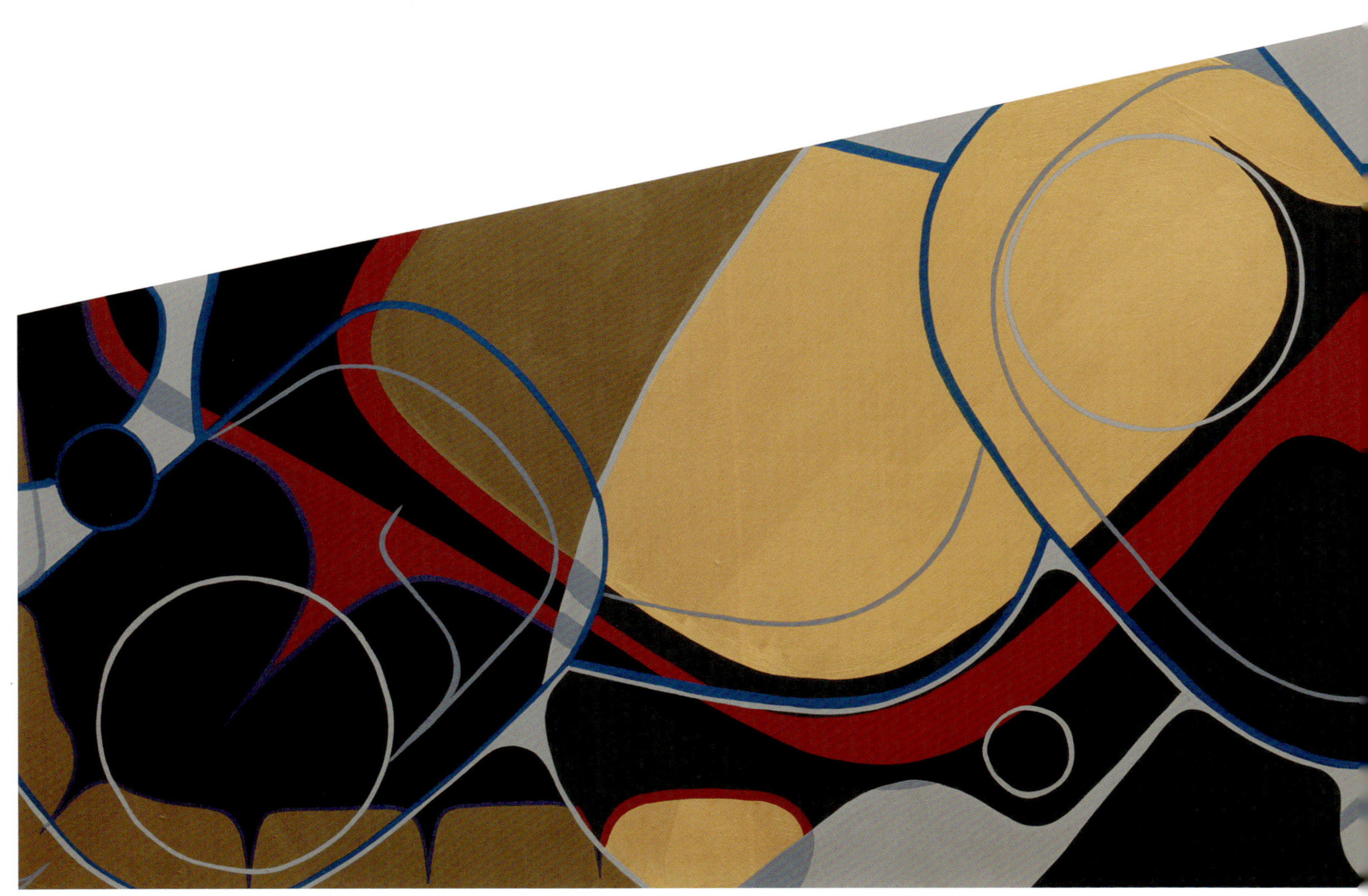

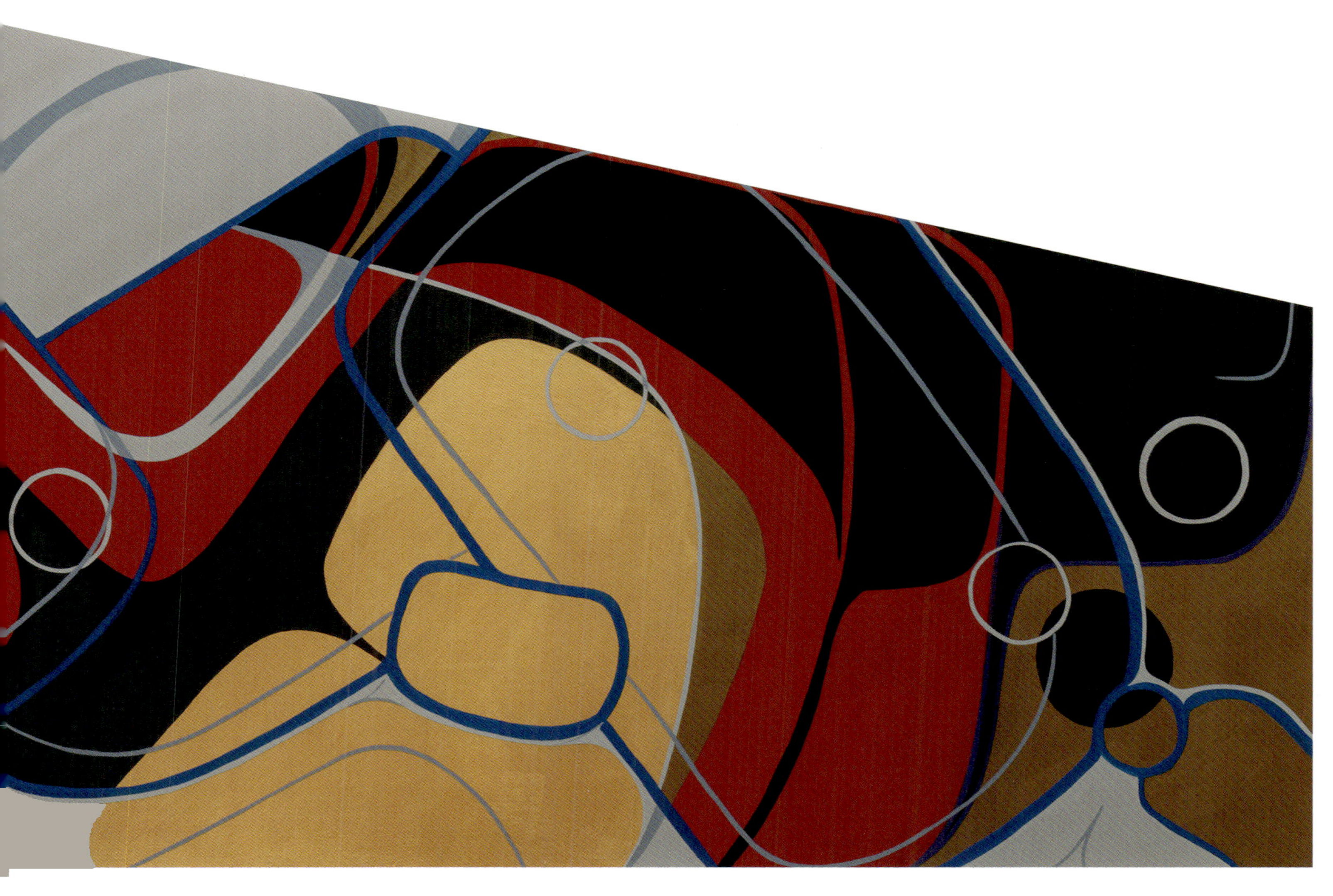

Sonny Assu
Dialect 2010

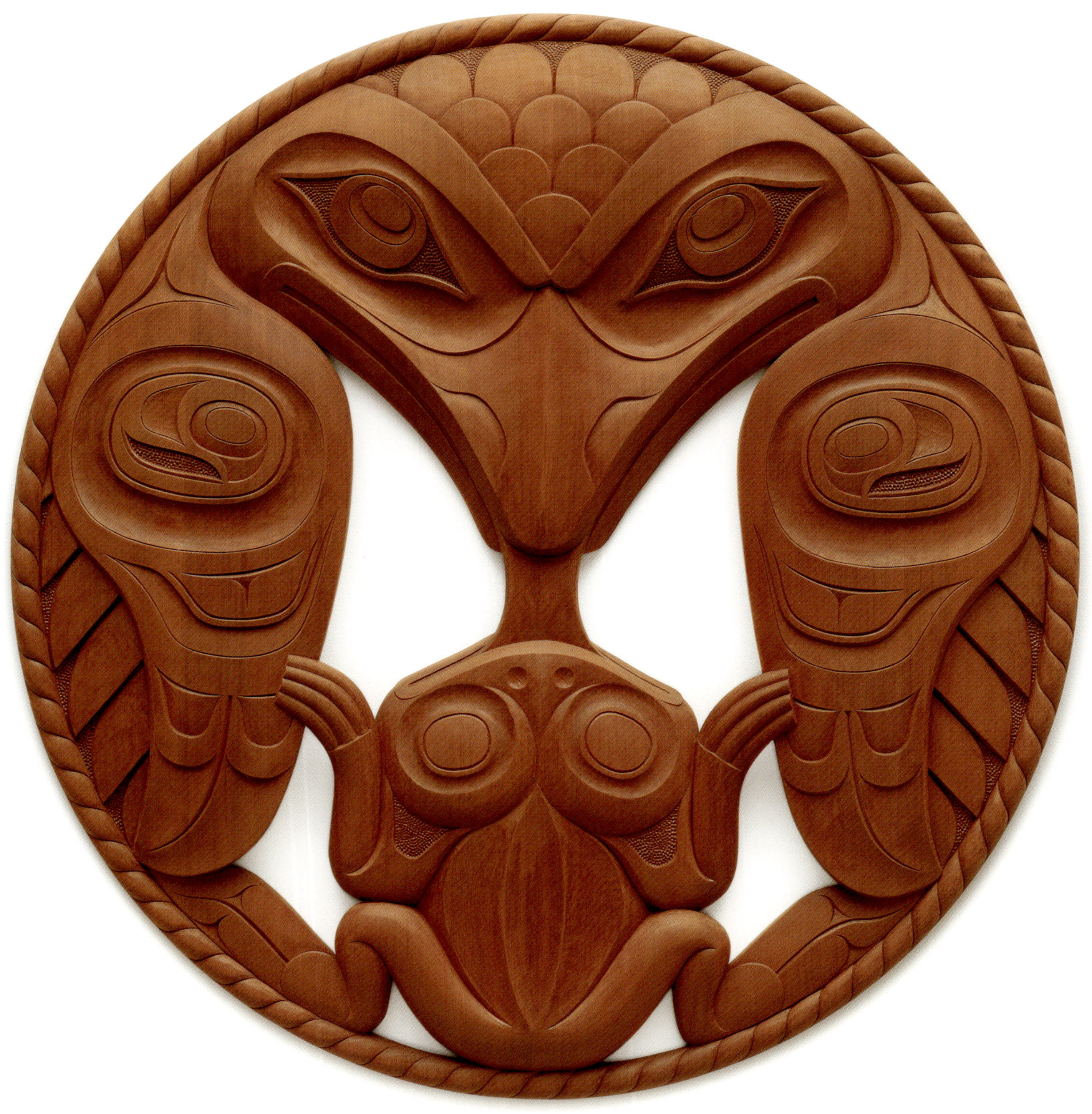

above

Don Yeomans

Raven and Frog

Panel 2006–07

facing

Brian Jungen

Variant 1

2002

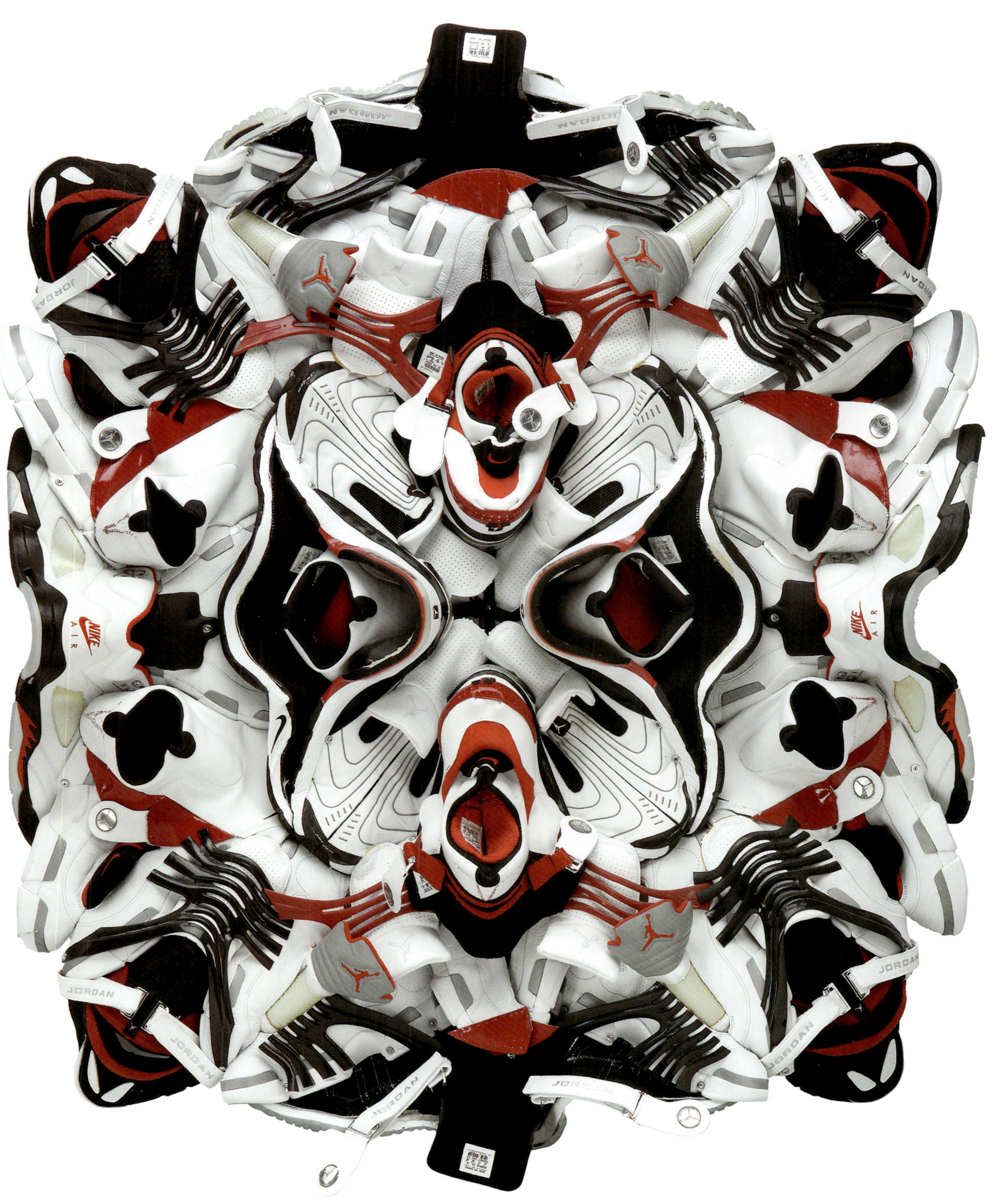
JORDAN
JORDAN
JORDAN
NIKE AIR
NIKE AIR
JORDAN
JORDAN
JORDAN

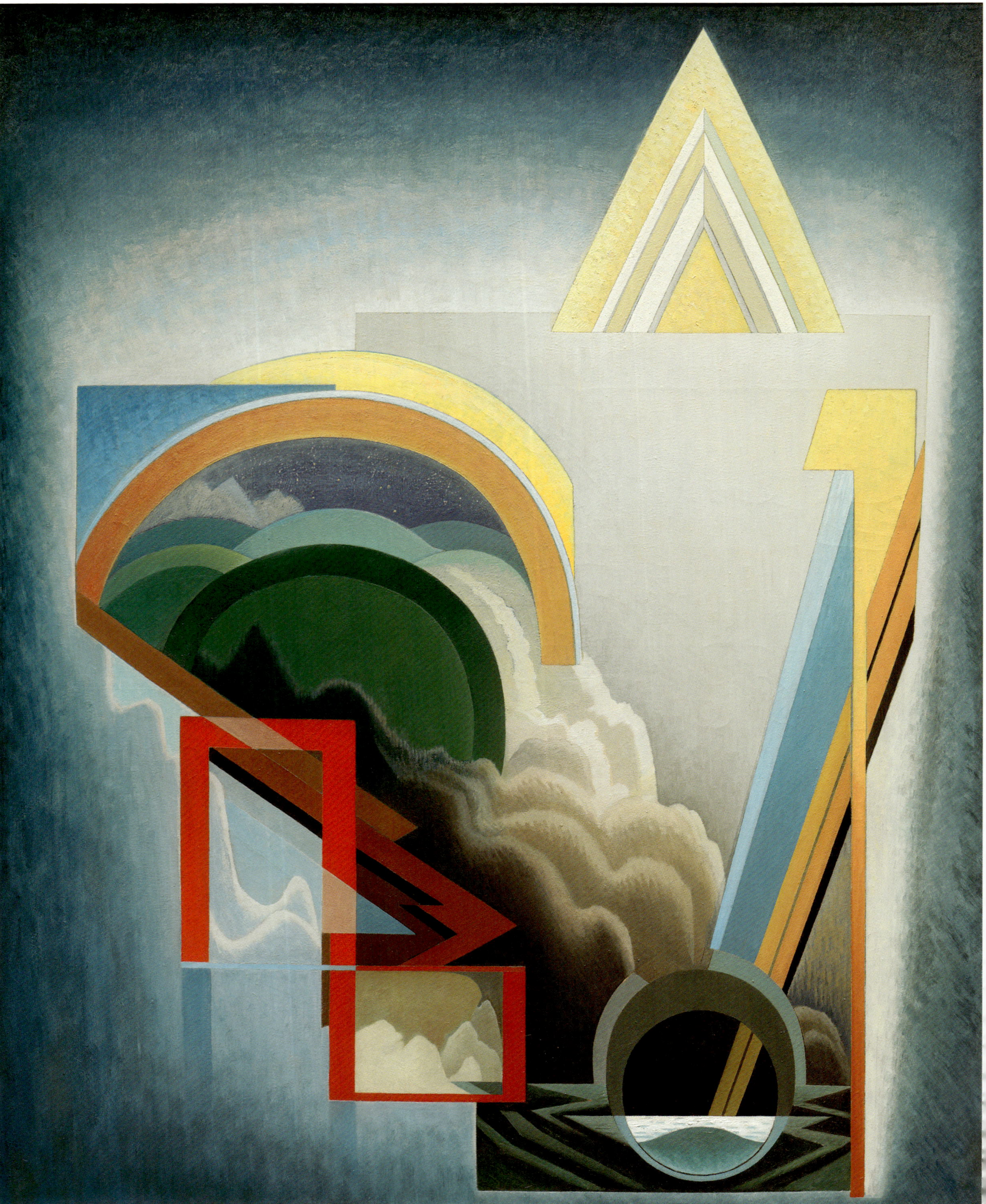

LEGACY

LAWREN HARRIS AND MODERNIST PAINTING IN BRITISH COLUMBIA

IAN THOM

ALTHOUGH THE HISTORY of Modernist painting in British Columbia is complex and varied, with figures such as Emily Carr, Frederick Varley and Jock Macdonald all playing their part, there is little doubt that Lawren Harris was a figure of primary importance. One of the original members of the Group of Seven, Harris was a passionate believer in the power of abstract art to express the truths of the human spirit and imagination. His friendship with Emily Carr, which began when they met in 1927, was pivotal to her progress as a painter. His advice as laid out in their long correspondence, which Carr saved and clearly valued, provides fascinating glimpses into her struggles, both spiritual and pictorial. Harris did not arrive in B.C. until 1940, but he remained a life-long champion of her work, playing a key role in establishing the strong Emily Carr collection that is now one of the treasures of the Vancouver Art Gallery. His own work, both the earlier landscapes and his later abstractions, was a significant catalyst for the Modernist visions that flourished within this province.

Harris's paintings reflect his aesthetic, spiritual and philosophical beliefs. Although *Abstraction,* c. 1945 (page 86), was painted as the Second World War was ending, it barely hints at the turmoil of that time. Interestingly, in this ambitious work there are scant reminders of his early interest in the landscape; he is more concerned with creating a complex composition that at once confirms and denies illusory space.

Harris had no direct followers among the artists of British Columbia but he was a keen supporter of the efforts of the next generation. In his role as a trustee of the Estate of Emily Carr, he awarded scholarships to artists such as E.J. Hughes and Takao Tanabe that enabled them to travel and further their careers. He was also a key figure in the life of the Vancouver Art Gallery and encouraged the work of B.C. Binning, Gordon Smith and many others. At a time of minimal support for the visual arts in this province, he helped to place works by several of these artists in both private and public collections.

Bertram Charles (B.C.) Binning, a dedicated Modernist who began to paint seriously in 1947–48, was a unique figure in B.C. history. An important teacher, he founded the Fine Arts Department (now Art History, Visual Art, and Theory) at the University of British Columbia as well as its art gallery (now the Morris and Helen Belkin Art

facing
Lawren Stewart Harris
Abstraction c. 1945

Gallery). His own work, which shows his dedication to form and design, is also marked by a keen colour sense and a love of the nautical life of the coast. *Triptych of Nautical Symbols,* 1956 (page 89), in which he transforms the inspiration of Renaissance art altarpieces into a contemporary work, reveals him at his best. The fact that these works remain engaging more than fifty years after they were painted demonstrates his impressive command of composition. Like his friend and colleague Lawren Harris, Binning's international view of the world influenced the careers of many younger artists and architects by encouraging them to look to Japan, the United States and Europe for inspiration.

Another respected artist who became a significant teacher at the Vancouver School of Art (now Emily Carr University of Art and Design) was Jack Shadbolt. His work represents a more expressive strain of Modernism than the work of either the elder statesman Harris or his contemporary Binning. In many ways, Shadbolt was an iconoclast who sought to assert his independence from B.C.'s two dominant artistic figures, Carr and Harris. Inflected by many of the major threads of twentieth-century art—the influence of Pablo Picasso and the Mexican muralists, to name only two—much of his work nevertheless remains connected to the natural world. Fascinated by ideas of transformation, Shadbolt intensively studied the masks of First Nations people and examined life and death cycles in nature, often expressing this interest through images of butterflies. *Butterfly Transformation Theme 1981* (pages 28–29), one of the most important examples of this recurring motif, reveals his skills as a colourist and his complex use of form.

British Columbia painting in the last few decades has been characterized by a wide variety of approaches. This collection includes very fine examples of the work of Claude Breeze, Arabella Campbell, Gathie Falk, Graham Gillmore, Attila Richard Lukacs, Toni Onley, Gordon Smith, Lawrence Paul Yuxweluptun and others, each of whom has produced striking and vivid work through a careful approach to image making. The coolly cerebral balance of Toni Onley's *Juno,* 1962 (page 90), is to a degree defined by the process of its making, something that finds echoes in the work of Arabella Campbell. The astringent narratives of Claude Breeze's work can be related to those of Attila Richard Lukacs and, interestingly, to the equally pungent work of Lawrence Paul Yuxweluptun. The latter three artists engage directly with the social issues of their times whereas Gordon Smith, in *P4,* 1994, and other works, reveals a deep understanding of Modernist ideas and the power of paint yet never loses contact with the wonders of nature. Graham Gillmore addresses language, form and colour in poetic and beautiful works still mindful of the power of formalist composition. Gathie Falk's role in the history of painting in this region is unique; in works such as *22 Apples,* 1997 (page 93), she encourages us to see the world in new and provocative ways.

While none of these images can be directly related to Lawren Harris's work, it was his example and encouragement that fostered the greater freedom of expression that marks the recent painting history of this region.

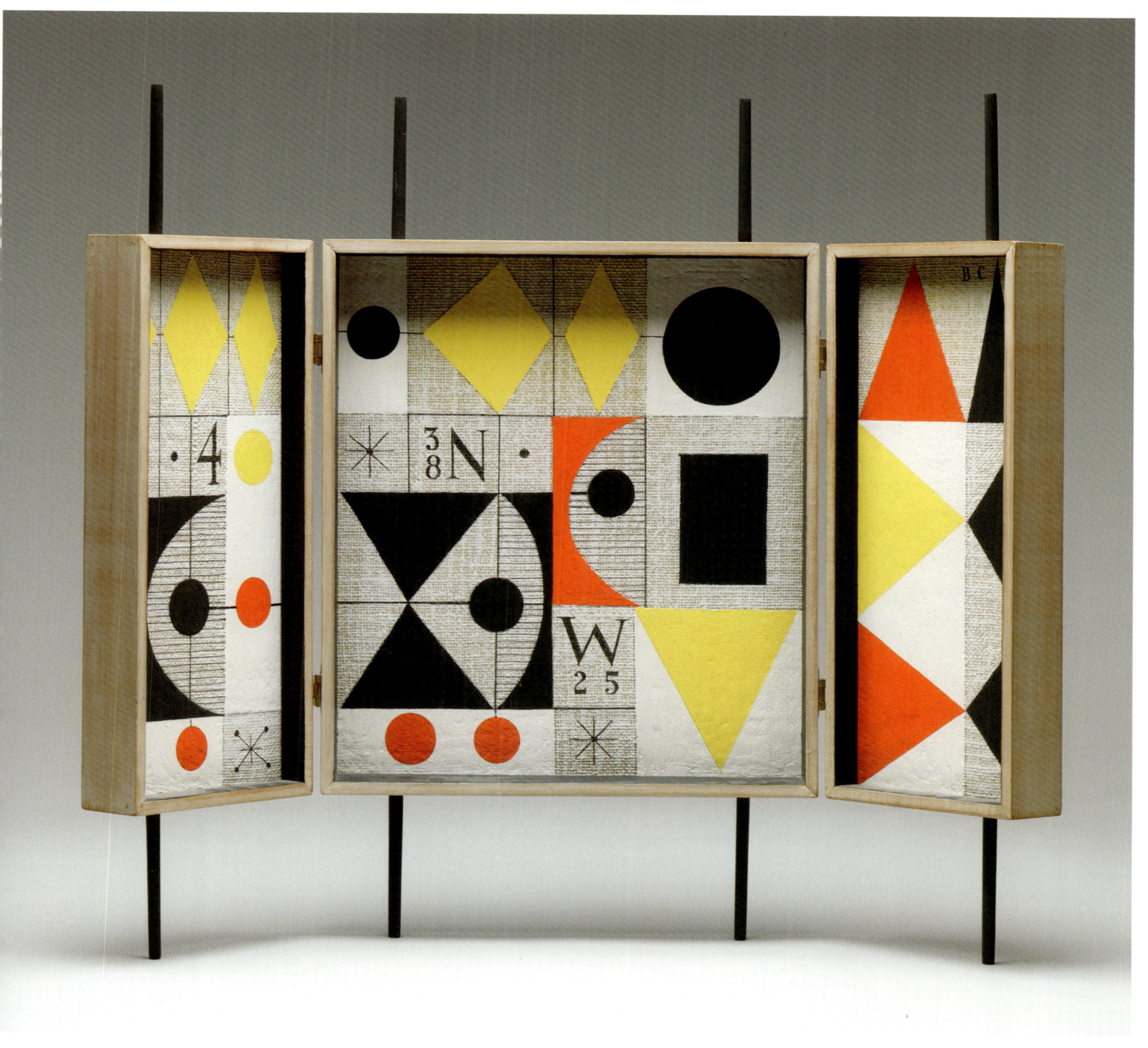

Bertram Charles Binning
Triptych of Nautical
Symbols 1956

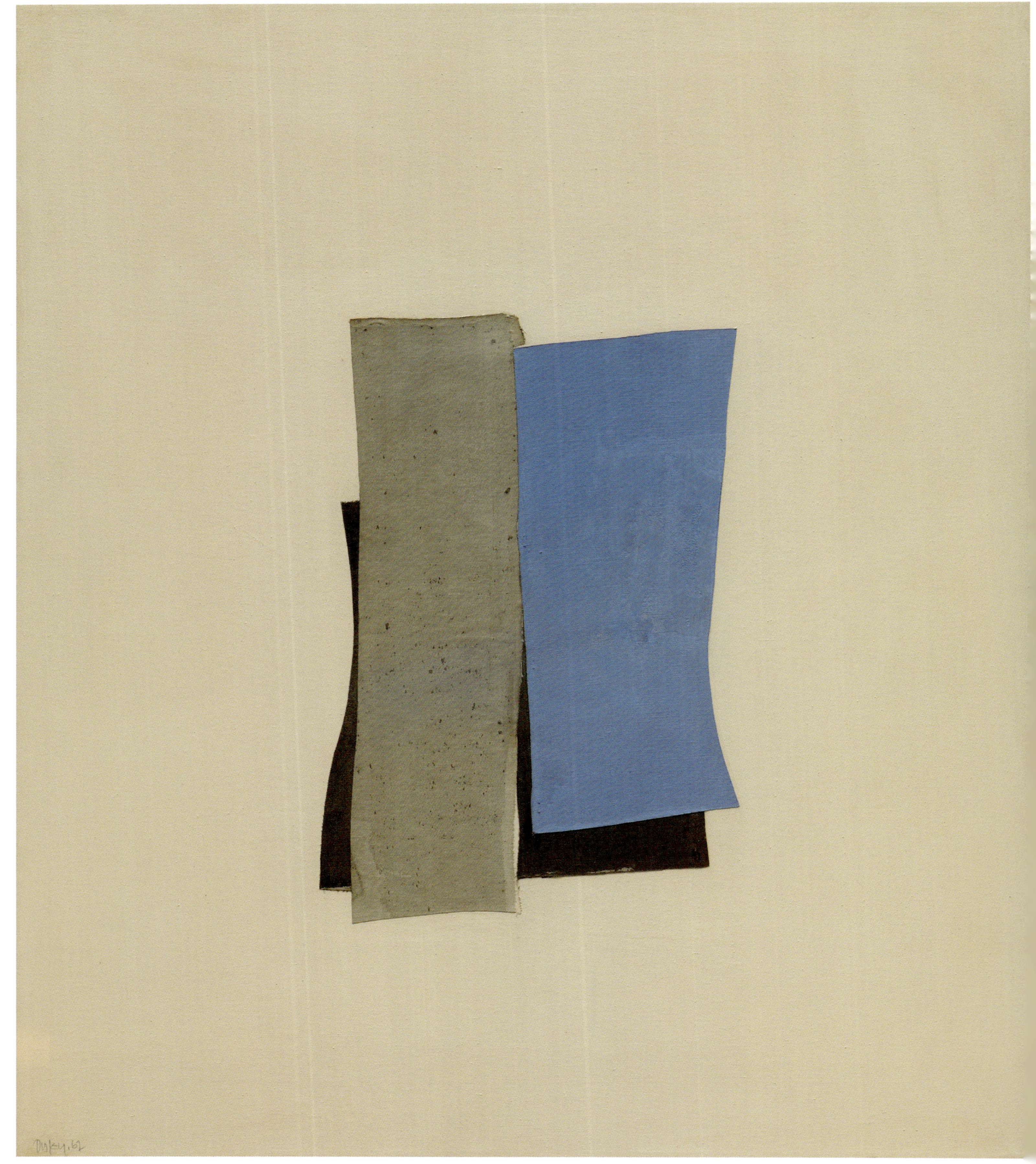

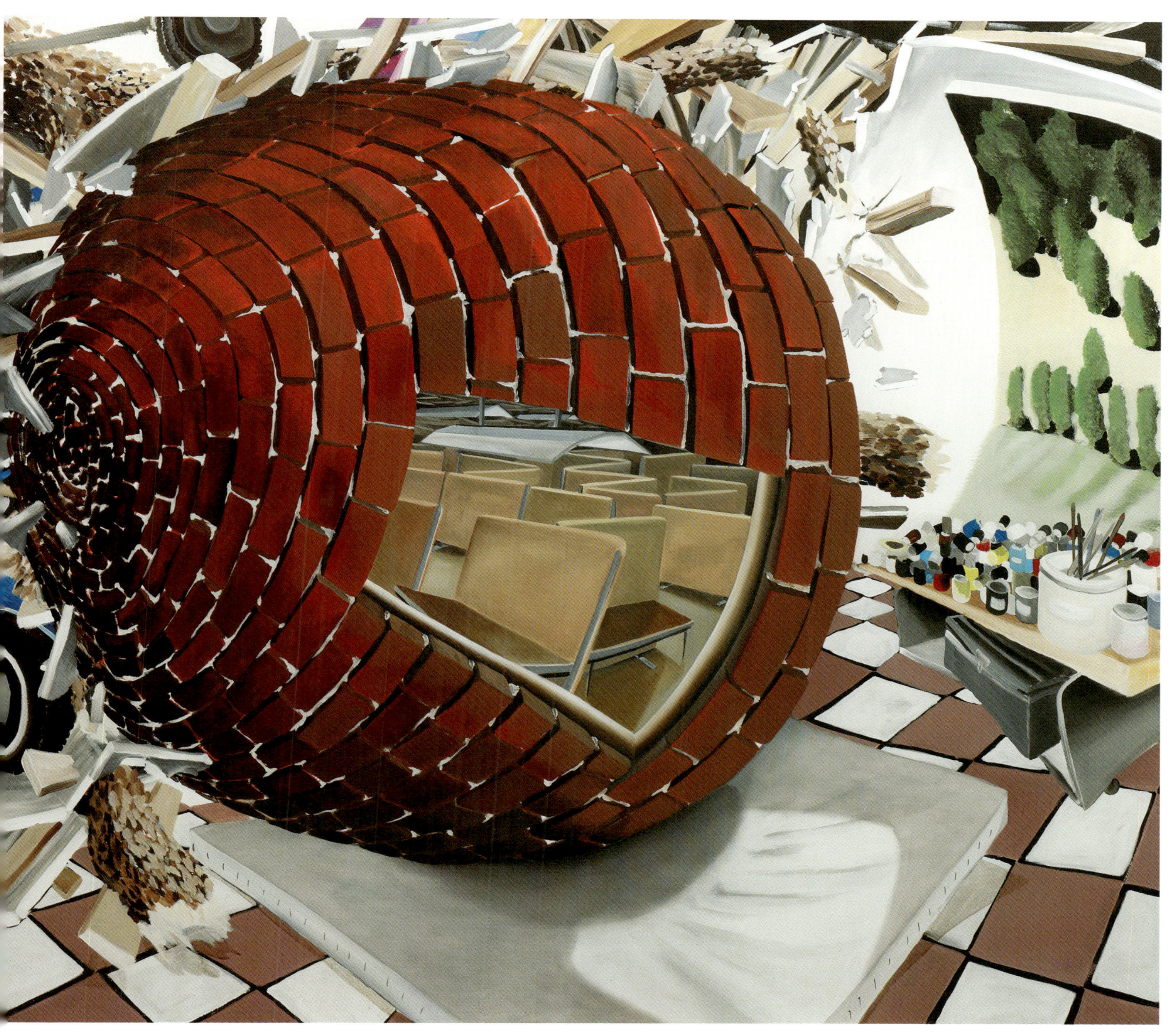

facing
Norman Antony (Toni) Onley
Juno 1962

above
Etienne Zack
Innerworks 2007

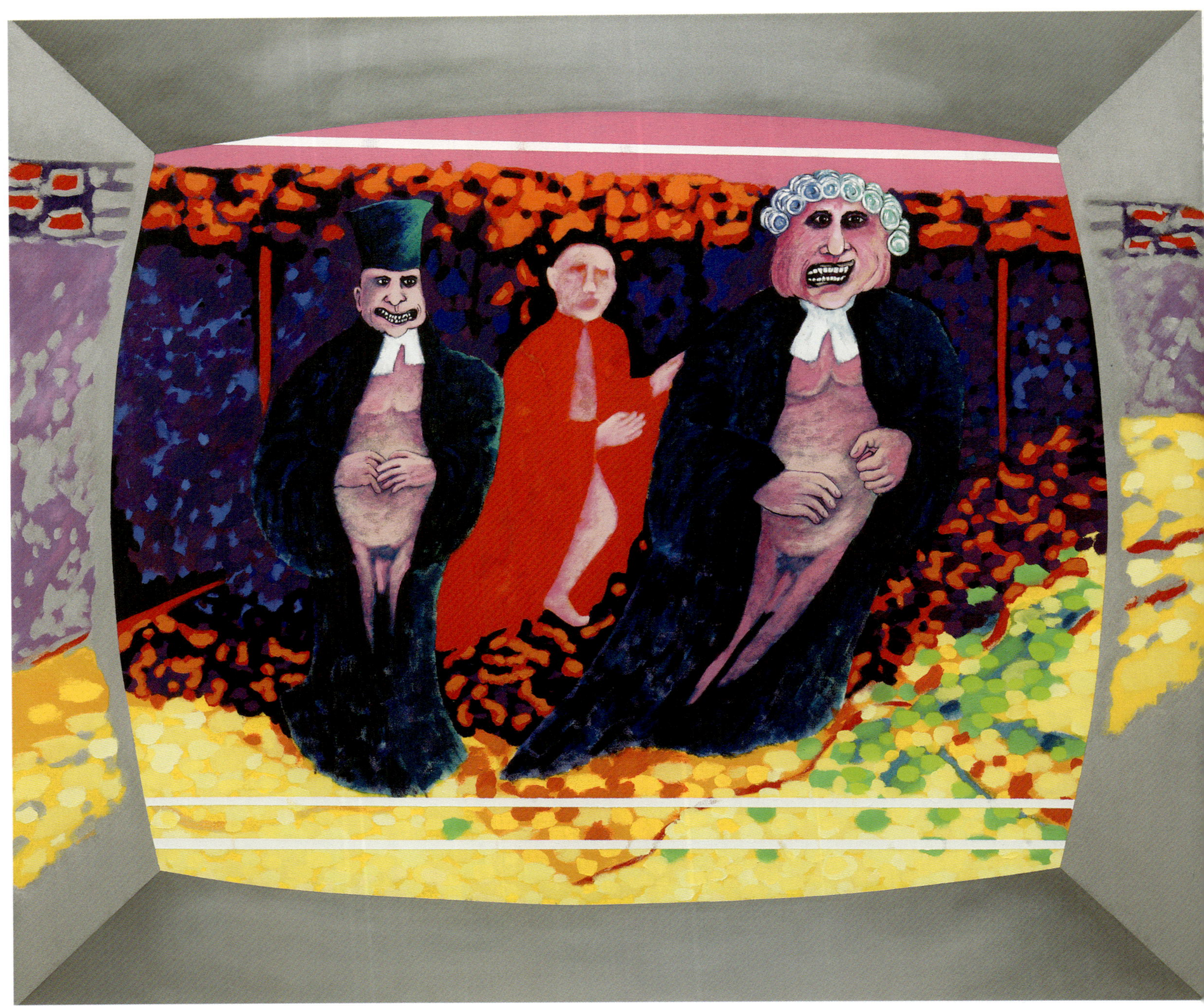

above
Claude Breeze
Transmission Difficulties:
The Dignitaries 1968

facing
Gathie Falk
22 Apples
1997

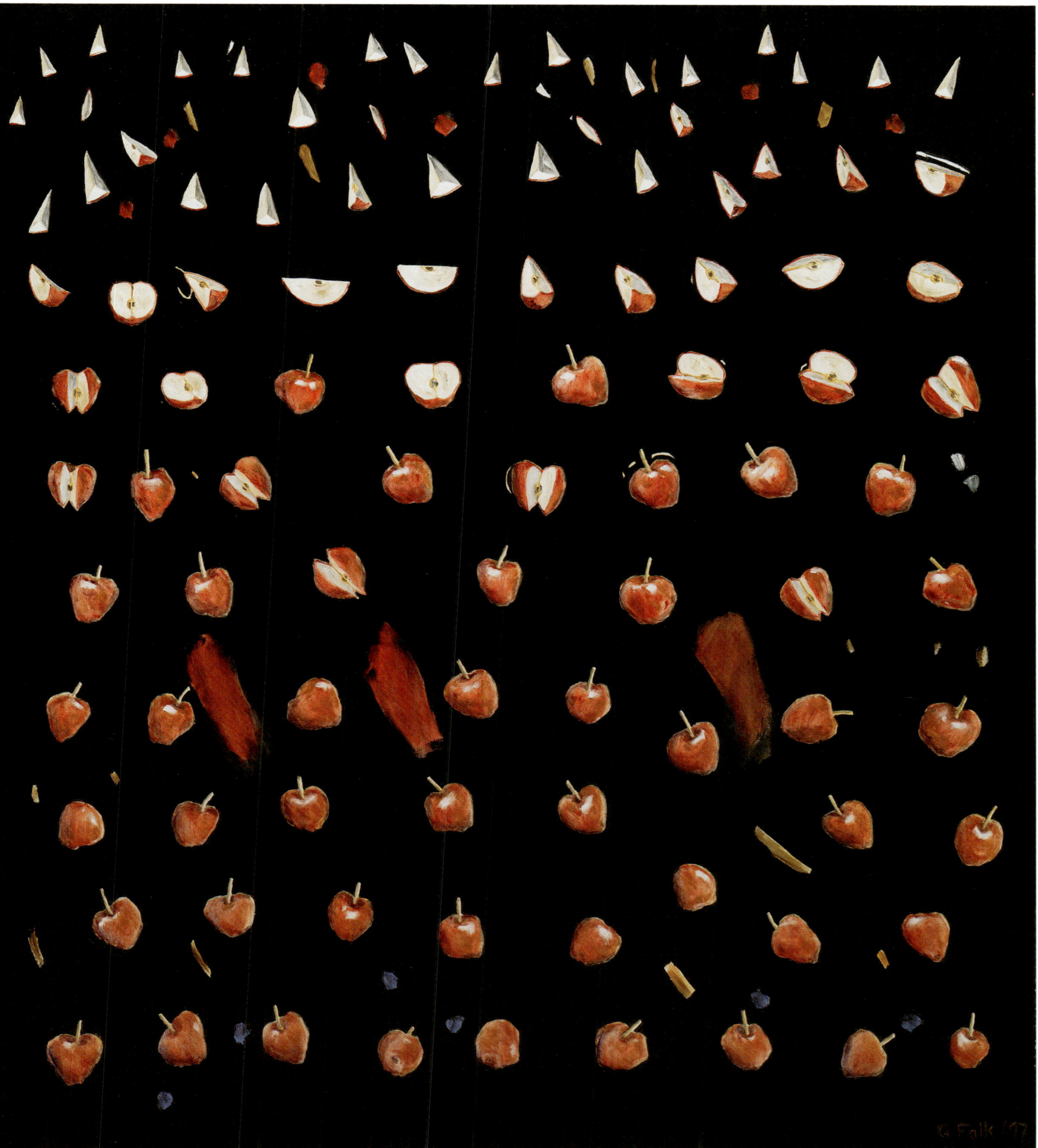
G Falk '97

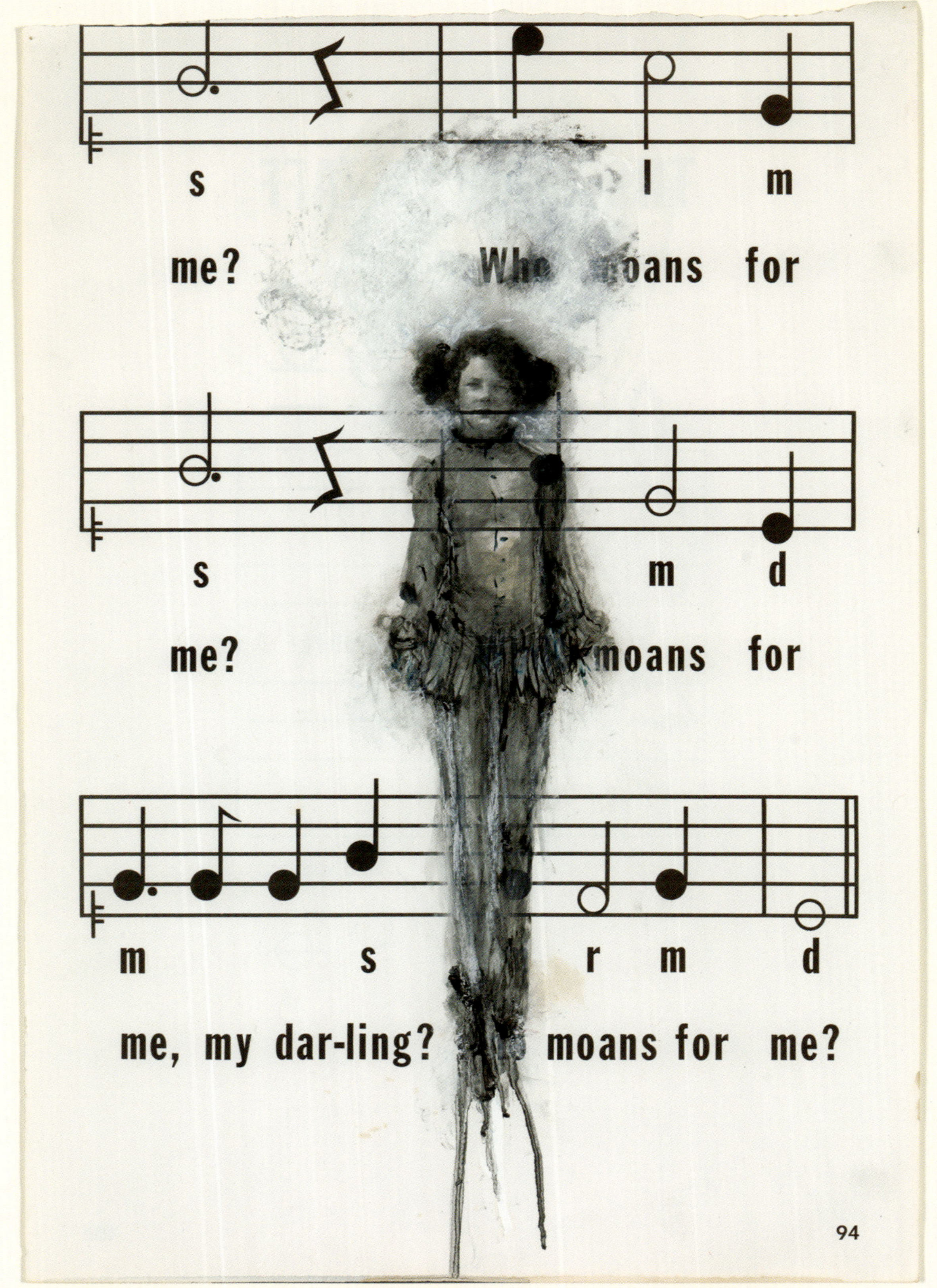

s l m
me? Wh oans for
s m d
me? moans for
m s r m d
me, my dar-ling? moans for me?
94

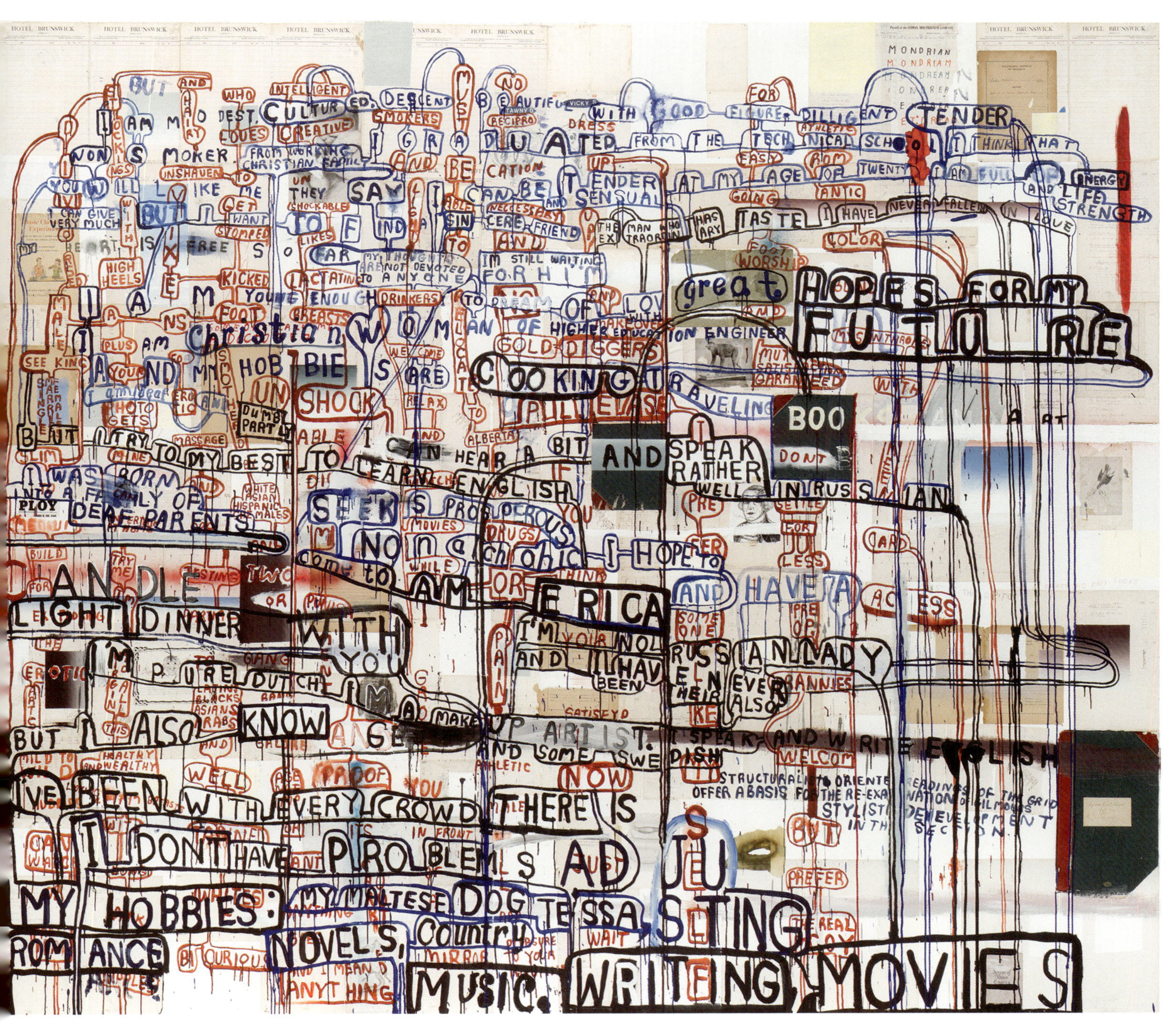

facing
Angela Grossman
Musical Notes 2007

above
Graham Gillmore
Ploy 2003

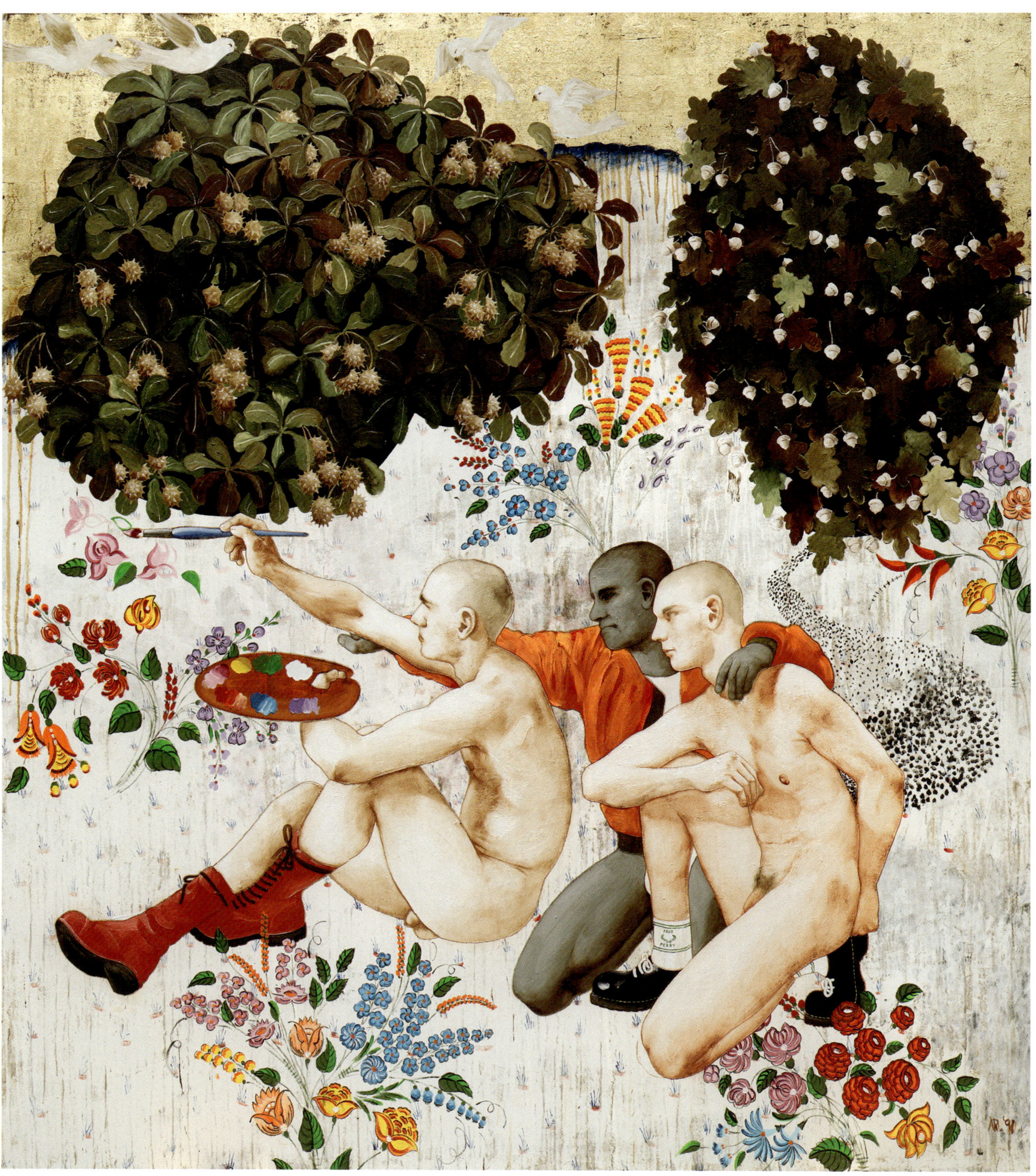

above
Attila Richard Lukacs
Varieties of Love: Painting the Lovers' Portrait 1991

facing
Laurie Papou
She saw her fallen clothes as a charity, a homage 2000

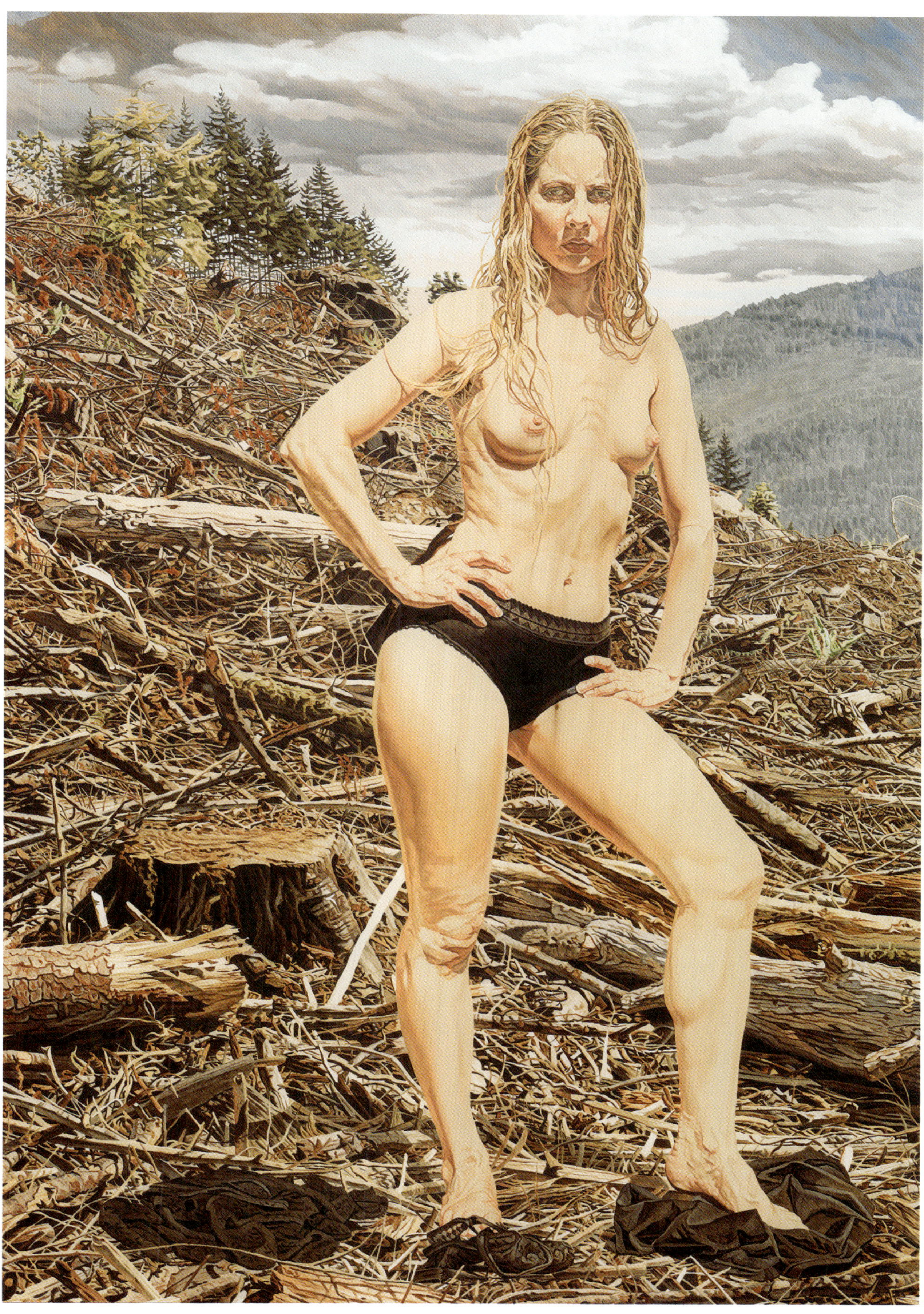

Arabella Campbell
Square Process Paintings:
Right Tilted, Left Tilted 2009

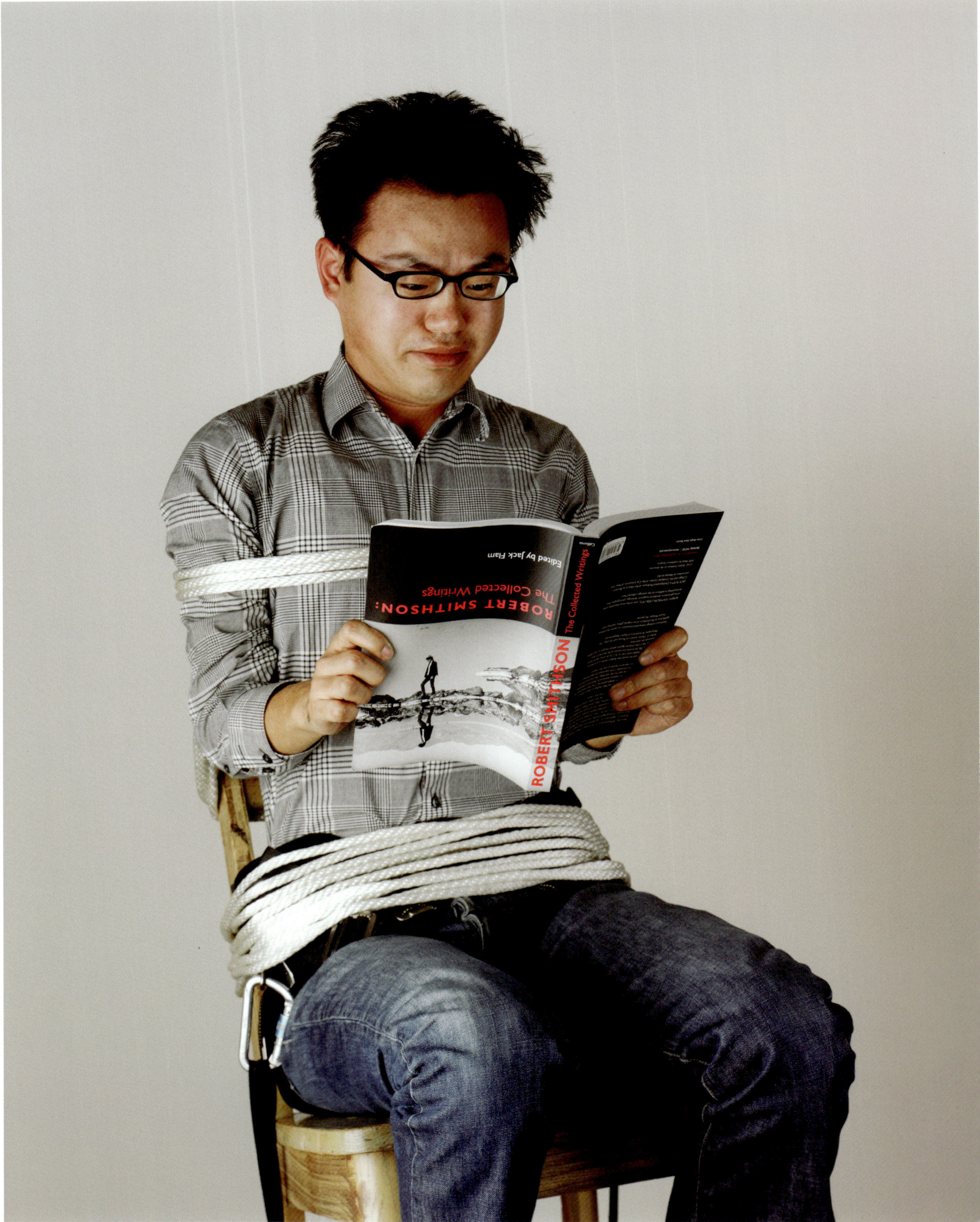
ROBERT SMITHSON:
The Collected Writings
Edited by Jack Flam
ROBERT SMITHSON
The Collected Writings

PHOTOCONCEPTUAL ART AND VANCOUVER

GRANT ARNOLD

THE PHOTOGRAPHIC WORK in the Audain collection is, for the most part, linked to Photoconceptualism, an idiom of artmaking that, over the past twenty years, has come to be closely associated with Vancouver in the psychic geography of the contemporary art world. This emphasis is not surprising, given Michael Audain's interest in art that is more overtly intentional than classical art photography and given the international attention received by Vancouver-based artists working in this idiom.

Photoconceptualism originated with the development of Conceptual Art in the 1960s. Photography was widely taken up in Conceptual Art as a link to the everyday, an index of the semiotics of the urban environment and a factual tool for documenting idea-based projects and performances. For artists working in geographically isolated places like Vancouver, Conceptual Art provided opportunities to escape a provincial condition. Its focus, on ideas that were easily transmissible and artworks that relied on technologies of reproduction, held out new possibilities for participating in the international art world's most current debates.

In keeping with an emphasis on the context that framed the production and reception of the artwork over its visual presence, the photographs used in Conceptual Art were small in scale, deliberately crude and consciously artless. This deadpan antiaesthetic stance informed the early work of Vancouver artists such as Christos Dikeakos, Jeff Wall and Ian Wallace, which took the defeatured landscape—representations of banal urban spaces that can be found throughout the industrialized world—as a central motif. Photography played a critical role in the development of a new art that eschewed personal expression and presented a direct challenge to the lyrical Modernism that dominated in Vancouver, and many other regional centres in the Western world, from the early twentieth century through to the late 1960s.

Beginning in the late 1970s, Conceptual Art's focus on subject matter and ideological critique extended into work that reasserted photography's descriptive power but also drew upon representational techniques prevalent in mass culture. Wall's large-scale lightbox entitled *The Destroyed Room,* 1978 (page 102), with its cinematic character and citation of early modern art history, is a key example of this paradigm. Over the following decade, this move away from Conceptual Art's iconophobia was

facing
Tim Lee
Upside Down Water Torture Chamber, Harry Houdini 1914 2004

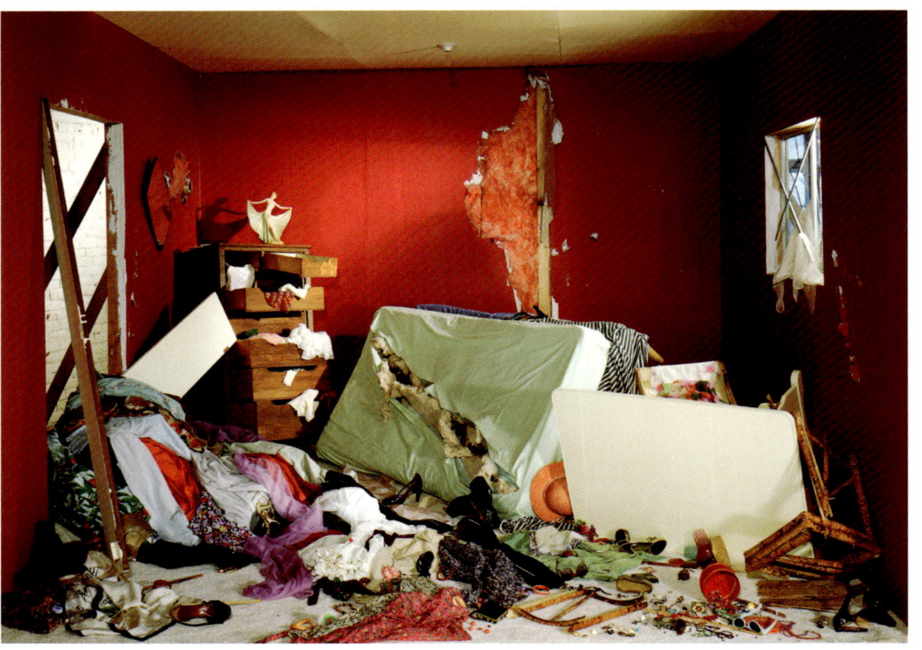

taken up by other Vancouver artists, including Wallace, Ken Lum and Rodney Graham, who produced large-scale, technically sophisticated and visually arresting photographically based artworks. These differed from more traditional photographs in their scale, their combination of the photographic image with text, their motifs drawn from mass culture and/or their overtly staged character—the sense that the recorded scene was constructed and performed for the camera. On the one hand, these practices presented a critique of Modernism through an emphasis on subject matter, a disavowal of medium-based purity and an interest in locating the image as a language-like construction. At the same time, they challenged the ahistorical character of certain versions of Postmodernism, especially the rise of neo-Expressionist painting and its break with the transformative ambitions of the Modernist avant-garde. As Wallace put it, Photoconceptualism's link to Modernism's avant-garde traditions was in opposition to a postmodern logic of consumption, in which "any 'free-floating' signifier can be substituted for another," and any image can be "integrated into an indeterminate flow of shifting ahistorical processes."[1]

1. Ian Wallace, "Photoconceptual Art in Vancouver," in *Thirteen Essays on Photography* (Ottawa: Canadian Museum of Contemporary Photography, 1988), 111–12.

The parameters and themes established in Vancouver during this time have continued to inform much of the photo-based work made in the city up to the present. As the basis for its wealth has shifted from resource exploitation into a post-industrial information and tourist economy, Vancouver's transformation has been a central concern in the work of artists like Wall, Wallace, Roy Arden and Stan Douglas. In a reciprocal manner, the international recognition they have earned has been held up as a sign of the city's development into a more cosmopolitan urban centre.

Interest in the defeatured, interstitial zones at the city's edge can be seen in Wall's *River Road*, 1994 (page 13); questions about the individual's place in the city as the

Jeff Wall
The Destroyed Room 1978
transparency in lightbox · 159 × 234 cm
Collection of the National Gallery of Canada

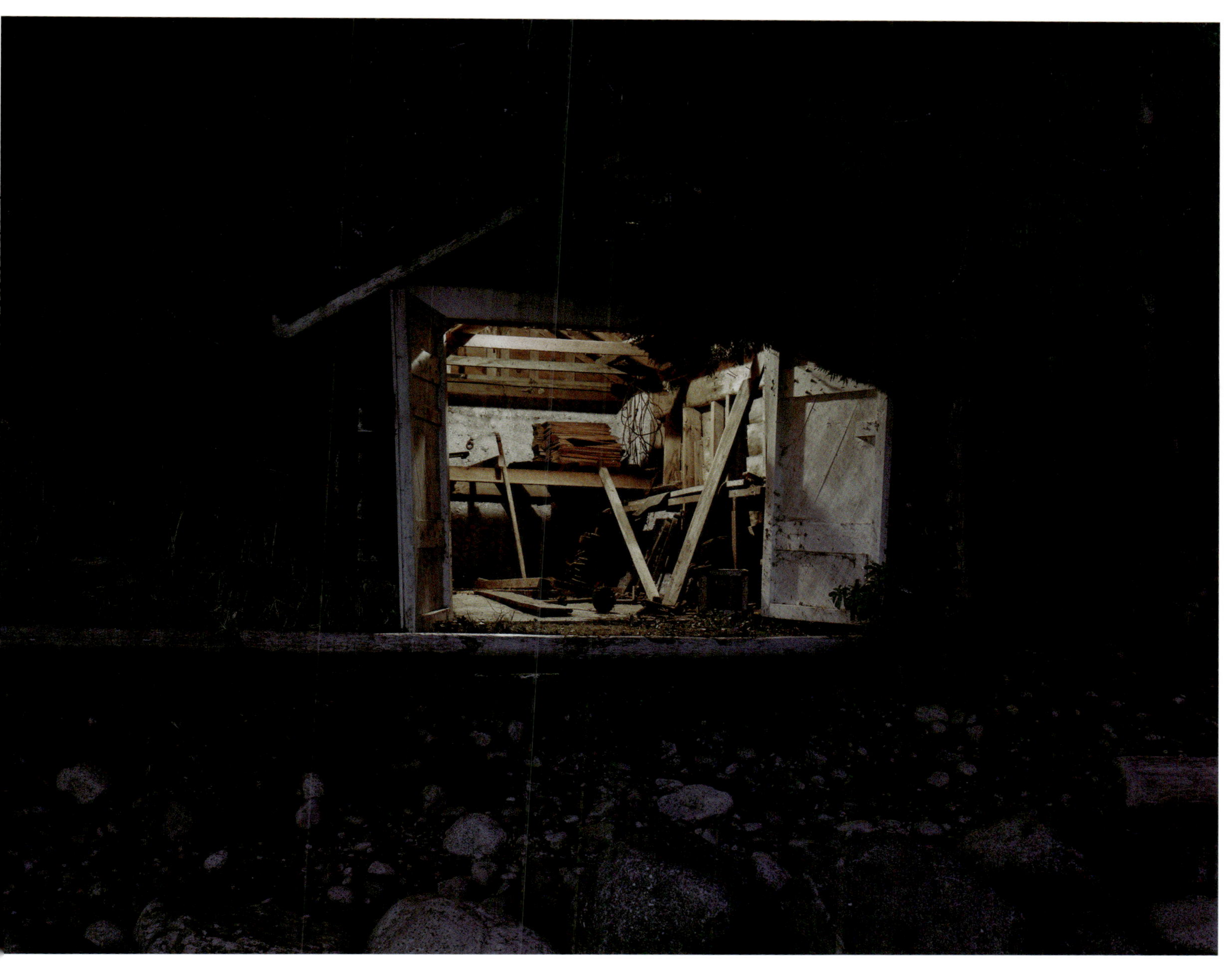

Scott McFarland
Boathouse with Moonlight
2003

paradigmatic space of modernity underpin Wallace's *Times Square, NYC* 2003 (page 22) and Stephen Waddell's *Stazione de Termini,* 2008 (page 117); the ongoing processes of displacement and development that lie at the heart of modernity inform Arden's *Condominium Advertisement, Vancouver B.C.,* 1992 (page 116); Dikeakos's *250 Northern Street,* 2009 (page 110–11); Douglas's *Downtown Eastside,* 2002; Danny Singer's *Calder,* 2005 (pages 114–15) and Greg Girard's picture of Shanghai, *Shanghai View 4,* from 2002 (page 112), while the way in which images mediate our understanding of the world and our place in it is pivotal to Graham's *Schoolyard Tree, Vancouver,* 2002 (page 113) and Lum's *Nancy Nishi, Joe Ping Chau, Real Estate,* 1990 (page 105).

By the late 1990s a number of Vancouver artists, both younger and more senior figures, were making work that addressed a complex matrix of patterns that flow through contemporary culture, while incorporating video, sculpture and other media into their practices. The work of Tim Lee, for example, has stressed the intersection of seminal moments from pop culture and art history, conflating high and low culture in an investigation of issues of transmission and translation. Steven Shearer has addressed youth culture, and the forms through which its alienation is expressed, in photo-collages assembled from hundreds of images found on the Internet, as well as in paintings, text-based work and sculpture. Working with painting, signage, photography and sculpture, Ron Terada draws attention to existing cultural forms, ranging from the television show *Jeopardy* to Conceptual Art to the instrumental structures in which art is presented and categorized. Dana Claxton, who became known for her film and video work in the early 1990s, has recently been working with large-scale photographs, such as *Paint Up #1,* 2010 (page 8), that examine the way images of First Nations are formed and commodified, while also pointing at ways in which these images can be resisted and transformed.

The work of Scott McFarland, as well as that of Lee, Shearer and Singer, demonstrates the role digital technology has played in photographically based work over the past decade. In an attempt to emulate human vision on a level that is technically beyond traditional photography, McFarland produces images such as *Boathouse with Moonlight,* 2003 (page 103) using multiple exposures of a given scene that are then digitally combined. This technique allows the viewer's eye to move continuously over the image, its scrutiny of the scene unhindered by the limitations of single-exposure, analog materials. Most of Fred Herzog's evocative images depicting Vancouver street life, a project he began in the 1950s, were photographed long before the arrival of digital materials and methods. However, the development of this new technology has enabled Herzog to print his photographs to standards that were difficult and expensive at the time the images were originally made, allowing him to make contemporary prints that more closely follow his original visualization. Thus, if digital methods have become central to new photographic work that draws upon the legacy of Conceptual Art, they can now also affect the appearance of the classical photography that preceded it. This technical convergence is one indication of the partial dissolution of the boundaries that were seen to demarcate classical photography and Photoconceptualism during the closing decades of the twentieth century.

facing
Ken Lum
Nancy Nishi, Joe Ping Chau,
Real Estate 1990

overleaf
Fred Herzog
Bogner's Grocery
1960

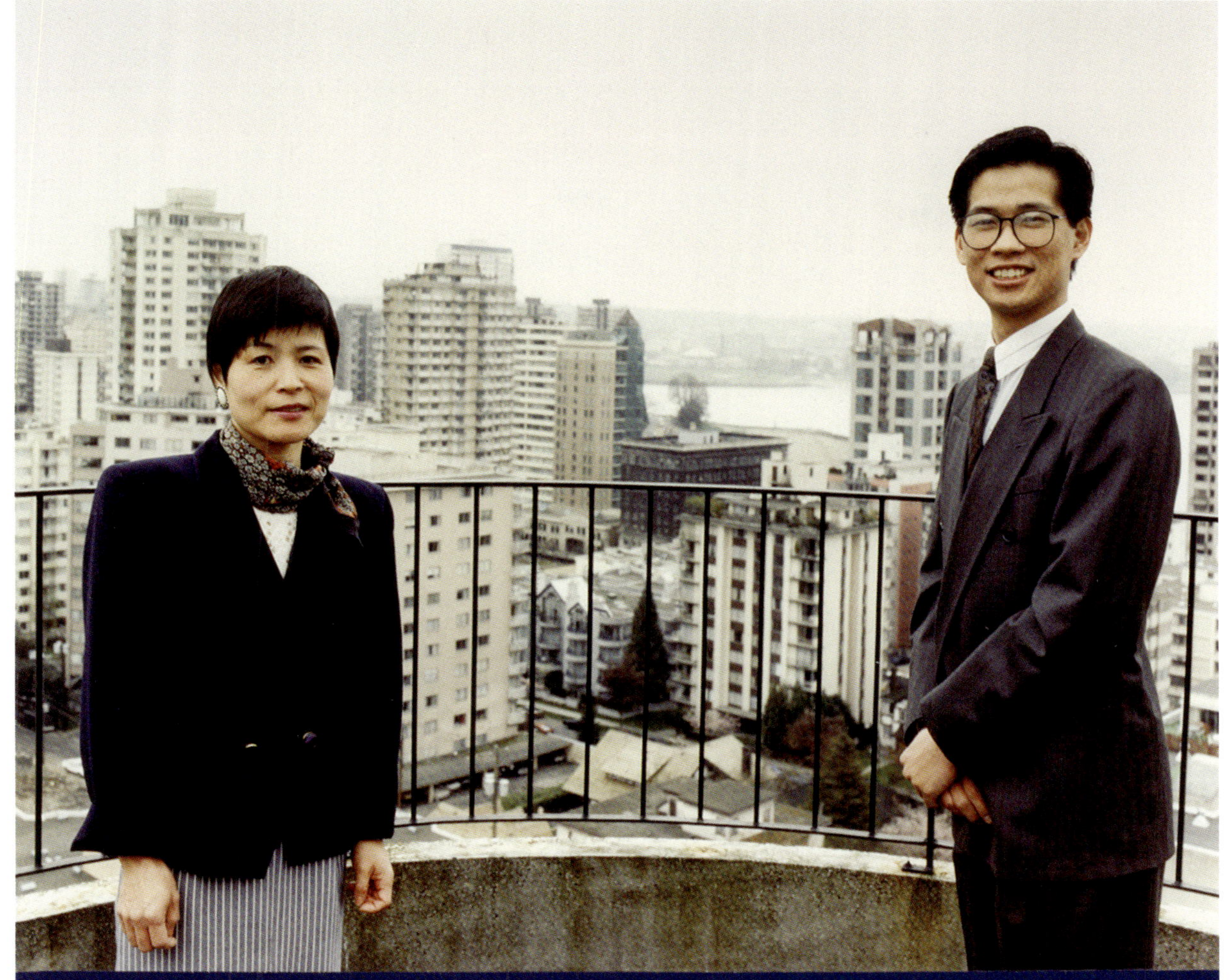

Nancy NISHI

Joe Ping CHAU

REAL ESTATE

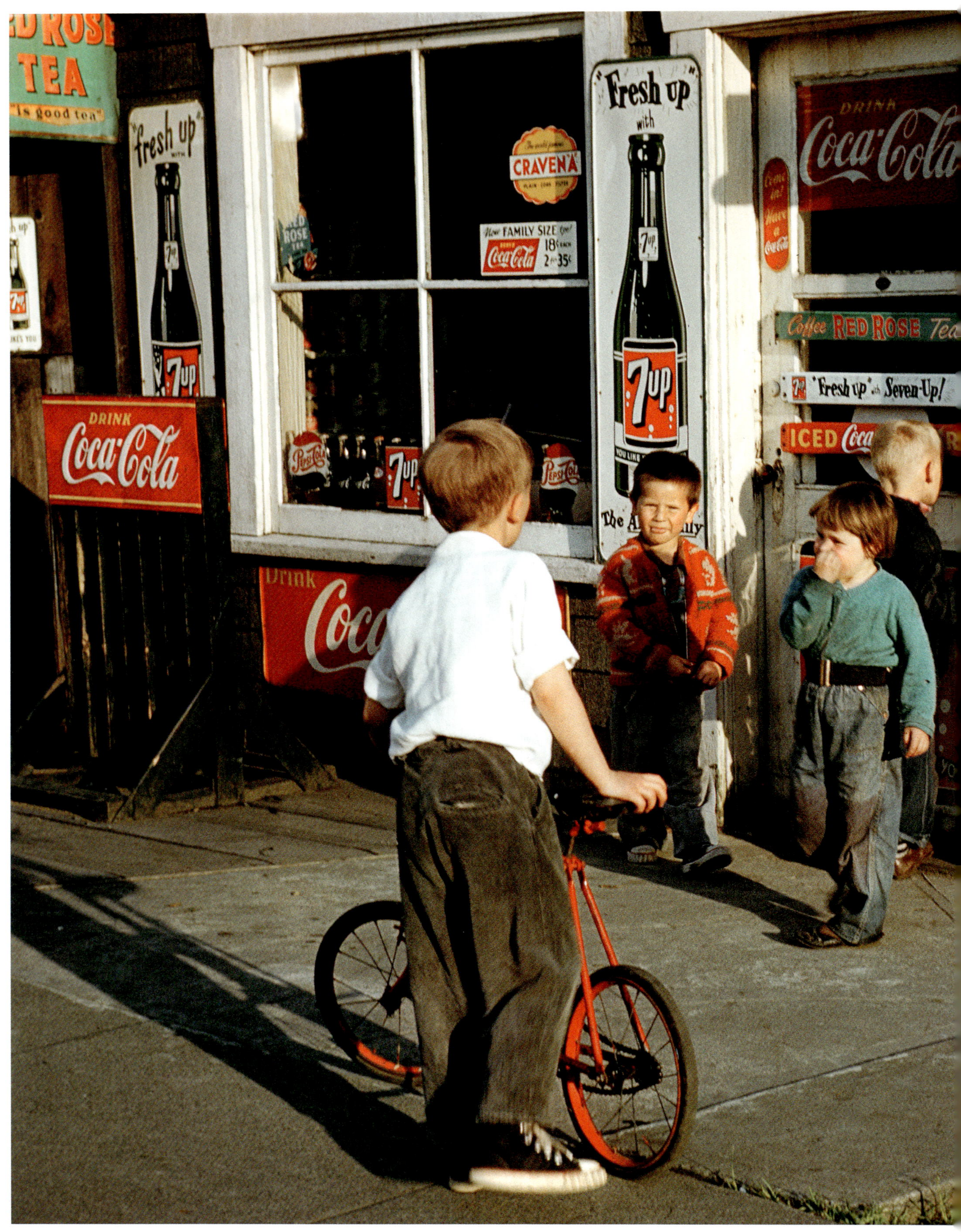

TEA
"is good tea"
"fresh up"
7up
DRINK
Coca-Cola
CRAVENA
New FAMILY SIZE
Coca-Cola
18¢ EACH
2 for 35¢
Fresh up
with
7up
DRINK
Coca-Cola
Coffee RED ROSE Tea
"Fresh up" with Seven-Up!
ICED
Drink
Pepsi-Cola

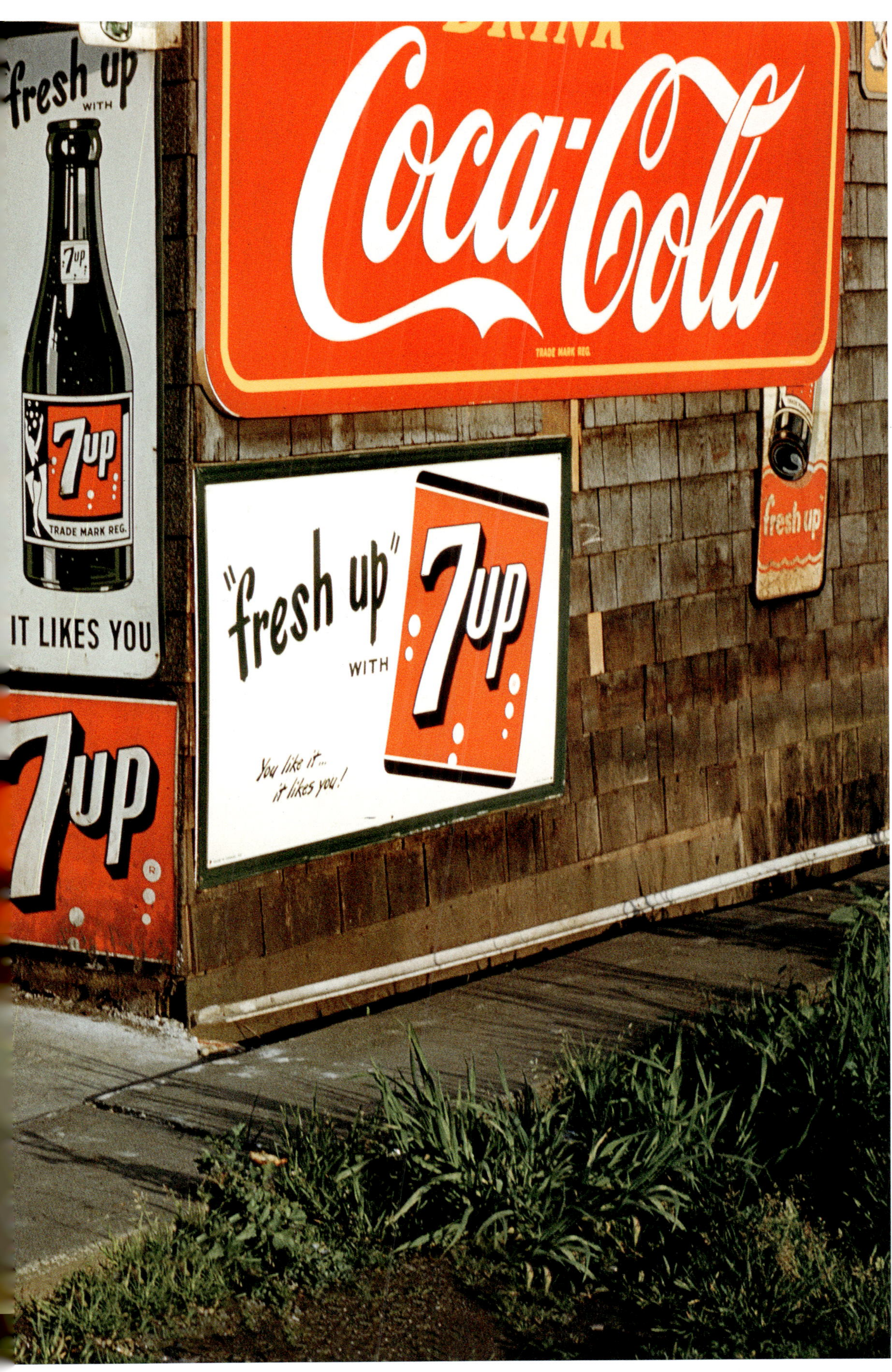
fresh up
WITH
7up
TRADE MARK REG.
IT LIKES YOU
7up
Coca-Cola
TRADE MARK REG.
"fresh up"
WITH
7up
You like it...
it likes you!
fresh up

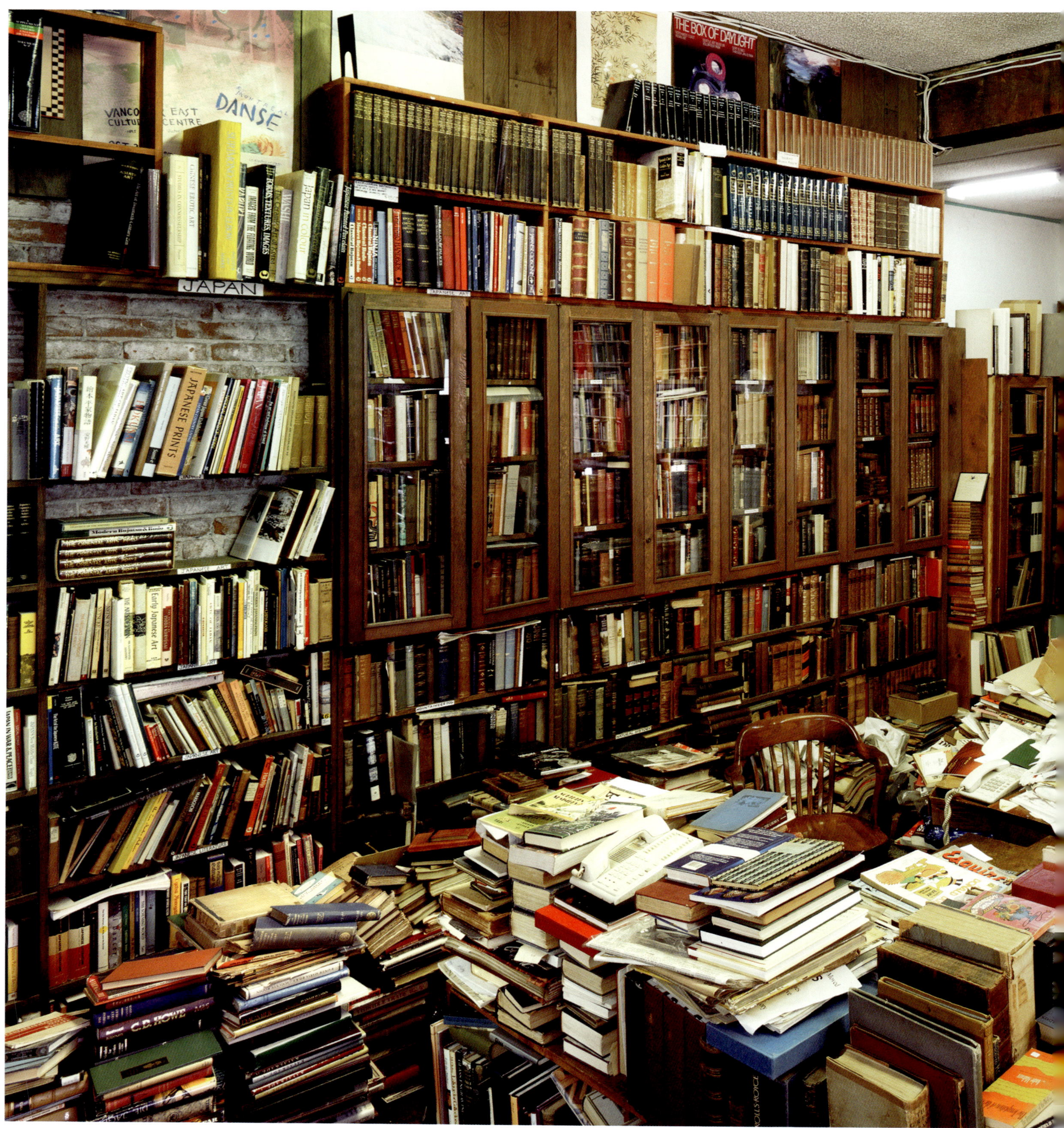
THE BOX OF DAYLIGHT
DANSE
JAPAN
JAPANESE PRINTS
Early Japanese Art
C.D. HOWE

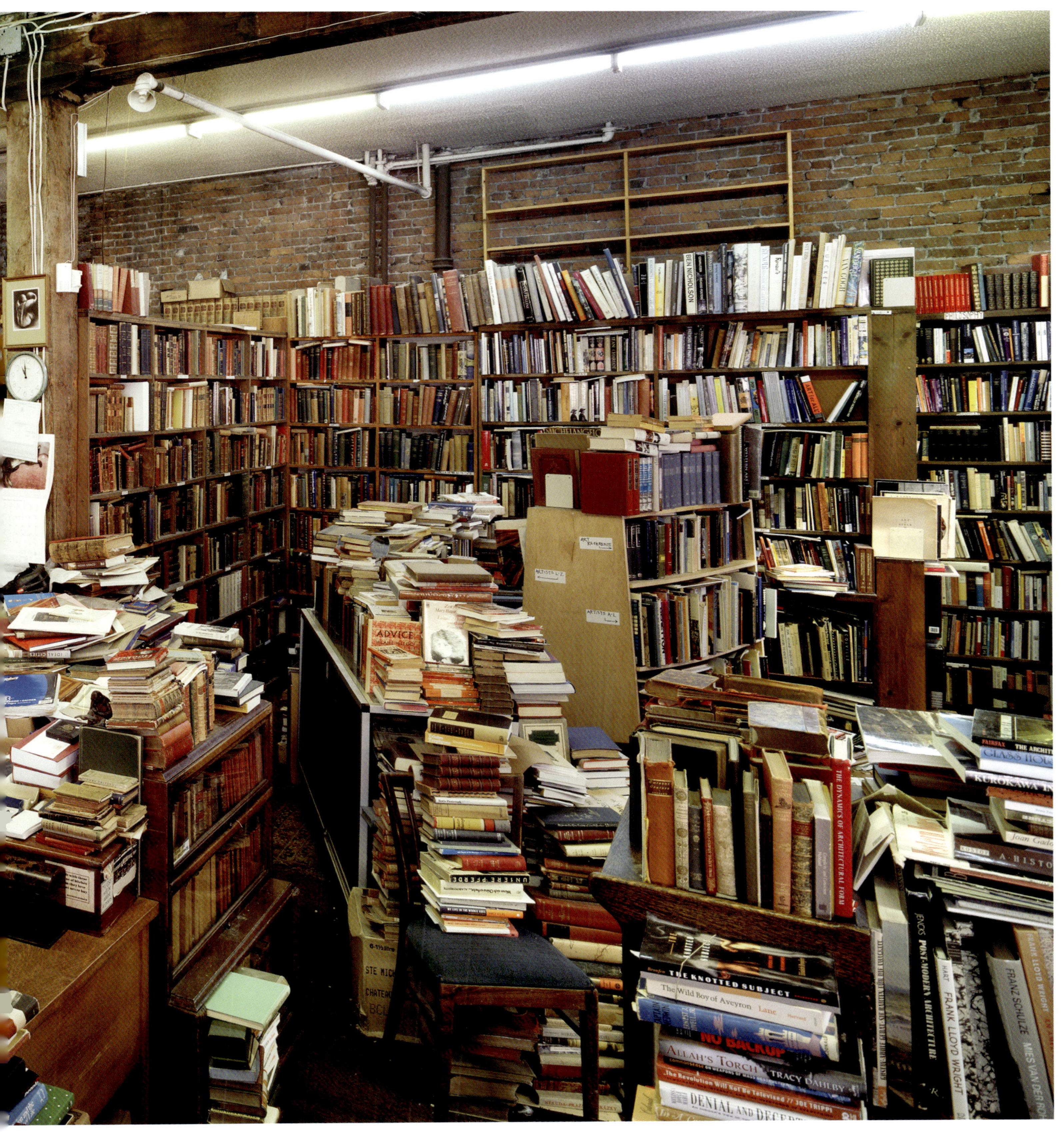
BEN NICHOLSON
ADVICE
THE DYNAMICS OF ARCHITECTURAL FORM
THE KNOTTED SUBJECT
The Wild Boy of Aveyron
ALLAH'S TORCH
TRACY DAHLBY
The Revolution Will Not Be Televised // JOE TRIPPI
JENCKS
POST-MODERN ARCHITECTURE
FRANK LLOYD WRIGHT
FRANZ SCHULZE

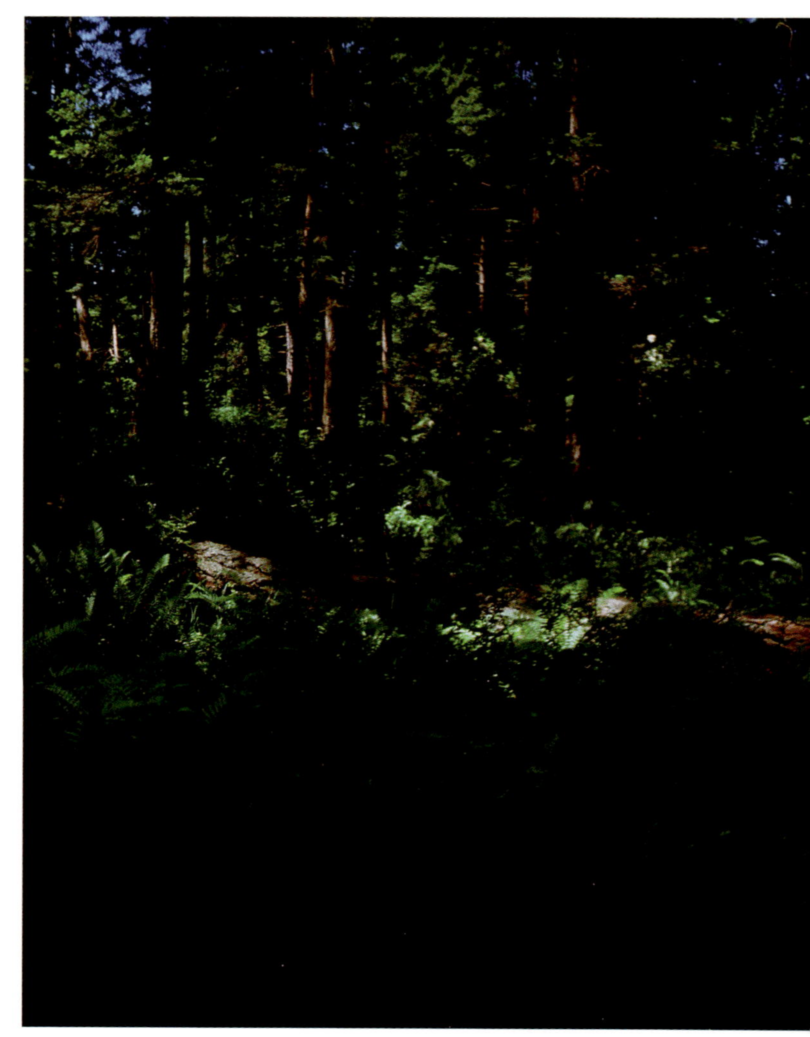

previous spread
Stan Douglas
McLeod's Books, Vancouver
2006

above
Christos Dikeakos
Windfall, Hornby Island 1994

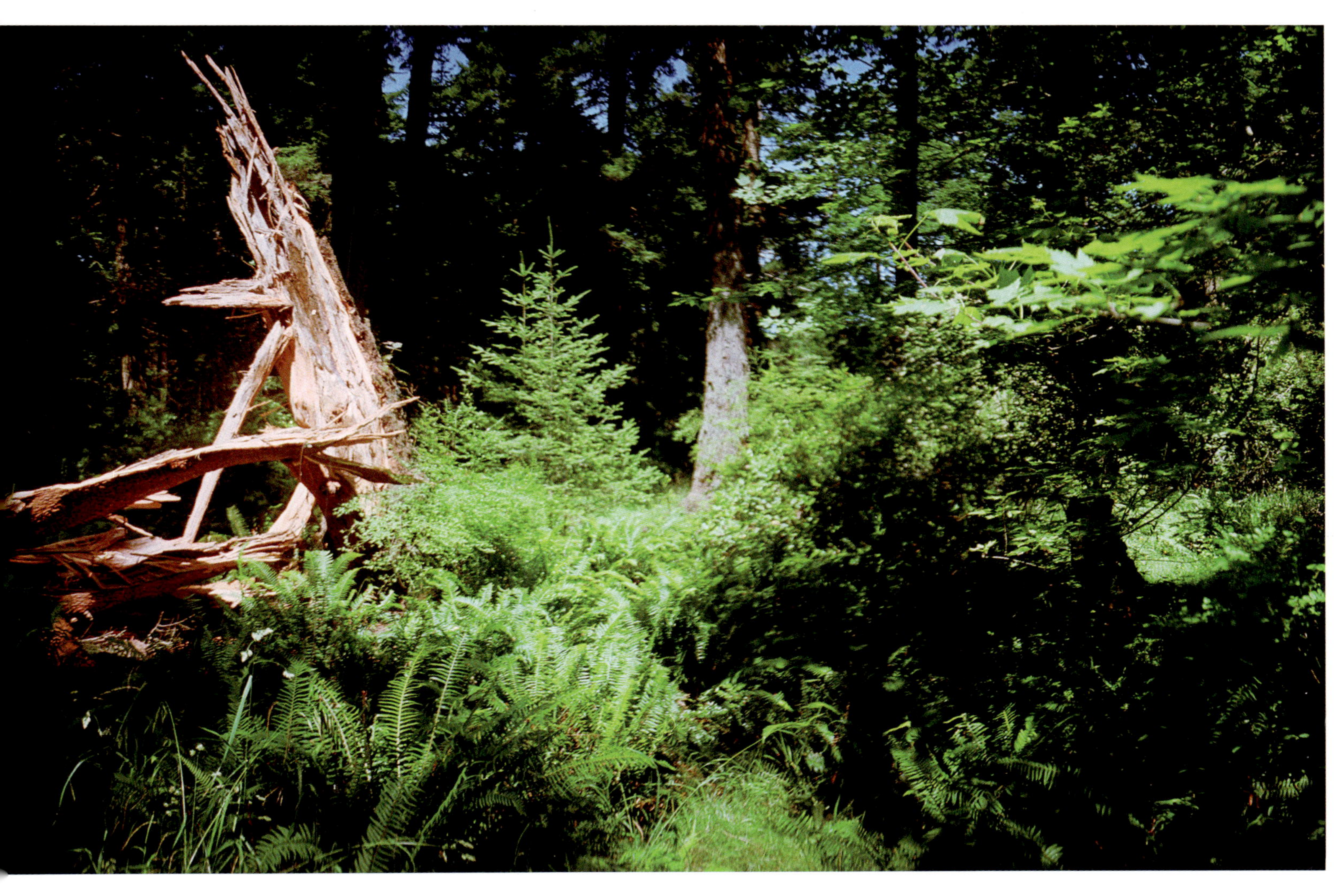

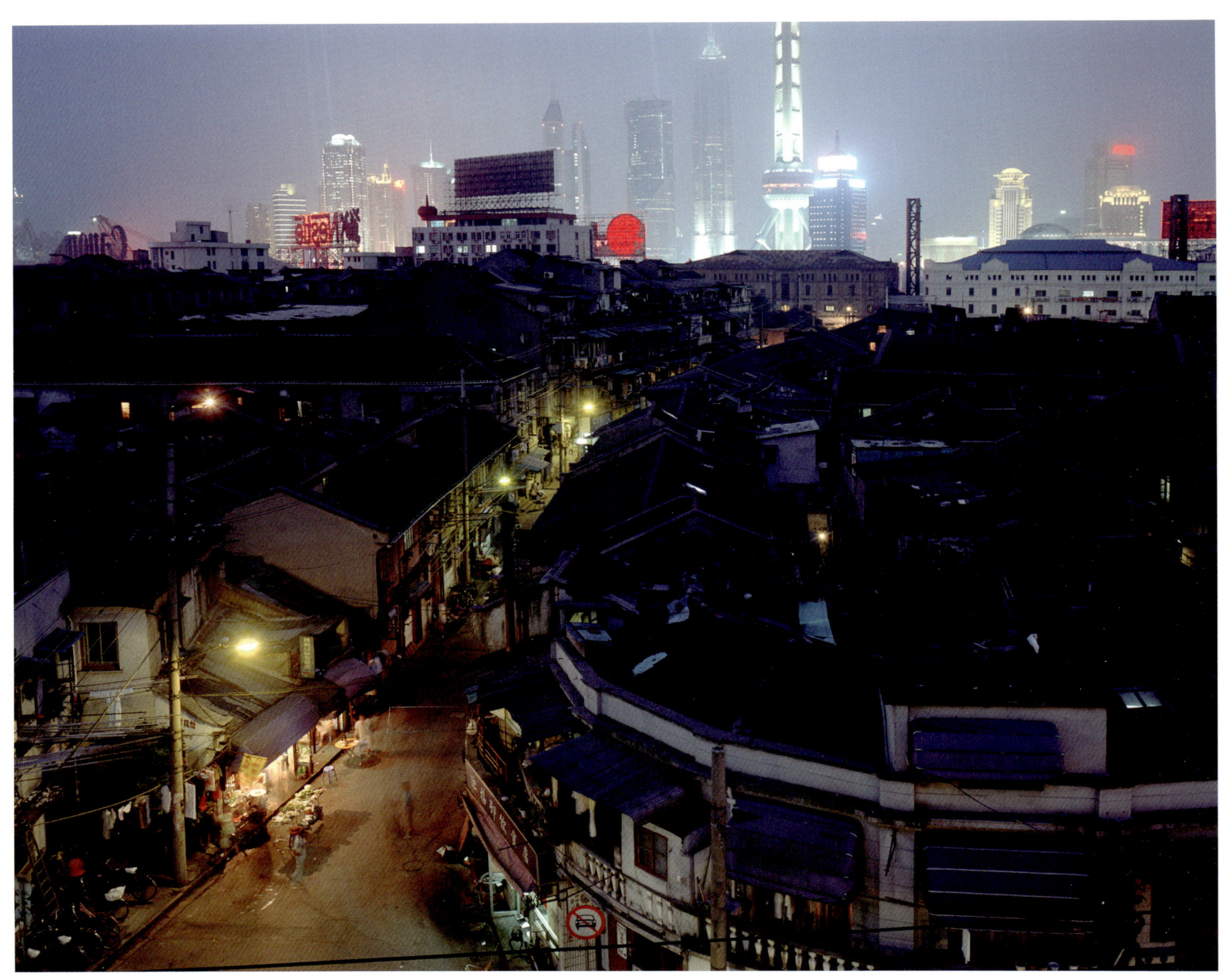

Greg Girard
Shanghai View 4 2002

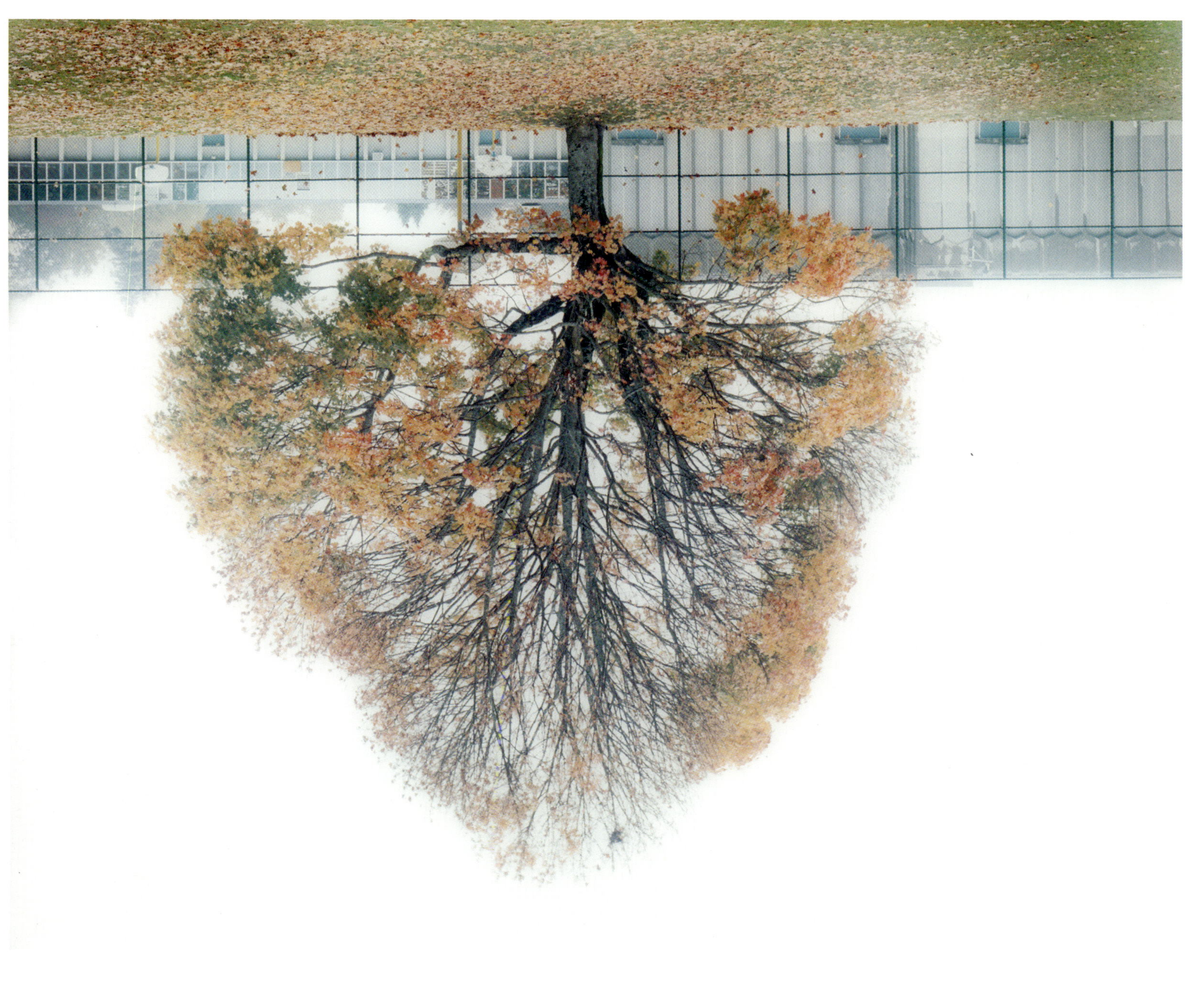

Rodney Graham,
Schoolyard Tree, Vancouver
2002

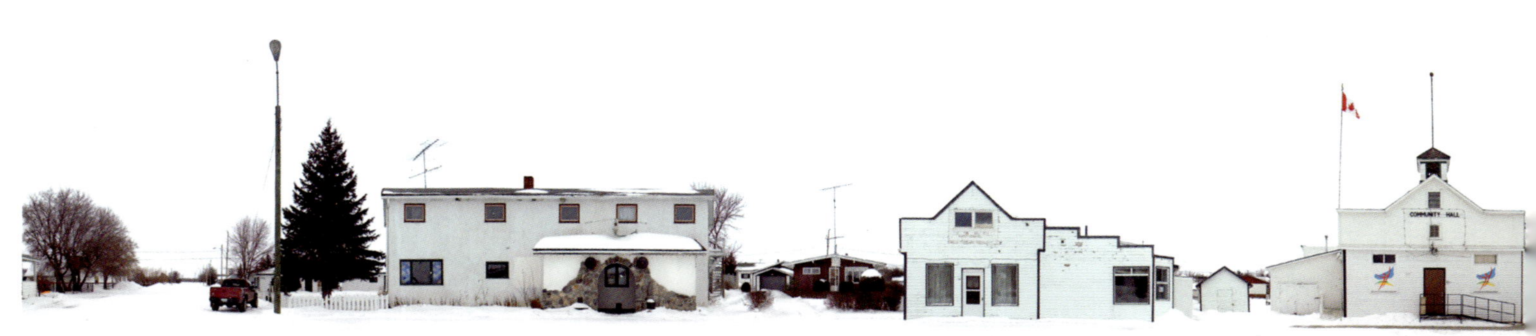
COMMUNITY HALL

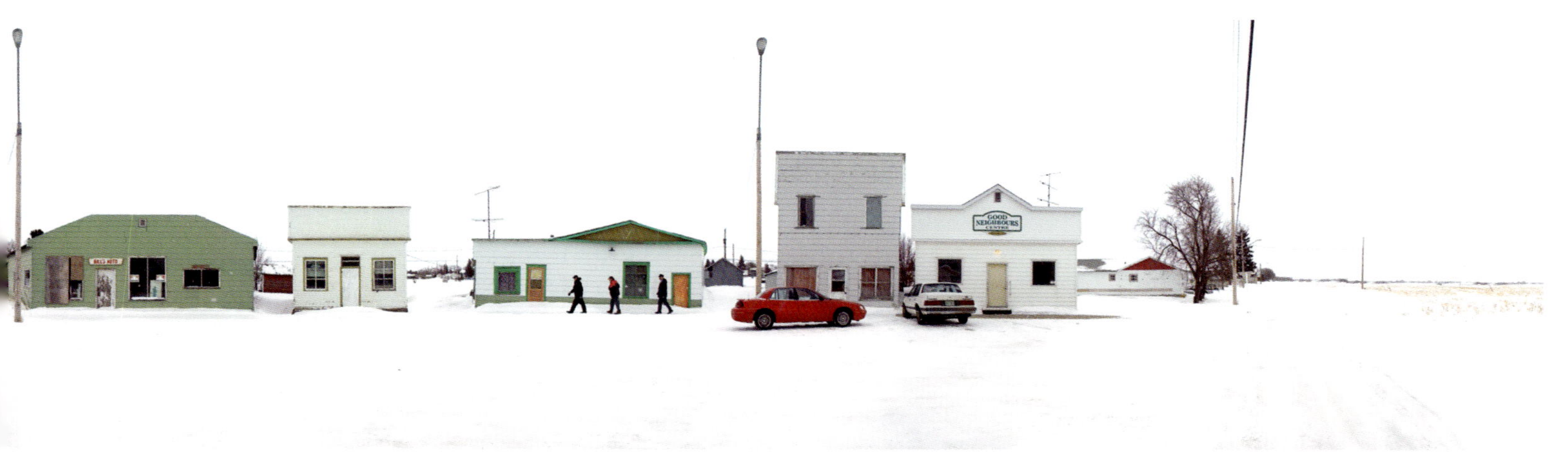

Danny Singer
Calder 2005

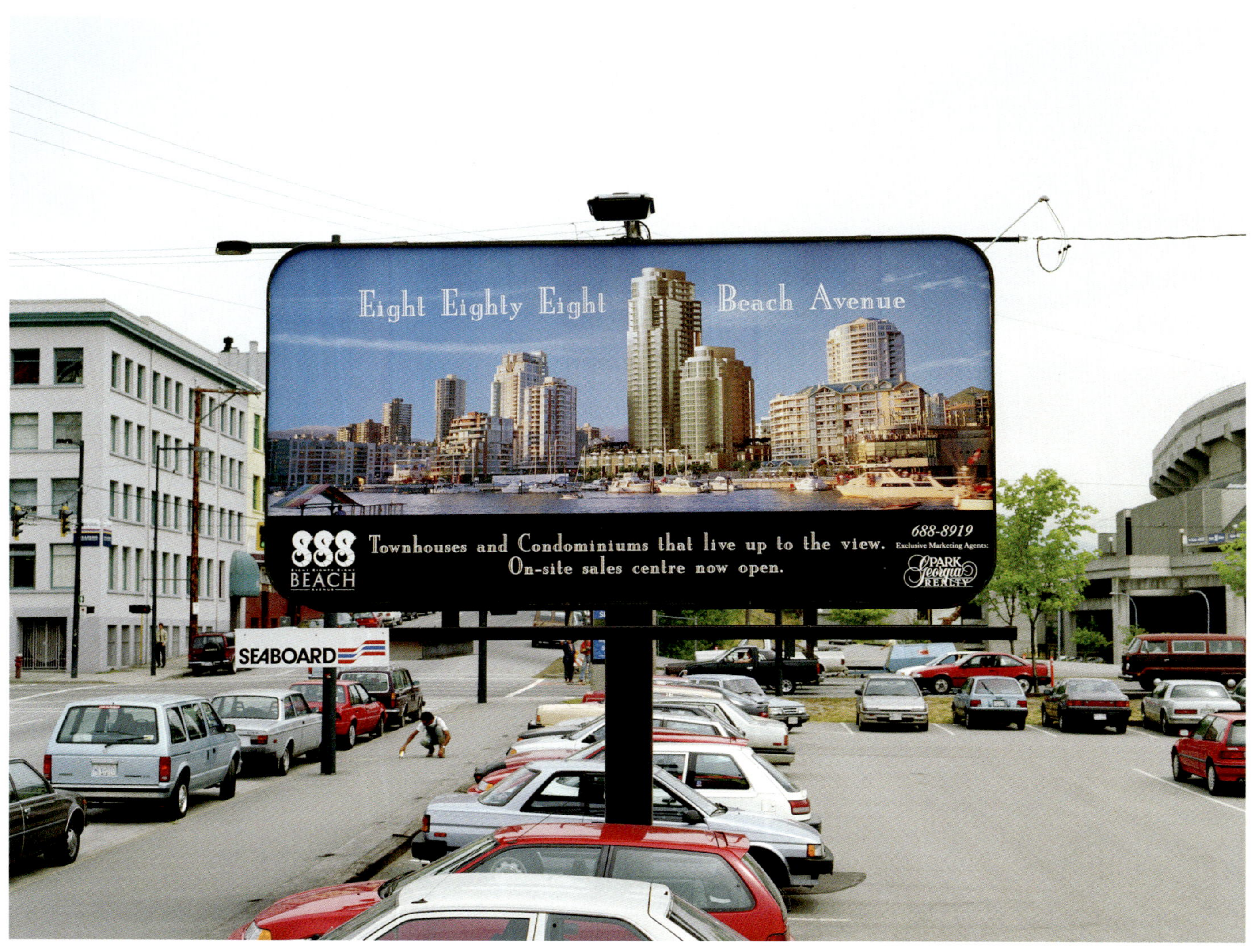

Roy Arden
Condominium Advertisement,
Vancouver, B.C. 1992

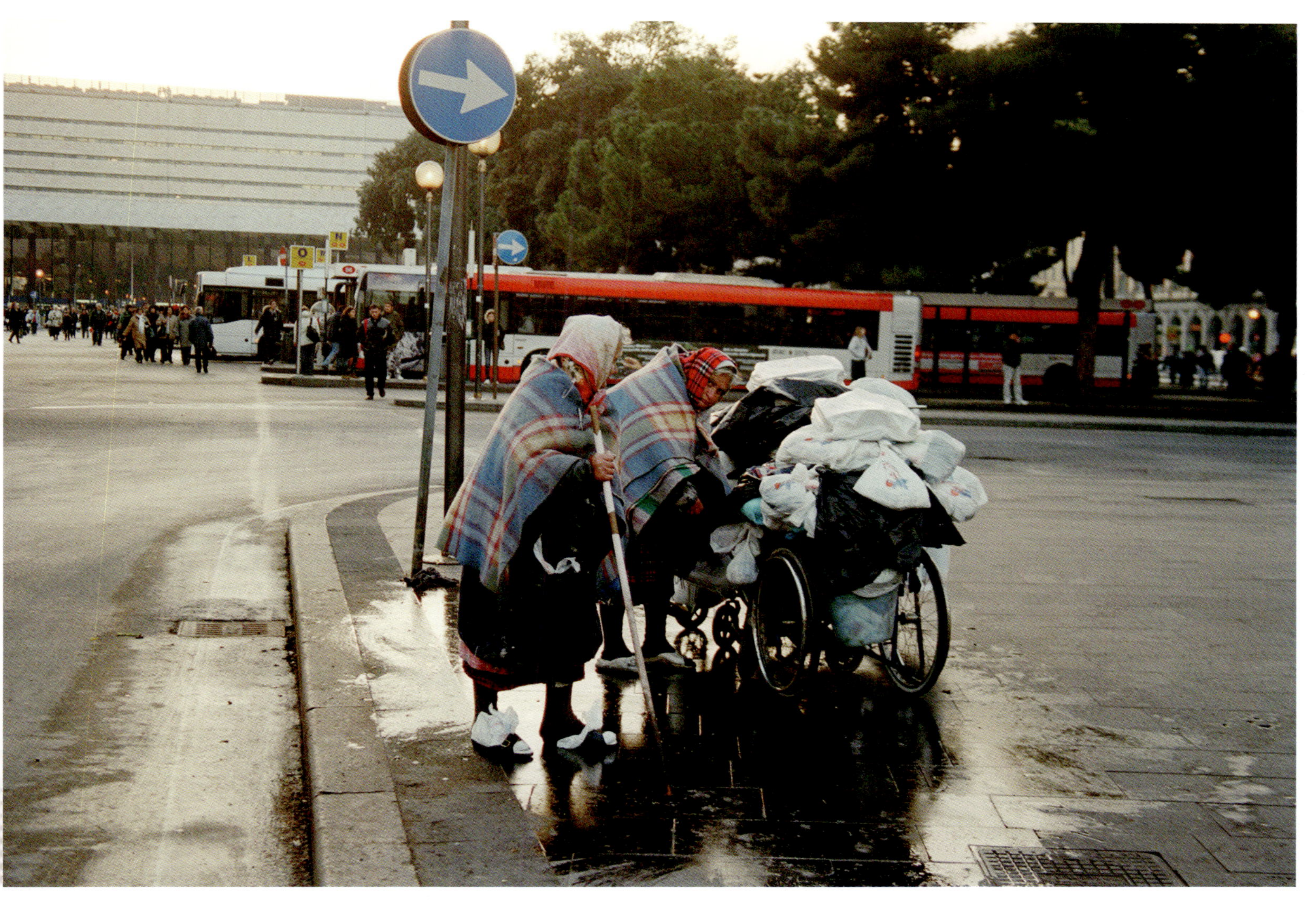

above
Stephen Waddell
Stazione de Termini 2008

overleaf
Steven Shearer
Guitar #5 2002–03

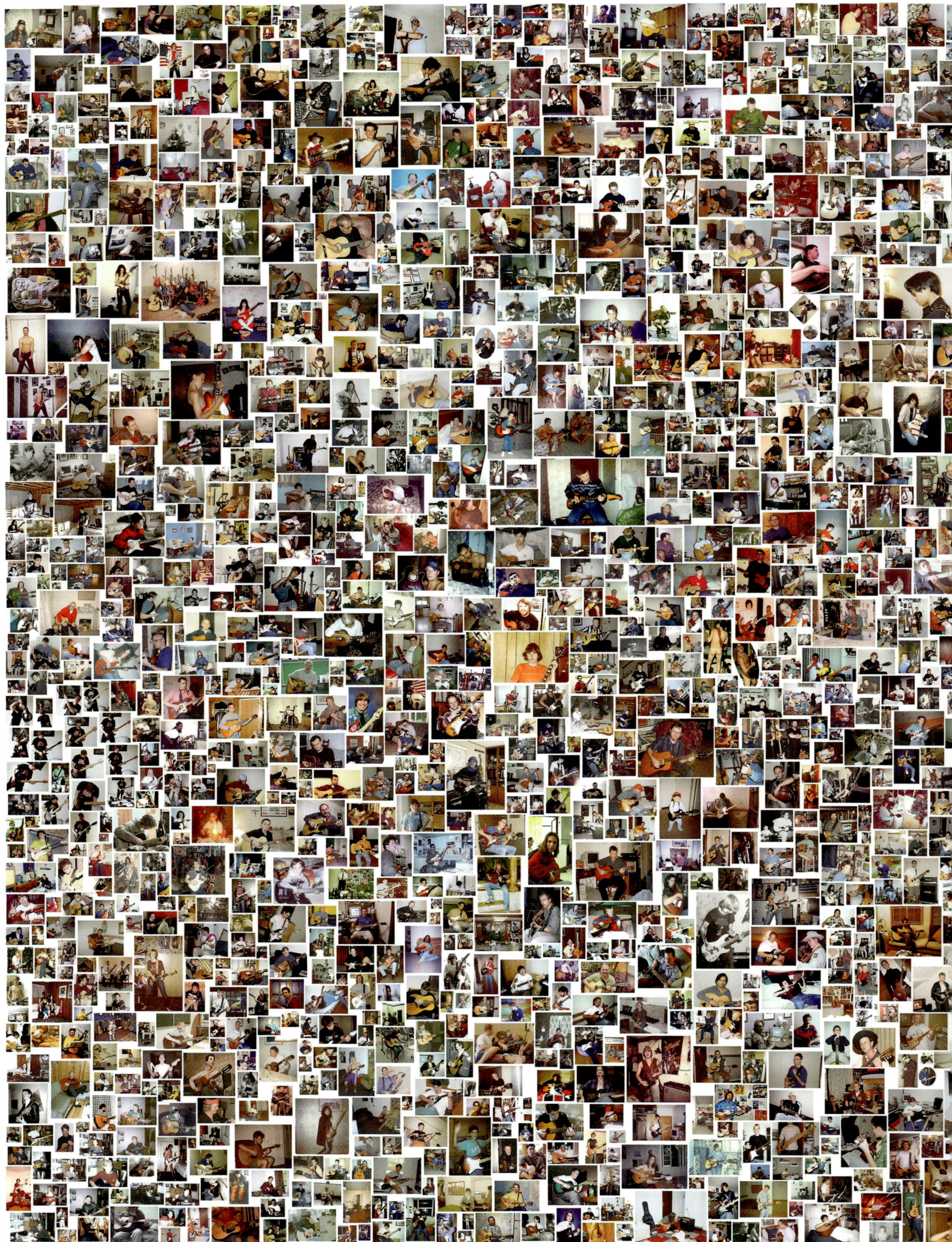

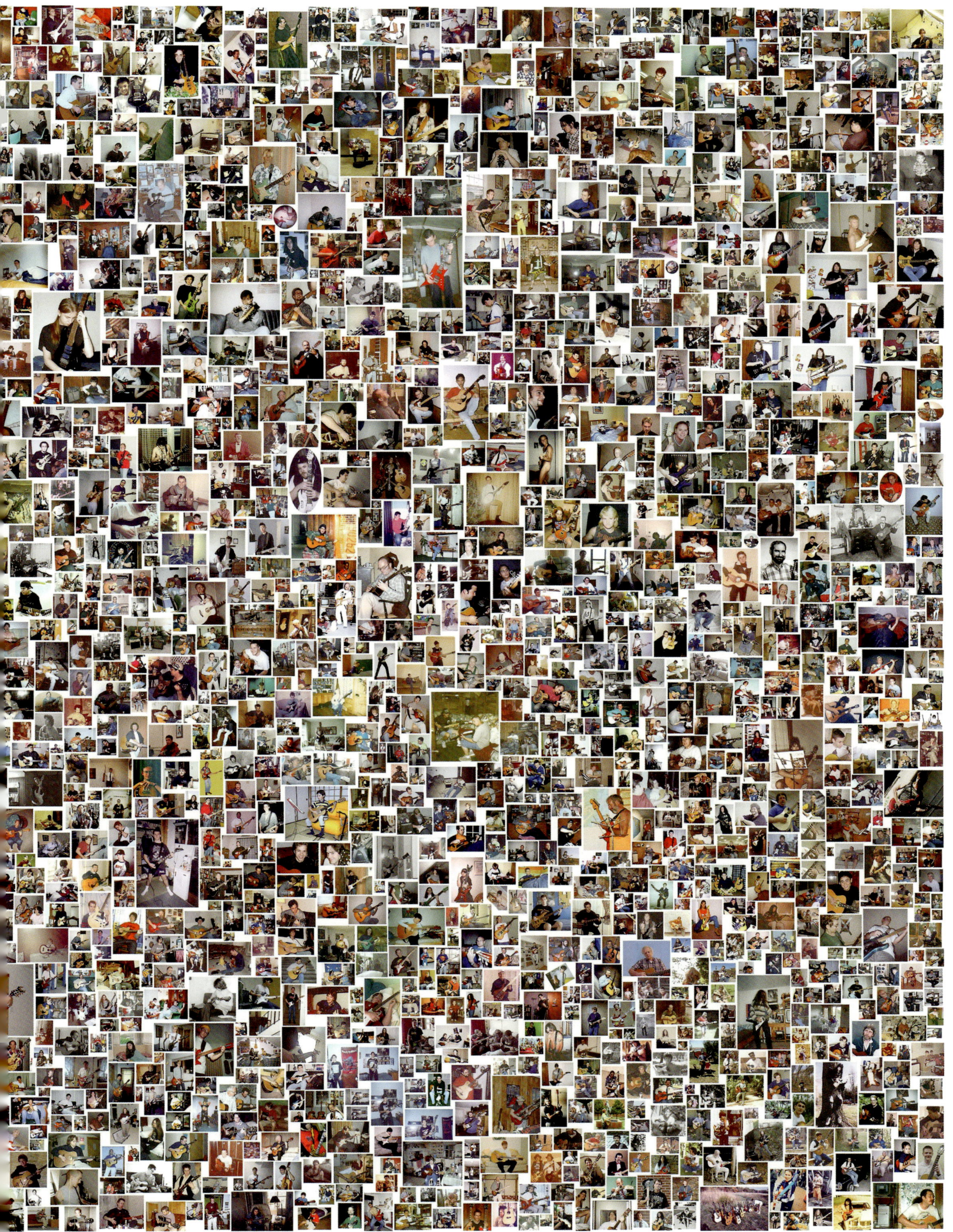

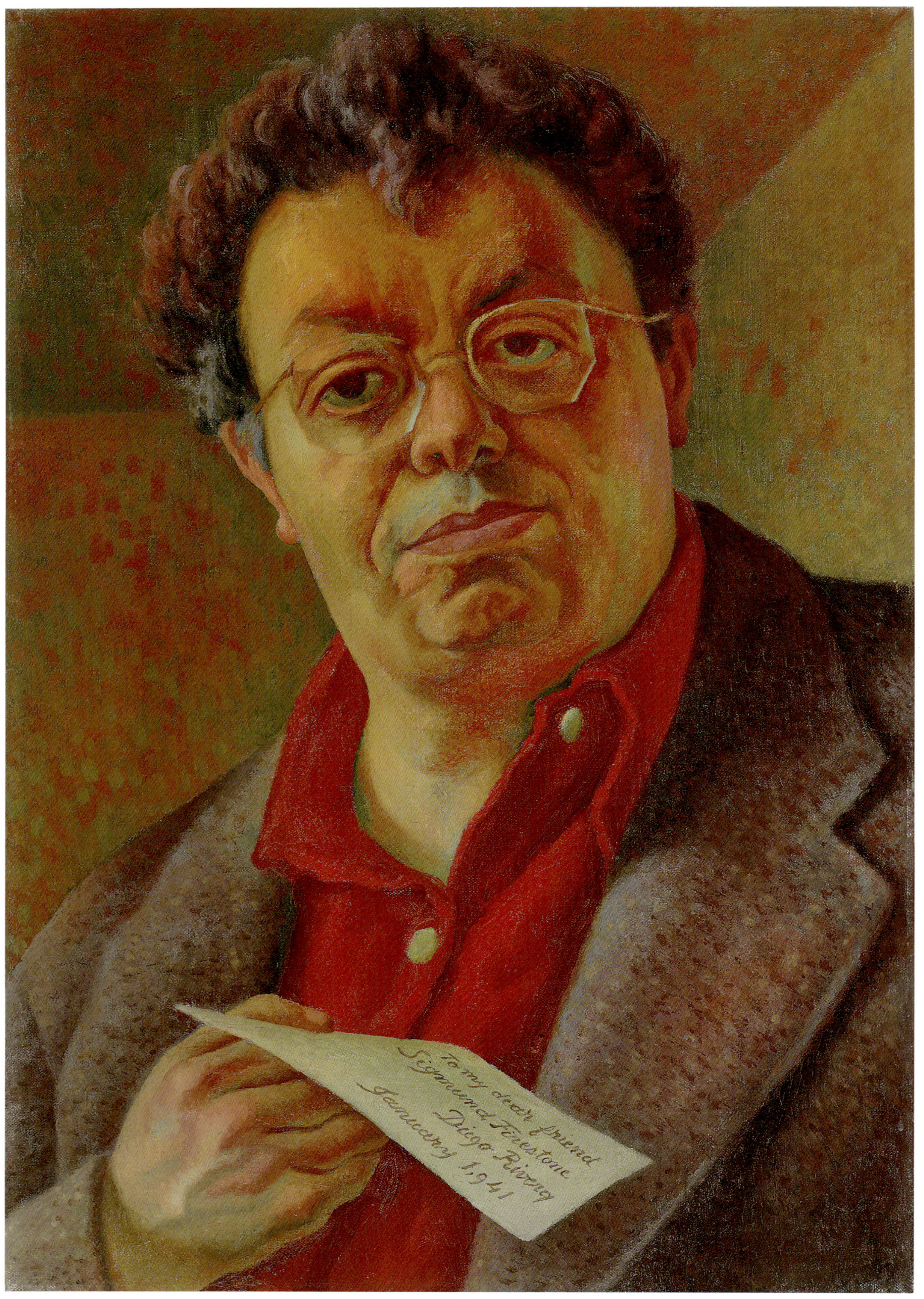
To my dear friend
Sigmund Firestone
Diego Rivera
January 1,941

THE MEXICAN SCHOOL OF PAINTING

IMAGES FOR REVOLUTIONARY TIMES

JESSICA BERLANGA TAYLOR
WITH JULIA SOTO MARTÍNEZ

THE WORK CARRIED out by artists of the Mexican School of Painting during the first decades of the twentieth century—exemplified by the painter Rufino Tamayo and the great Mexican muralists Diego Rivera, David Alfaro Siqueiros and José Clemente Orozco—invites reflection on the avant-garde influence of their work on art history and its active and polemic presence up to the present day.

The movement combined tradition with the experience of the Mexican Revolution, which redefined society and provided workers and peasants with the opportunity to become prominent protagonists. These factors produced the physical and emotional spaces in which to express *el Mexico profundo,*[1] a term coined by Mexican ethnologist and anthropologist Guillermo Bonfil Batalla, and gave it legitimacy. Until then, the underprivileged classes had been depicted as romantic and picturesque. The search for a new identity provoked the depiction of these groups from a powerfully renewed, more dignified, perspective.

The social and political events that led to the Russian Revolution, the First and Second World Wars and the Spanish Civil War strengthened the international position of the new artists in Mexico. Intellectuals and artists who shared the same political ideology, such as André Breton, Leon Trotsky and Sergei Eisenstein, visited Mexico in order to meet these creators and experimenters. Artists across America shared in and strengthened this vigorous change. The legacy of this international exchange has been an emphasis on artists working in public spaces and on the importance of breaking rules in order to create new artworks with avant-garde, revolutionary plastic elements.

The social revolution generated a revolution within the arts. One hundred years later, the experiments of these four great Mexican artists, the philosophical and political ramifications of their far-reaching ideas and in particular their relevance to contemporary Latin America, have proved to be one of the triumphs of the Mexican Revolution.

1. This term literally means "the profound Mexico" and implies that Mesoamerican civilization is undeniably present in contemporary Mexican life.

THE ARTISTS AND THEIR WORK

Tamayo, Rivera, Siqueiros and Orozco are bound together by the historical specificities mentioned, but these, combined with their commanding personalities and the logics

facing
Diego Rivera
Autorretrato [The Firestone Self-Portrait] 1941

of resistance each configured, also differentiate them. While Orozco's work contains a "Promethean fatalism"[2]—the idea that humankind is caught in a spiral of suffering—and Rivera's painting is "pedagogical, circumstantial and narrative,"[3] David Alfaro Siqueiros's oeuvre is a field of emotional forces that contains his political, social, physical and artistic strengths. Rufino Tamayo, who refused to join in the political activities of the other three, created his own expression of Mexico. Mexican writer and Nobel Prize winner Octavio Paz said, "If I could express with a single word what it is that distinguishes Tamayo from other painters, I would say without a moment's hesitation: Sun: for the sun is in all his pictures whether we see it or not."[4]

Among the Mexican works in the Audain collection is *Autorretrato,* 1941 (page 120), commissioned by North American businessman Sigmund Firestone, which is also known as *The Firestone Self-Portrait.* It depicts an Apollonian Diego Rivera, the artist as a wise, mature man who has observed himself throughout turbulent years. In his hand he holds a note: "To my dear friend Sigmund Firestone, Diego Rivera, January 1, 1941." The painting's commission, together with Firestone's request to Frida Kahlo for a self-portrait, detonated a series of intimate letters between the three that tell of the artists' intense relationship. Two further examples of Rivera's talent for individual and intimate portraiture are *Luz hilando [Light Spinner],* 1936 (page 4) and *Retrato de Gladys March,* 1946 (page 126). The first gracefully captures a young woman—one of Rivera's favourite models, called Luz—as she weaves. This is a classic illustration of Rivera's commitment to visually narrating the daily activities of the Mexican people. The second painting is the serene, thoughtful depiction of a young American journalist who co-wrote Diego Rivera's autobiography, *My Art, My Life,* based on her visits to his studio between 1944 and 1957. Of Rivera she noted, "He had an active and many-sided personality; his mind was quick, his imagination staggering."[5]

José Clemente Orozco is known for his highly expressive, violent syntax of form. One of the characters he reiterated was Prometheus, who in Greek mythology stole fire, a symbol of wisdom and enlightenment, from the gods and gave it to humankind. Prometheus was severely punished by Zeus, his great deed never fully appreciated by human beings concerned with their own mortality and corruptibility. This myth was depicted by Orozco and his assistant, Jorge Juan Crespo de la Serna, in a painting on the walls of Pomona College in Claremont, California, in 1930. Another of his Prometheus works, *Hombre de Fuego,* 1936–39, this one a mural at the Hospicio Cabañas, Guadalajara, Mexico, is a series of powerful images that tell of Orozco's concern for humankind's ignorance and suffering. Orozco painted his Prometheus series as liminal moments in his emotional and intellectual survival and that of his country's people. A more modest yet powerful depiction of this figure is *Prometheus,* 1945 (page 130), also in the Audain collection, whose caricature-like heads float in the atmosphere. Orozco's beginnings were as a social and political cartoonist for newspapers in Mexico. His political satire always appears in his works, combining the artist's anguish with a sarcastic sense of humour.

David Alfaro Siqueiros has been described as "not just a painter. He is a polemicist, theoretician of art, a politician and a revolutionary."[6] For him, art was all about

2. Mario de Micheli, *Siqueiros* (New York: Harry N. Abraham Inc.), 1968, 1–2.
3. Ibid.
4. Octavio Paz, *México en la obra de Octavio Paz. Vol. 3. Re/visiones: La pintura mural: ocultación y descubrimiento de Orozco: Rufino Tamayo: Transfiguraciones: Frida Kahlo y María Izquierdo* (México: FCE), 1998.
5. Diego Rivera, *My Art, My Life: An Autobiography* (New York: The Citadel Press), 1960, 225–26.
6. Mario de Micheli, *Siqueiros,* 2.

facing
Diego Rivera
Naturaleza muerta en ovalo
[Oval Still-Life] c. 1915–16

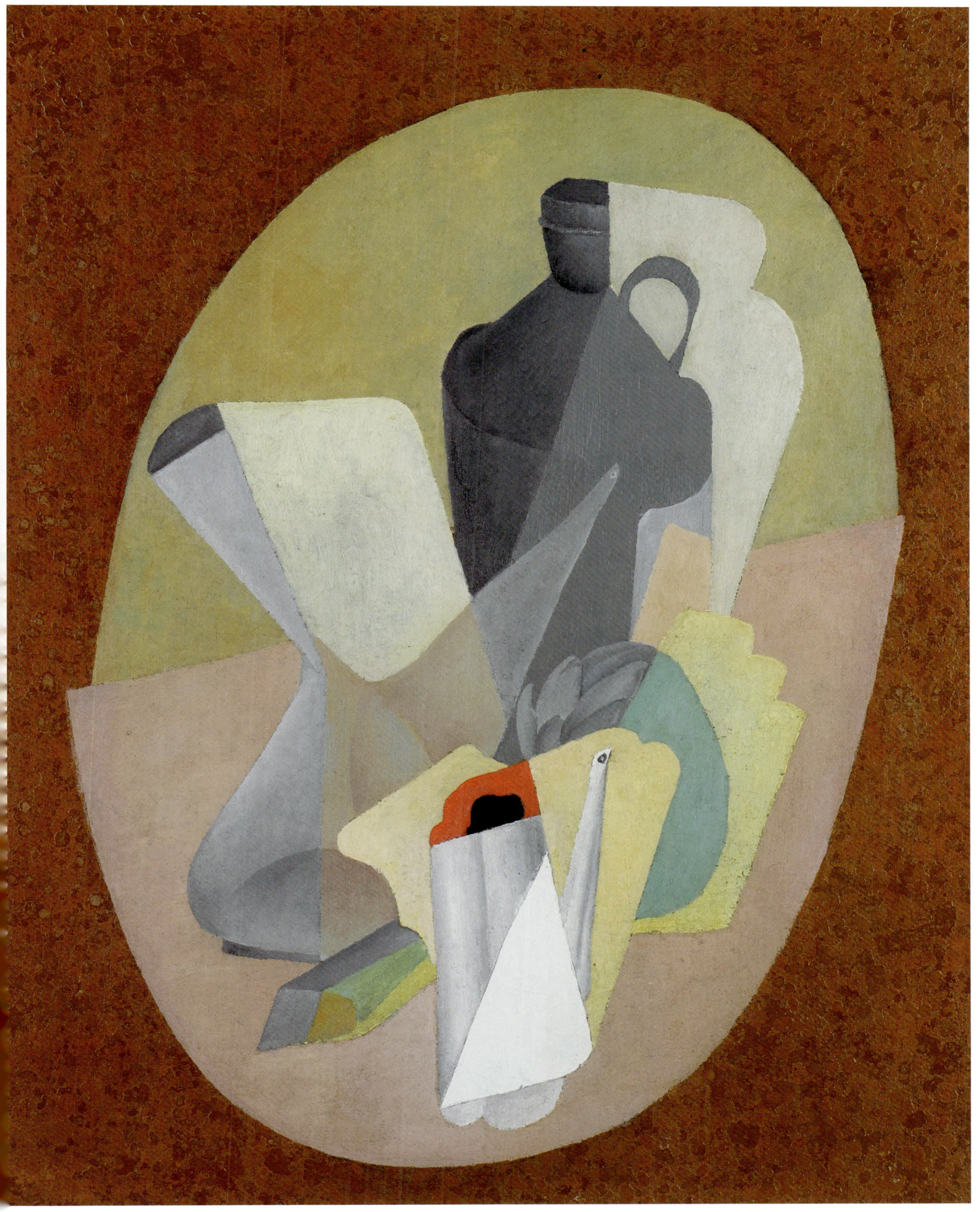

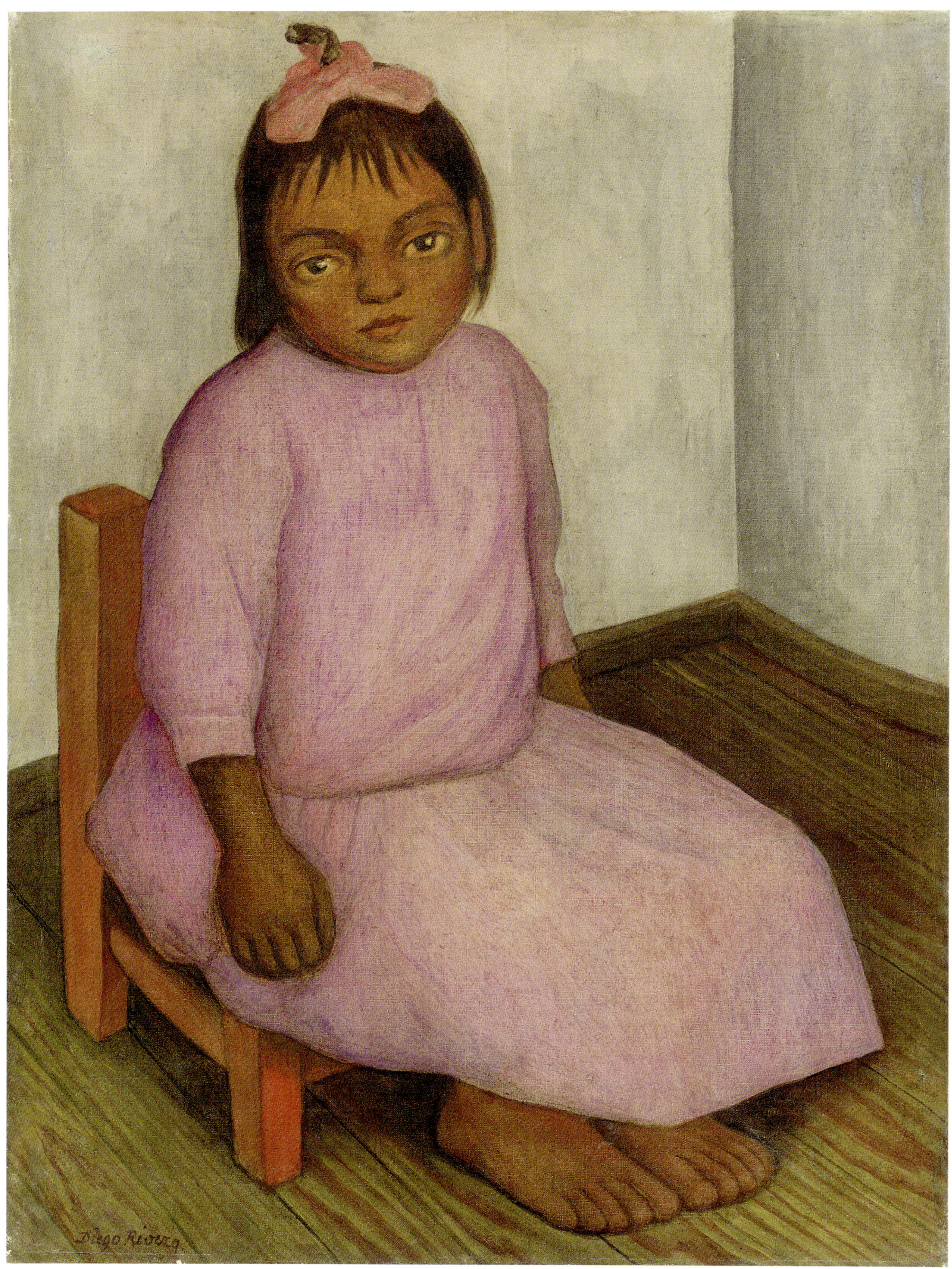
Diego Rivera

creating volume in space. Among Siqueiros's most valuable legacies are his experiments with industrial materials such as spray-paint guns, pyroxylin, silicate paints and masonite. He continued his investigations into these materials and into spotting, dripping and automatic gestures when he was in Argentina and New York, where he founded the Experimental Workshop, attended by Jackson Pollock. An endearing example of Siqueiros's use of such materials and techniques and of his relationship to Christ as a politically significant yet persecuted man, is *Los Dos Davides,* 1963 (page 133), dedicated to his adopted daughter Adriana on her birthday. "Siqueiros executed this painting based on the large production of images of Christ as Man of Sorrows, mothers fleeing with children in their arms, and Trees of Life in twisted shapes looming behind crosses which he produced while he was in prison,"[7] from 1960 to 1964, at a time when he was accused of social disruption. It depicts the painter and his grandson, David Constantino, as his own version of the Madonna and Child, yet here he offers the figure of paternal[8] love, his big, strong hands (seen throughout his iconography) clutching the baby. Minimal brushstrokes, automatic gestures and empty faces are reminiscent of his other works.

Rufino Tamayo's paintings are deeply rooted in his Zapotec heritage, and in Fauvism, Impressionism and Cubism. Tamayo's expert use of light and colour produce vibrant pictorial planes, significantly textured, as seen in *La Constelación [Constellation],* 1947 (page 136). By using geometric colour abstraction and minimal gestures, he created colossal, yet delicate, lyrical figures that usually stand alone. One example is *Hombre contra un muro,* 1975 (page 25): "The figure… summons not only the spectre of the country's recent violence, but might allude to Tamayo's sense of isolation against the cultural inundations he felt in Mexico at the time."[9]

7. Irene Herner, 2007, in www.christies.com/LotFinder/lot_details.asapx?intObjectID+4989324, consulted December 10, 2010.

8. Irene Herner notes that the viewer should understand the relationship between *father* and *pater/patria;* paternal love in Siqueiros refers to the fact that *patria* in Spanish comes from the Latin *pater,* meaning "father."

9. Deborah Cullen, 2008, in www.christies.com/LotFinder/lot_details.aspx?intObjectID+5139483, consulted December 10, 2010.

facing
Diego Rivera
Niña con vestido rosa
[Girl with Pink Dress] 1930

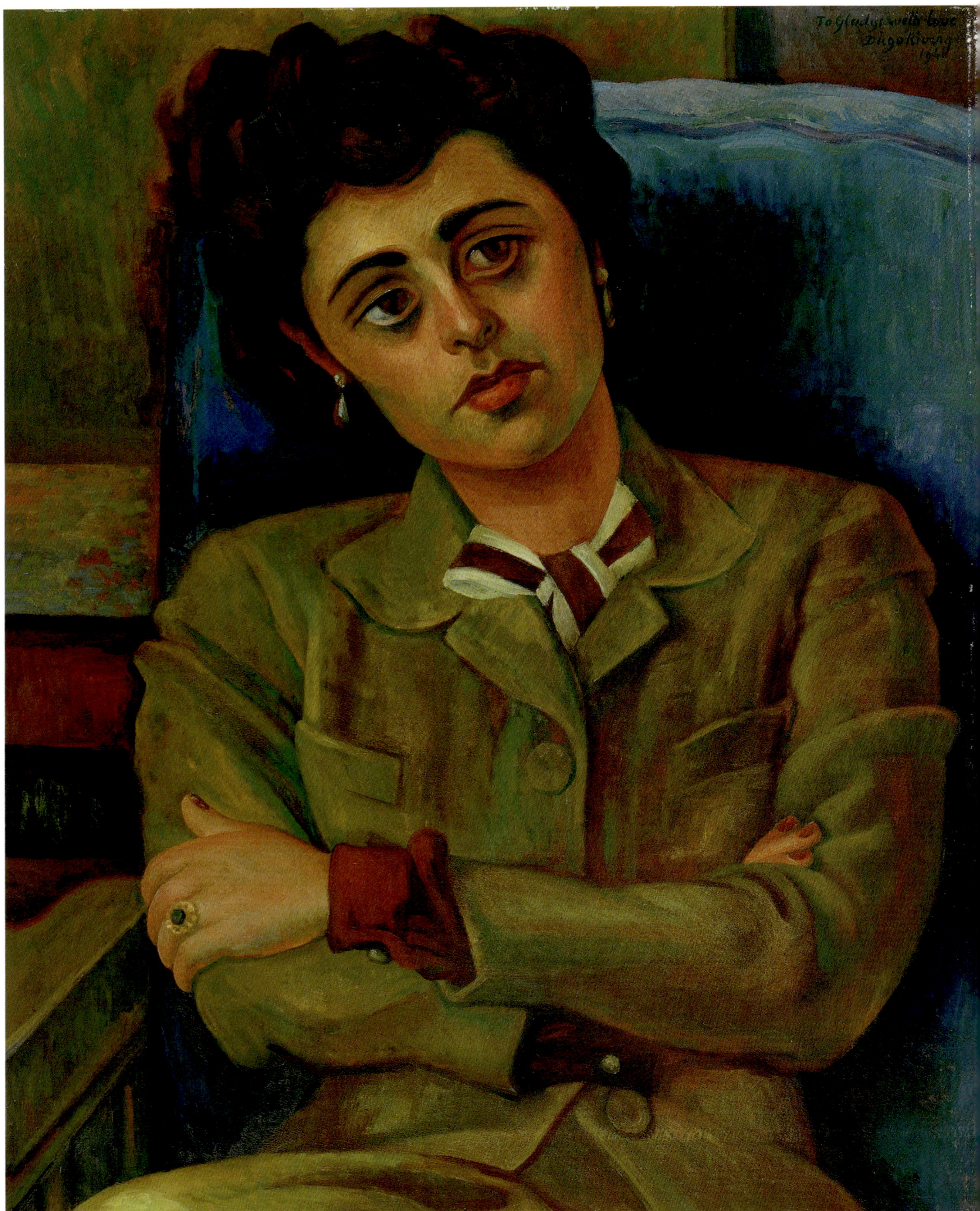
To Gladys with love
Diego Rivera

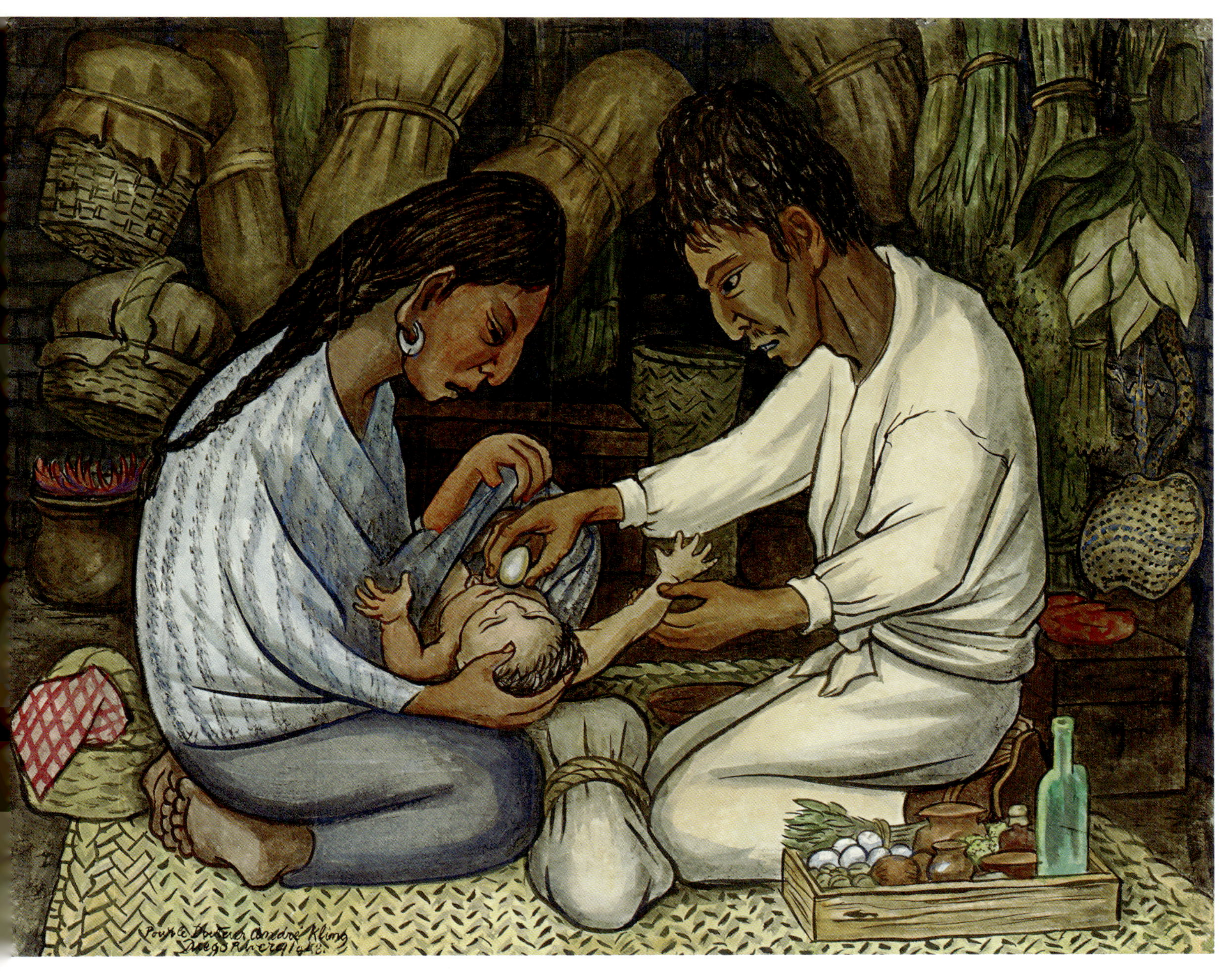

facing
Diego Rivera
Retrato de Gladys March
[Portrait of Gladys March]
1946

above
Diego Rivera
El curandero [The Folk
Healer] 1945

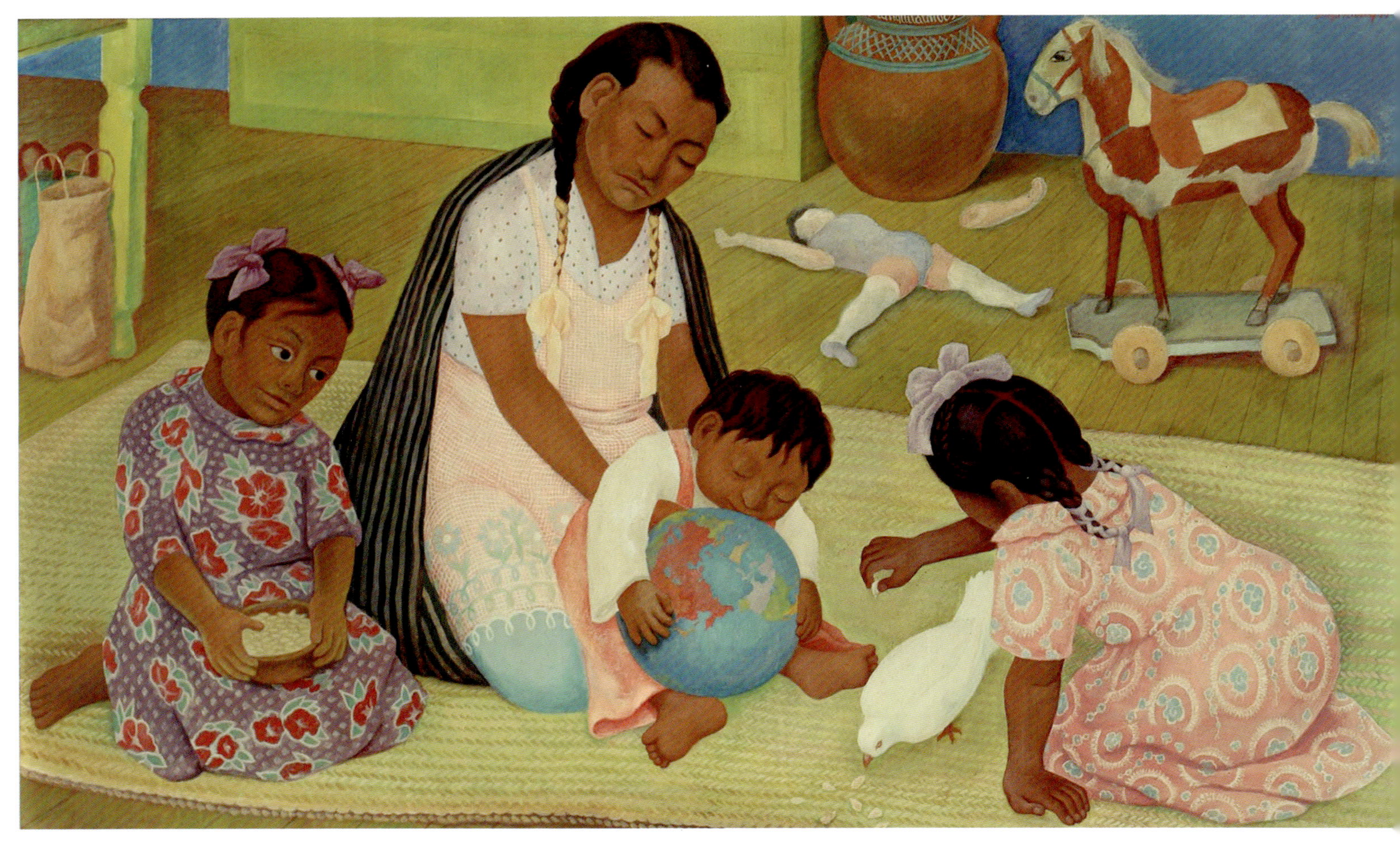

Diego Rivera
Maternidad [Motherhood] 1954

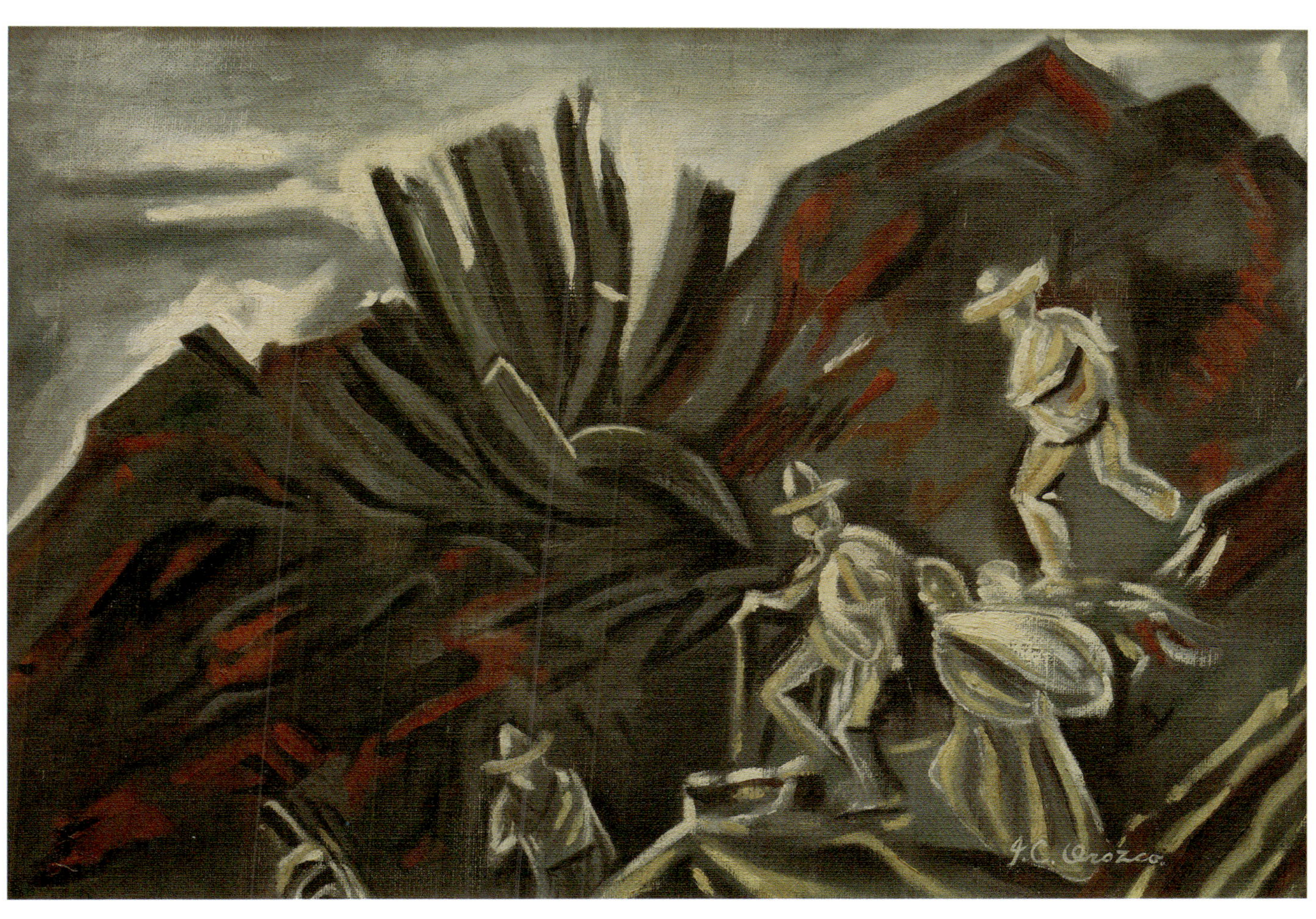

José Clemente Orozco
Pedregal [Stony Place] 1947

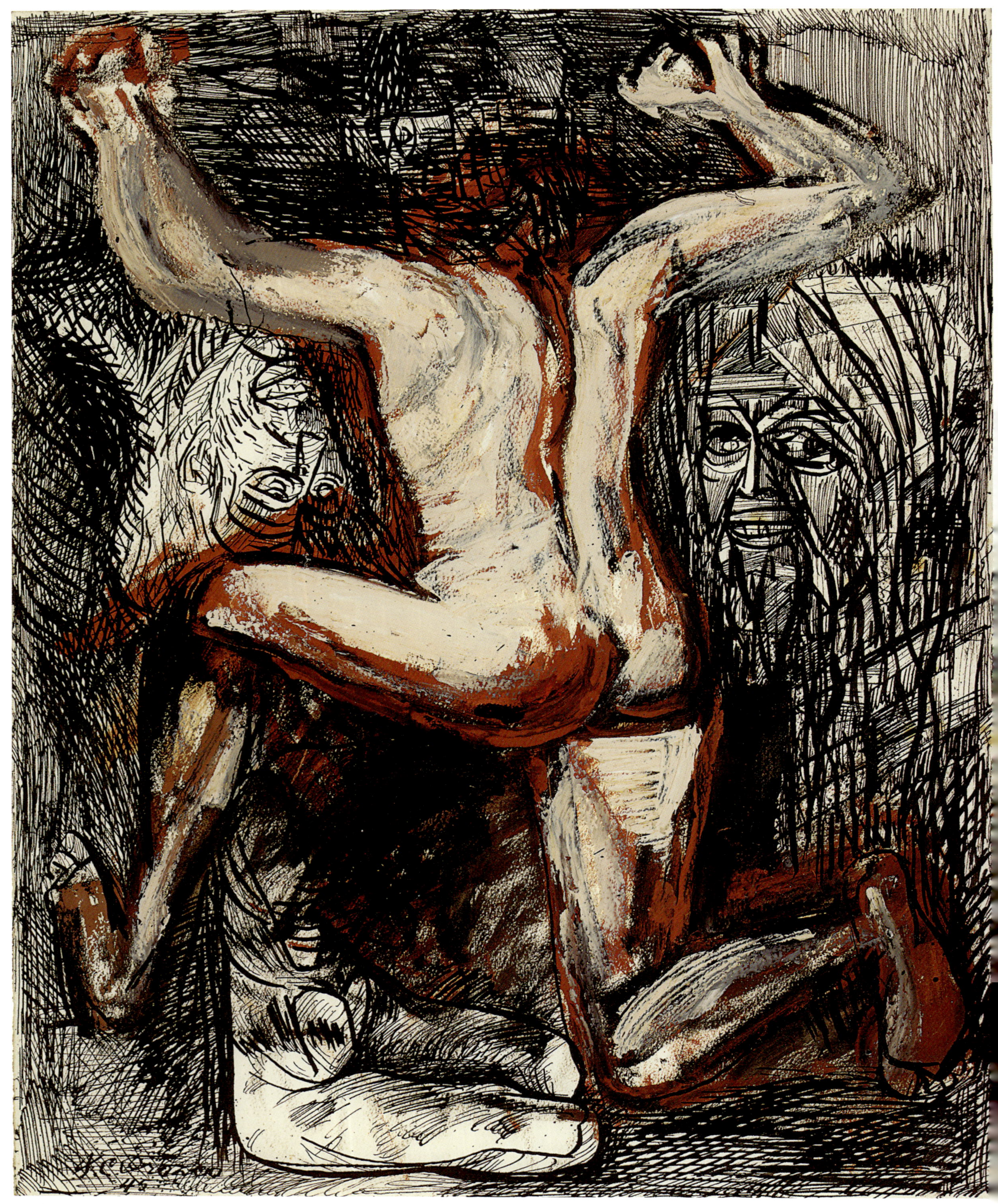

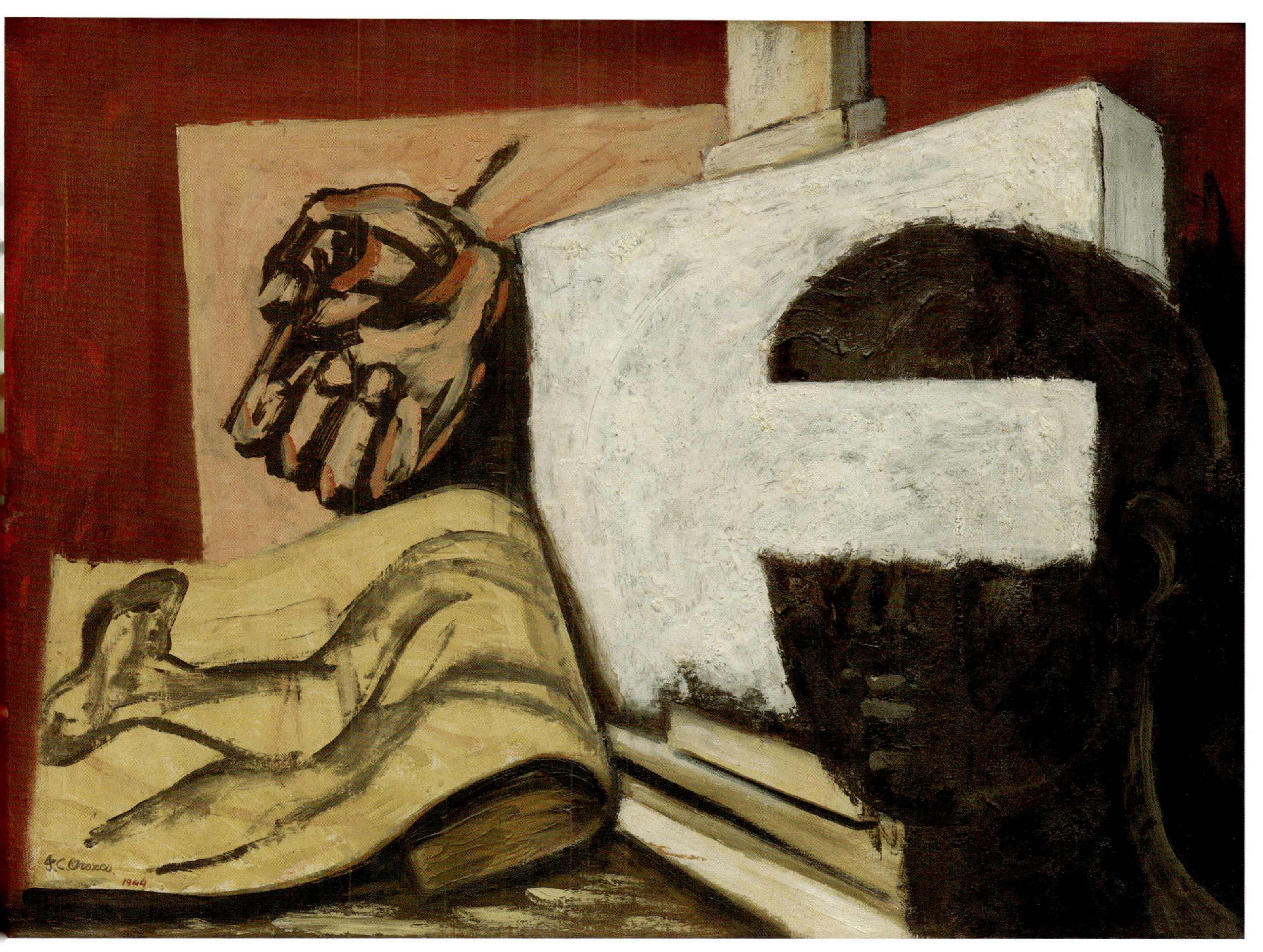

facing
José Clemente Orozco
Prometheus 1945

above
José Clemente Orozco
Naturaleza Muerta
(Autorretrato)
[Still-Life (Self-Portrait)] 1944

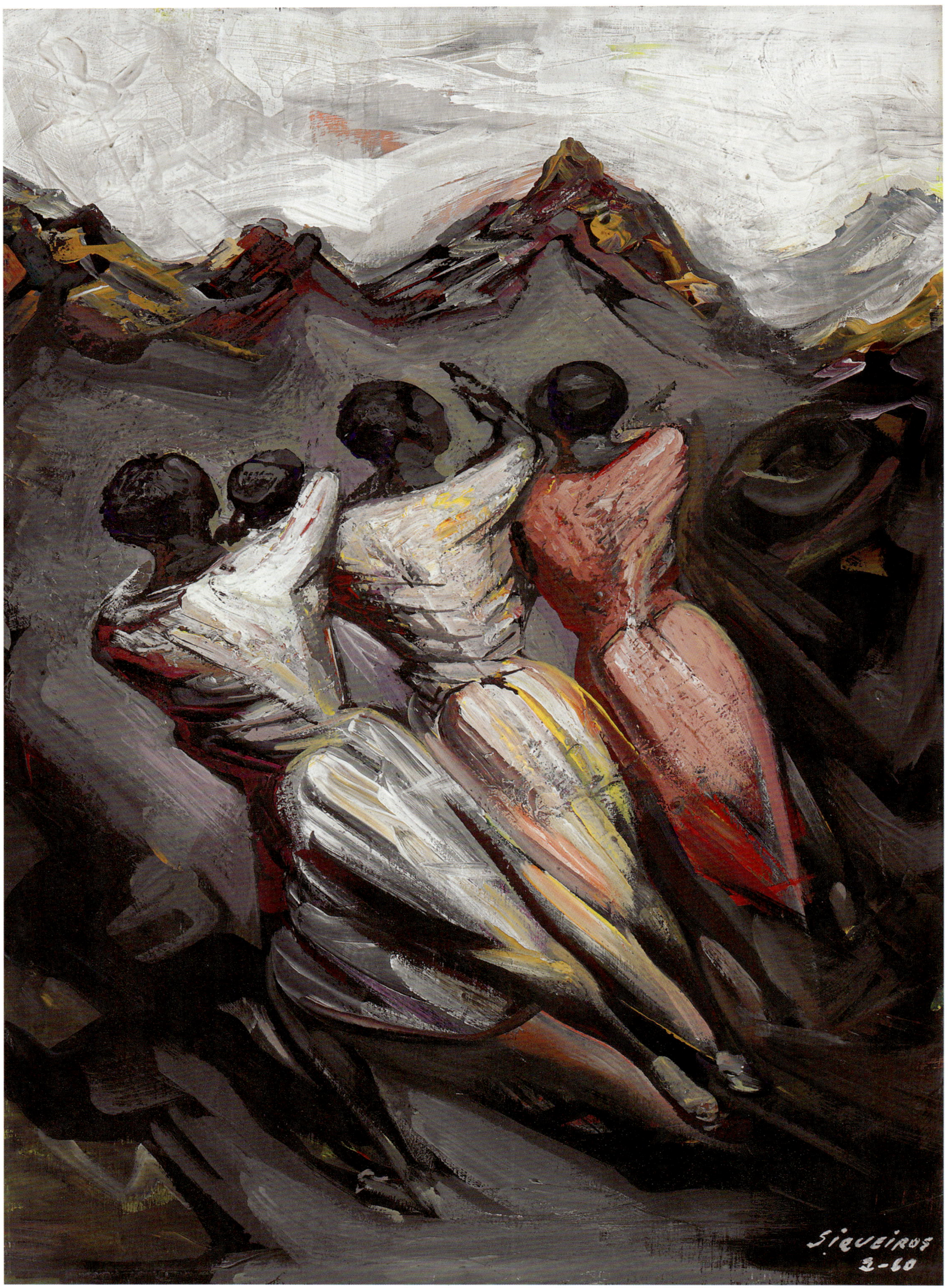
SIQUEIROS
2-60

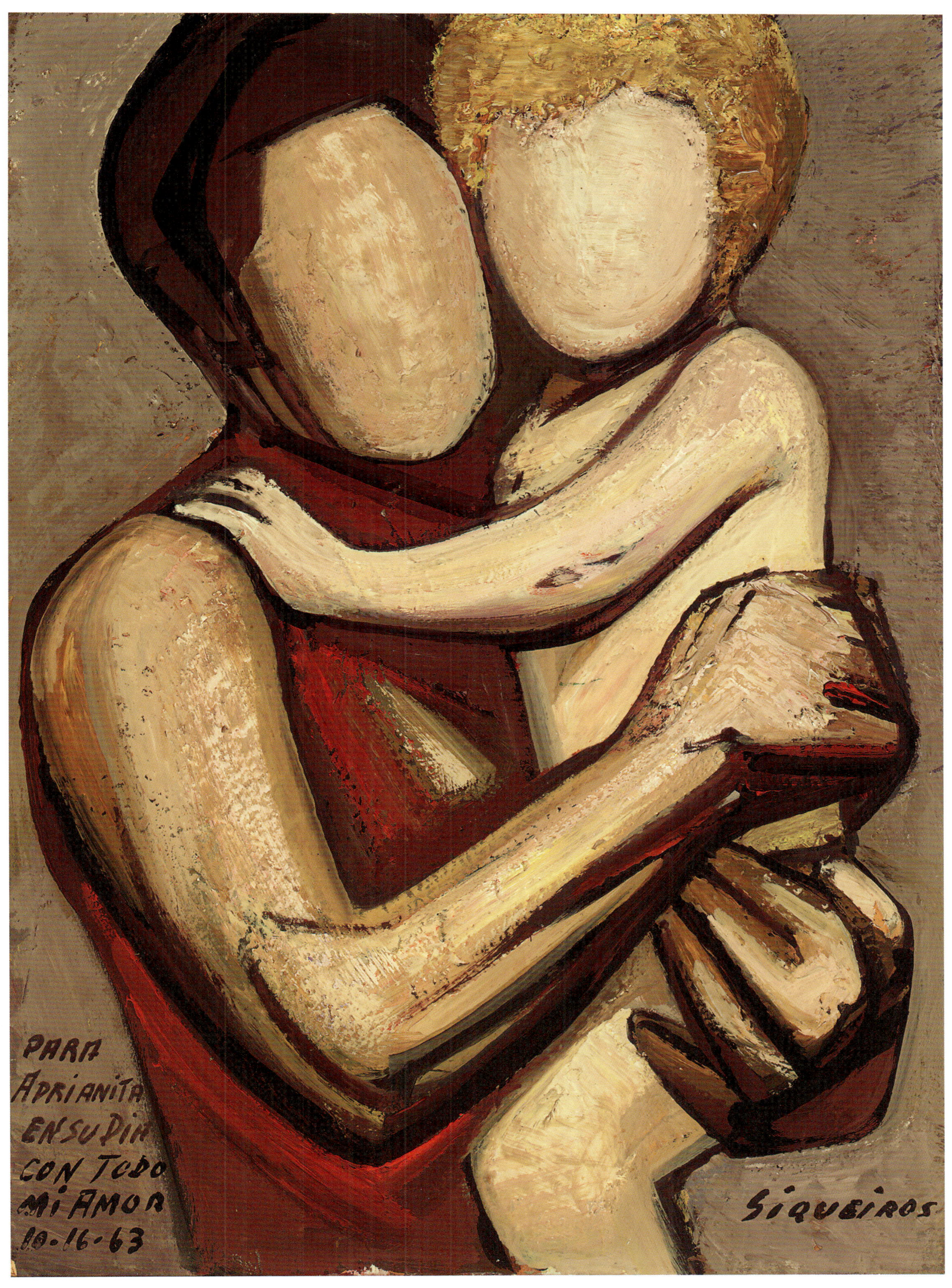
PARA
ADRIANITA
EN SU DIA
CON TODO
MI AMOR
10-16-63
SIQUEIROS

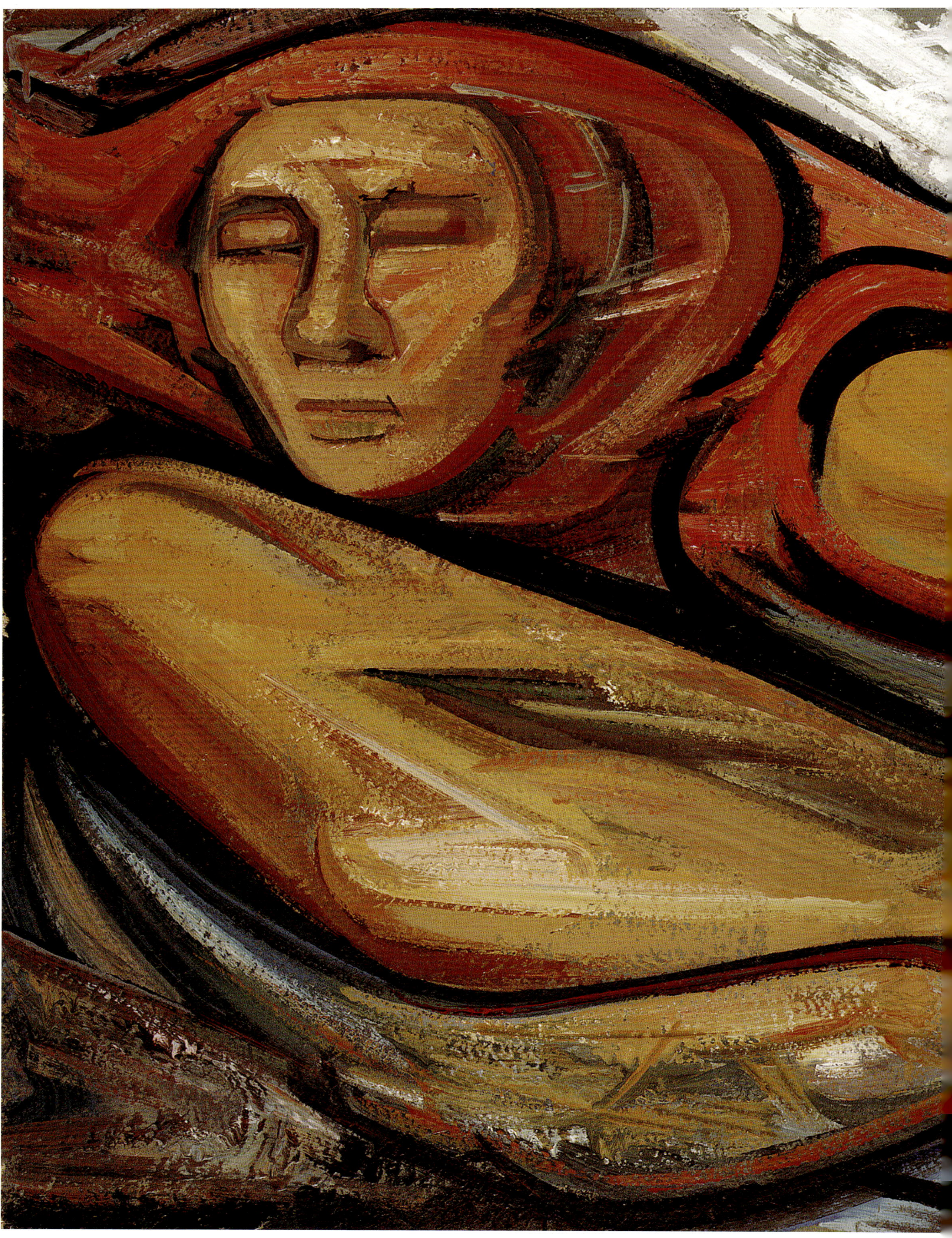

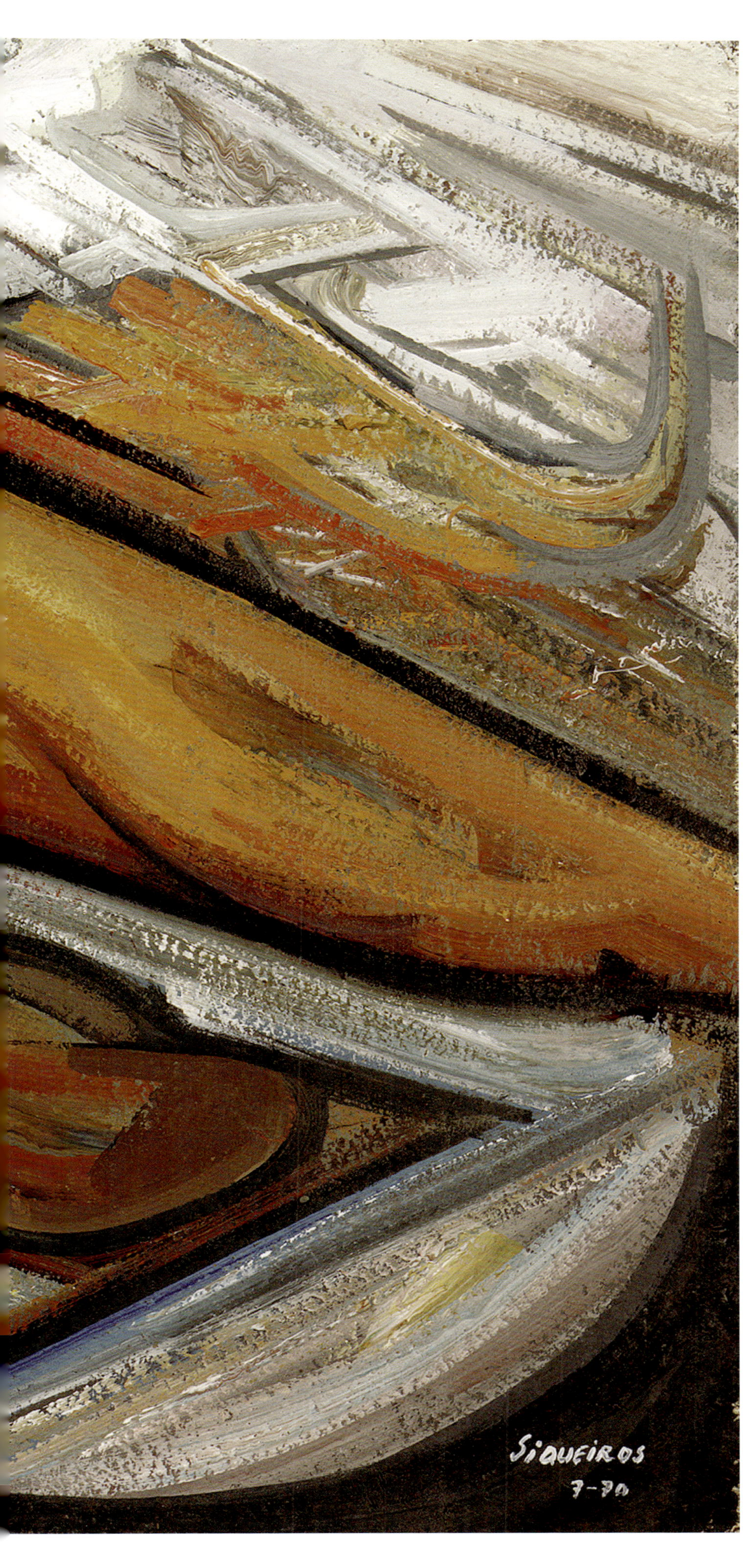

previous spread, left

David Alfaro Siqueiros
Hacia la cumbre!
[Towards the Top!] 1960

previous spread, right

David Alfaro Siqueiros
Los Dos Davides
[The Two Davids] 1963

left

David Alfaro Siqueiros
Sueño [Sleep] 1970

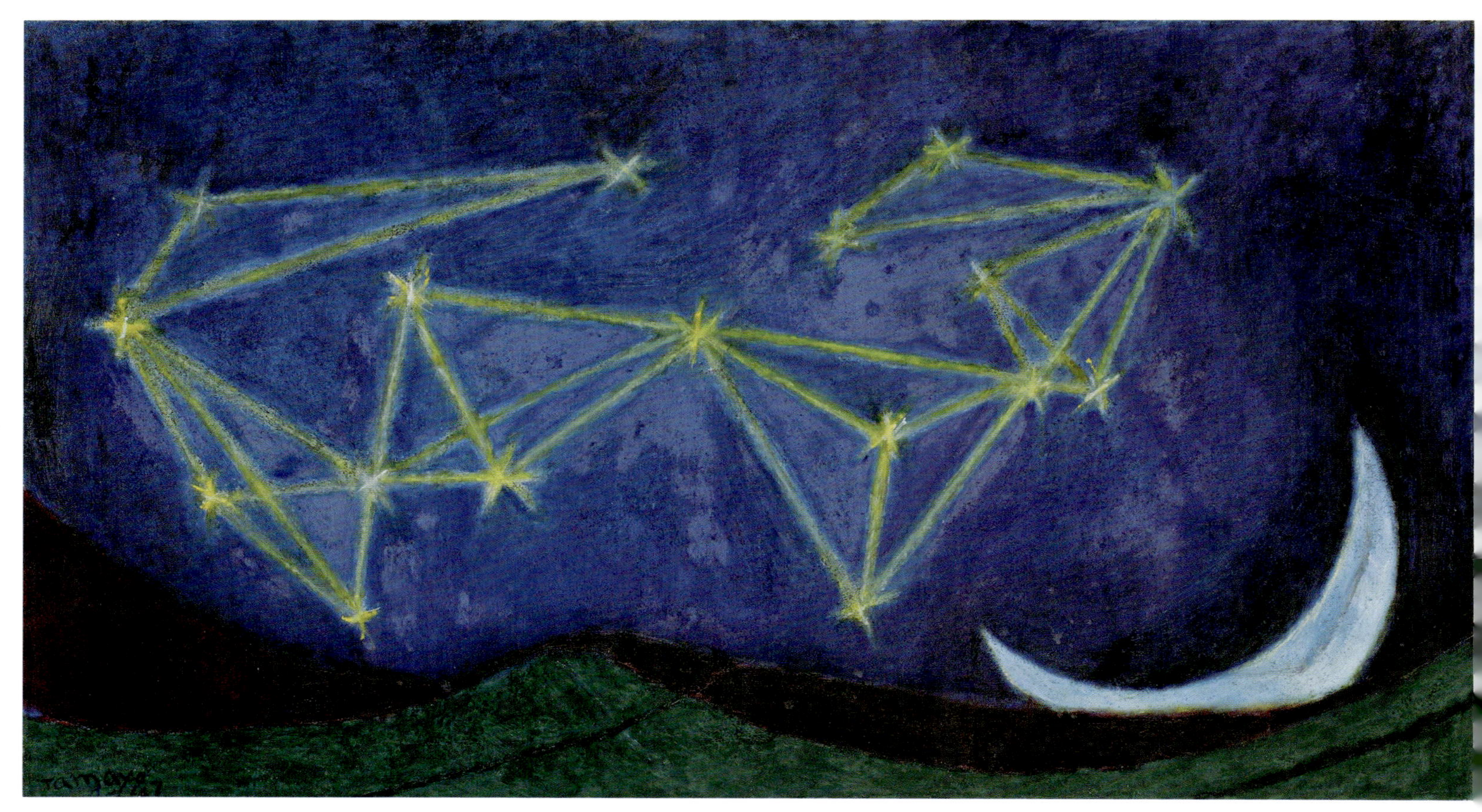

above
Rufino Tamayo
La Constelación
[**Constellation**] 1947

facing
Rufino Tamayo
Mujer llamando
[**Woman Crying Out**] 1941

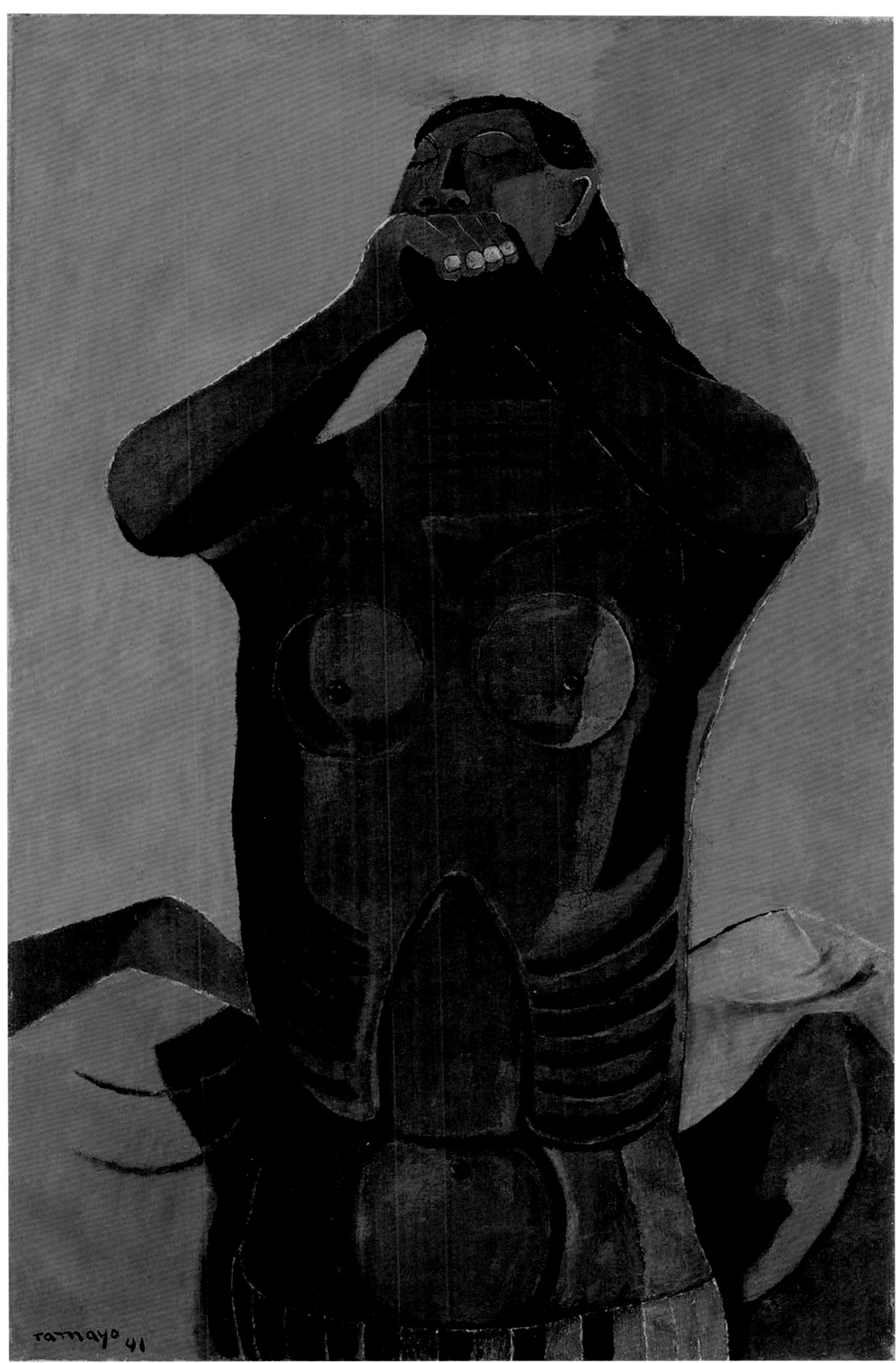
tamayo 41

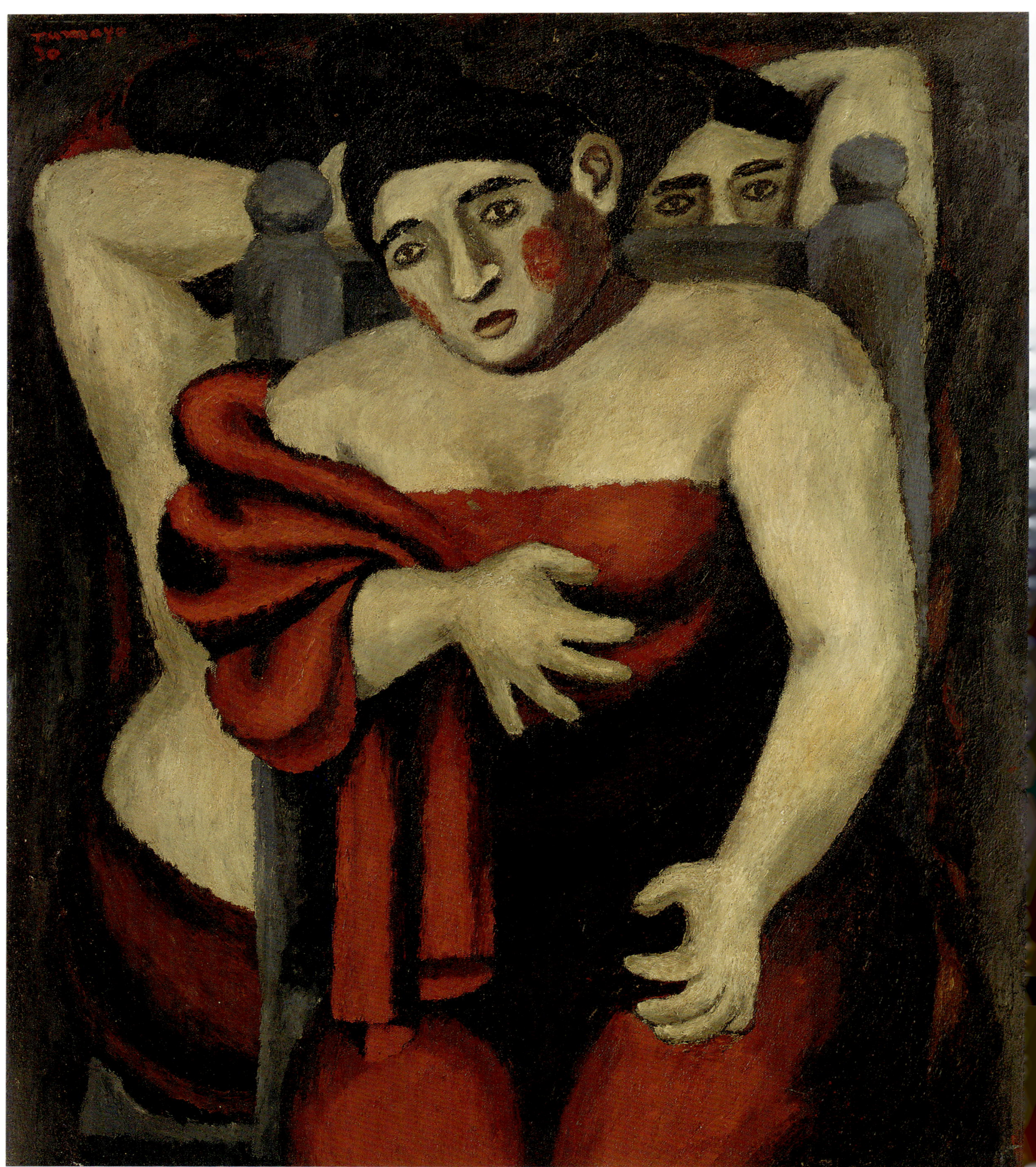
Tamayo
30

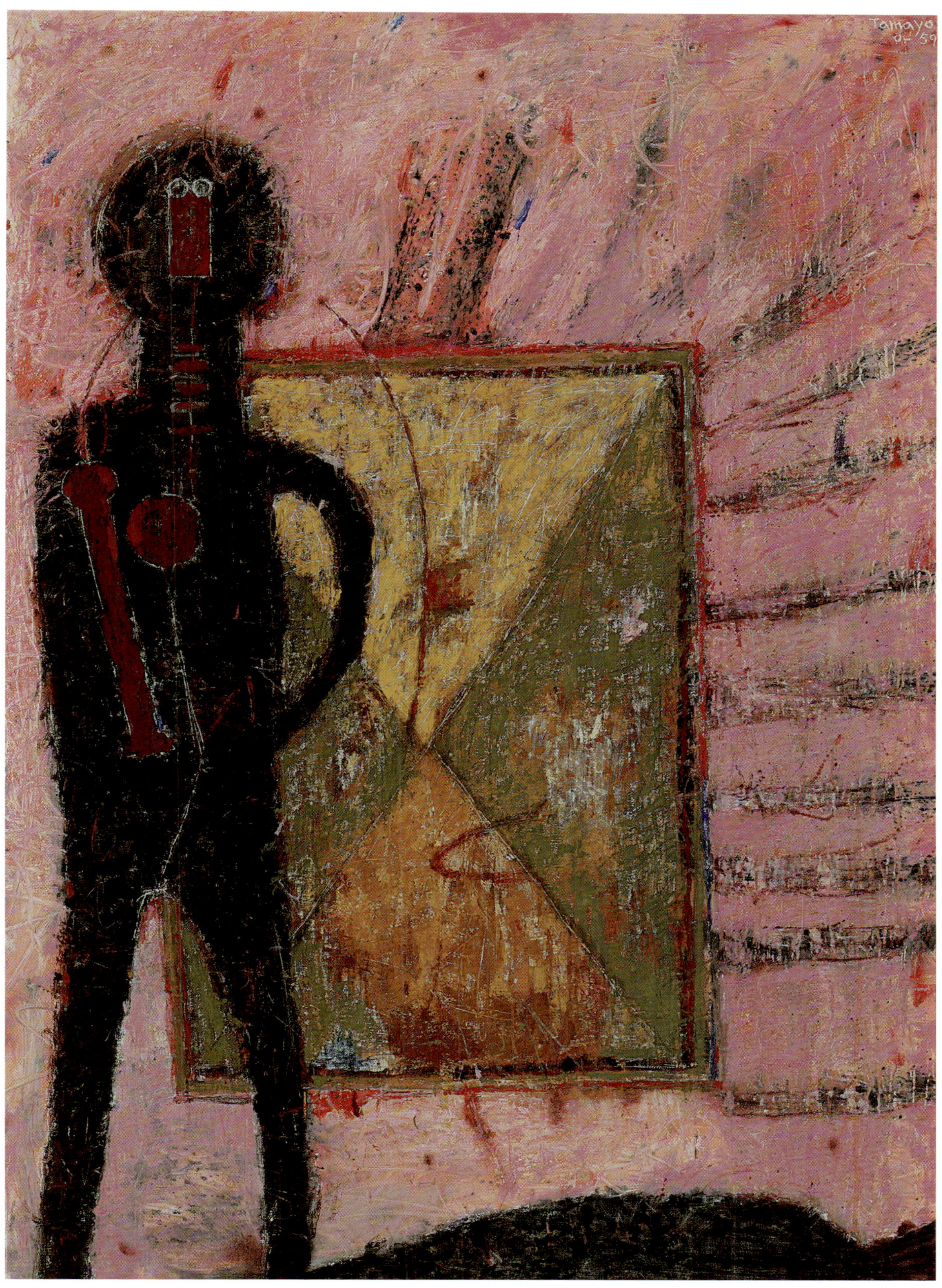

facing
Rufino Tamayo
Bañistas [Bathers]
1930

above
Rufino Tamayo
Figura de pie
[Pious Figure] 1959

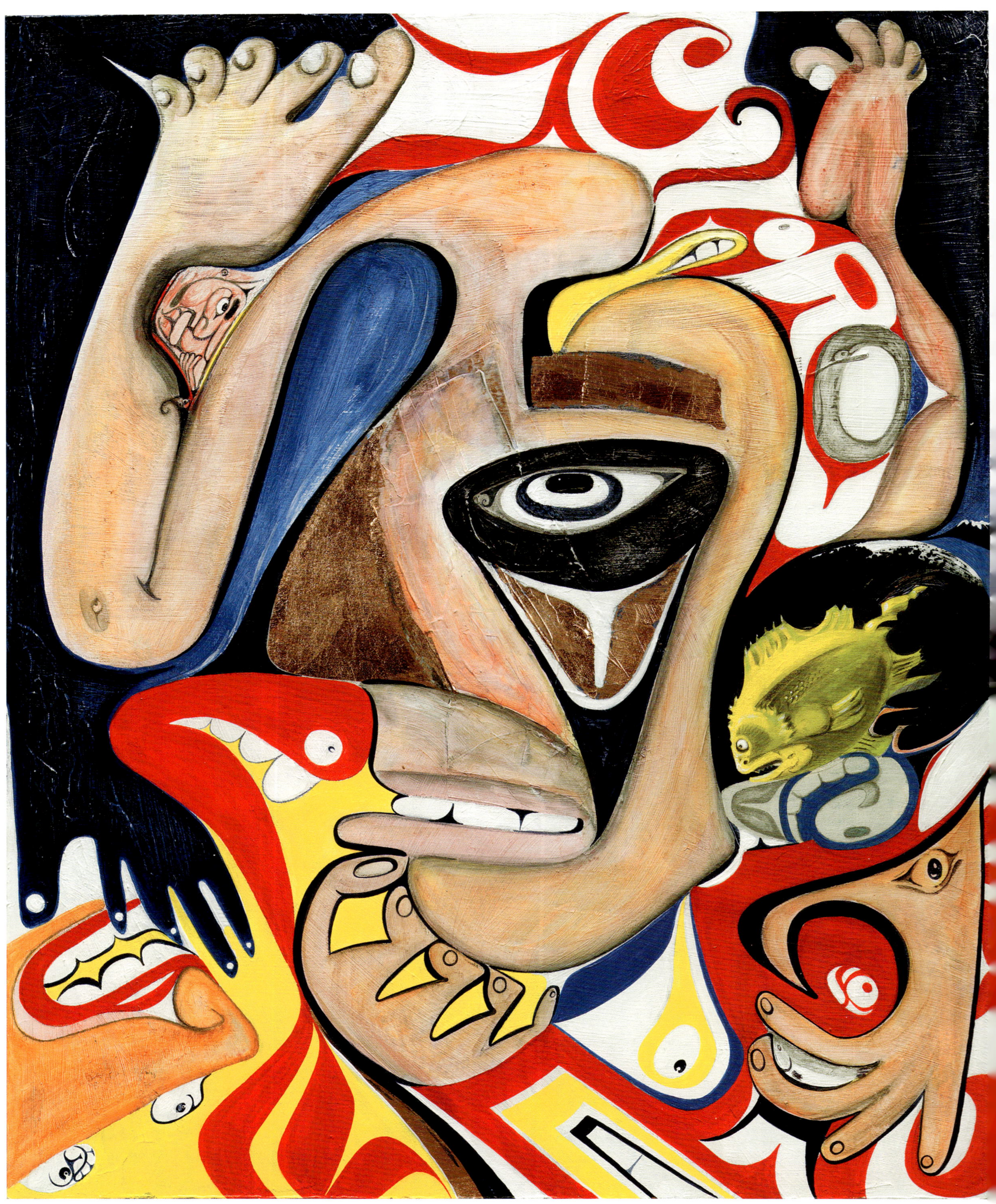

AFTERWORD

THE HONOURABLE **GORDON CAMPBELL**

MICHAEL AUDAIN BELIEVES that great works of art enrich our lives, broaden our horizons and should be accessible to everyone to enjoy. He is well known as an active supporter of artists and art institutions, yet until now the collection that he and his wife, Yoshiko Karasawa, have amassed over the years has been a private one. Now, through the Audains' generosity, the Vancouver Art Gallery offers the first public opportunity to view their extraordinary personal collection, one that reflects an evolving passion for the visual arts and recognition of artists at pivotal cultural moments, whether it was Vancouver photo-based artists on the cusp of the international scene, Mexican artists of early Modernism or First Nations artists whose legacy extends back over 150 years. Perhaps what is most extraordinary for us British Columbians, however, is the reflection of our own history in many of these works.

Michael resists common description. He balks at being called a collector and blanches at the term philanthropist, but what is clear is how his rich appreciation for the arts coalesces with his love for British Columbia and his belief in public service.

That this collection touches the spirit of our province is not surprising. Michael's roots here go deep. His great-great-grandfather Robert Dunsmuir discovered coal in Nanaimo in 1869 and as an industrialist, railroad developer and finally a Member of the Legislative Assembly helped build the province. Michael's great-grandfather, James Dunsmuir, was Premier and later Lieutenant-Governor of British Columbia. Now, tourists on Vancouver Island daily admire the first family home, Craigdarroch Castle, and students from around the world study at Royal Roads University in Hatley Castle, where James Dunsmuir once lived.

Inspired by a family legacy of public life, Michael showed his community conscience early on. As a young man he was arrested in Mississippi for participation in the civil rights Freedom Rides, and subsequently organized and participated in Ban the Bomb and anti–Vietnam War marches. When he was only twenty-five he hosted the first meeting of the B.C. Civil Liberties Association in his Vancouver living room. After earning a master's degree in Social Work at the University of British Columbia he worked at the Ontario Housing Corporation before helping to establish the B.C. Ministry of Housing in 1973. In 1980 he started the Polygon Group in Vancouver, overseeing the development of over 19,000 homes to date. Michael's social conscience endures: he is still the man who wants everyone to have a safe home.

facing
Michael Nicoll Yahgulanaas
Fishing 2008

The instinct that led Michael Audain to invest his considerable talent in home-building has also led him on a remarkable journey through the visual arts in Vancouver, across Canada and internationally. An avowed devotee of British Columbia artists, he sought out both established artists and the early masters of the craft with the same intensity he showed for social justice. As he shifted his activism to cultural issues, his patronage and encouragement of emerging artists has been a true public gift to us all.

In 1997 he established the Audain Foundation to support the visual arts, and has since given more than $25 million to regional and national arts endeavours. Recognizing that the next generation of artists must be nurtured, he has sponsored the Artists for Kids Trust, giving thousands of school children the opportunity to take part in art programs. He has served as a Chair and Trustee on the boards of the Vancouver Art Gallery and Canada's National Gallery. And in addition to his membership in the Order of British Columbia, Michael is the recipient of the Order of Canada—our country's highest honour.

In some ways, the greatest gift of this exhibition is to foster understanding of how art can inspire us to see others through different lenses.

The masks exhibited here remind us not just of the traditional cultures of Aboriginal peoples but also that we all wear masks that reflect the world we live in and the world to which we aspire. These traditional craftspeople and artists pass their culture, traditions and understanding of the world around them on to the generations that follow.

Michael's unerring eye and joy in discovery enabled him, with Yoshi, to collect works that personally appealed, but their appreciation for First Nations art and culture goes far beyond collecting. They have purchased pieces and repatriated them to their traditional First Nations bands to ensure that the ceremonial artifacts are never offered for sale again.

This exhibition is not finished when it leaves the Gallery. By sharing their insights and passion for art, Michael and Yoshi also show exemplary citizenship. British Columbia is fortunate that our artists have the support of private patrons like the Audains, who recognize and encourage artistic growth.

We had the unique opportunity to house the B.C. Pavilion in the Vancouver Art Gallery during the Vancouver 2010 Olympic Winter Games, exposing thousands of people from around the world to the staggering talent of B.C.'s artists. In 2008, the B.C. Government announced $50 million in support of a new art gallery to ensure that we continue to showcase our incredible artists. As British Columbians, we must all step up and acknowledge our responsibility as custodians of art, so that future generations are able to enjoy and study the rich legacy of our contemporaries.

With this exhibition, British Columbians, Canadians and art lovers from around the world will see an accomplished, eclectic collection. They will see in it a passion for beauty and come to appreciate the generosity of the Audains and the importance of their role as caretakers of our provincial art legacy.

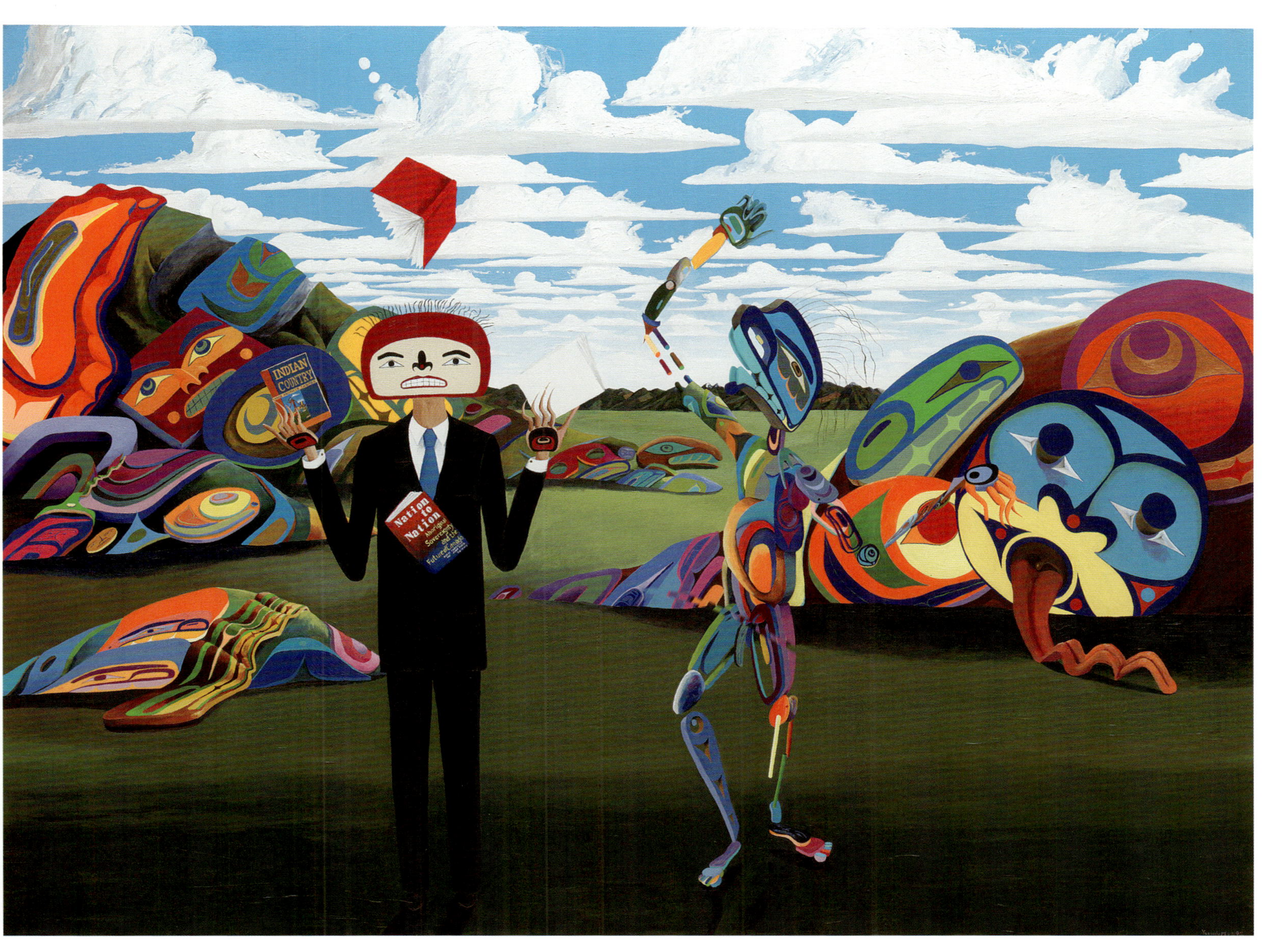

Lawrence Paul Yuxweluptun
An Indian Game
(Juggling the Books) 1996

LIST OF WORKS

All works, unless otherwise noted, are in the collection of Michael Audain and Yoshiko Karasawa. Measurements are height × width × depth.

Roy Arden
Condominium Advertisement, Vancouver, B.C., 1992
archival pigment print
101.6 × 116.8 cm
(page 116)

Sonny Assu
Death Blanket, 2006
Hudson's Bay blanket, akoya shell and red melton
172.5 × 216.4 cm

1884–1951, 2009
67 spun copper cups, Hudson's Bay blanket
dimensions variable
(page 81)

Dialect, 2010
acrylic on panel
76.2 × 242.7 cm
(pages 82–83)

Silenced #2, 2010
acrylic on hide
27.9 × 45.7 × 45.7 cm

Bertram Charles Binning
Comment on Horseshoe Bay, 1949
oil on board
45.7 × 60.9 cm

Triptych of Nautical Symbols, 1956
oil, gesso on burlap mounted on board
58.4 × 68.6 × 10.4 cm
(page 89)

Claude Breeze
Medallion (for R.K.), 1966
acrylic on canvas
208.3 × 137.2 cm

Transmission Difficulties: The Dignitaries, 1968
acrylic on canvas
152.3 × 182.8 cm
(page 92)

Arabella Campbell
Square Process Paintings: Right Tilted, Left Tilted, 2009
acrylic on canvas
60.9 × 60.9 cm (two panels)
(pages 98–99)

Emily Carr
The Quay, Alert Bay, c. 1908
watercolour on paper
26.3 × 36.5 cm

House with Slanted Roof—Brittany, 1911
oil on board
66.1 × 51.8 cm
(page 34)

Gitwangak, 1912
watercolour on paper
26.2 × 25.3 cm

Hazelton, 1912
oil on board
62.9 × 33 cm

Memkish, 1912
watercolour on paper
74.9 × 55.3 cm
(page 14)

Skidegate, 1912
oil on board
64.6 × 32.2 cm

War Canoes, Alert Bay, 1912
oil on canvas
63.4 × 81.3 cm
(page 35)

Emily and Lizzie, c. 1913
oil on board
48.3 × 66.7 cm
(page 33)

Arbutus Tree/Untitled Portrait, c. 1913–20
oil on canvas
56.5 × 46.3 cm
(page 3)

Oak Wood, c. 1913–27
oil on canvas
38.1 × 48.3 cm

Totem D'Sonoqua, c. 1928
watercolour, charcoal on paper
64.8 × 46.4 cm

At Beacon Hill Park, c. 1935
oil on paper
58.4 × 88.8 cm
(pages 36–37)

The Path, c. 1935
oil on canvas
111.8 × 68.6 cm

Coast Hill and Two Cabins, c. 1935–36
oil on paper
60.9 × 91.4 cm

Gaiety, 1935–37
oil on canvas
50.8 × 38.2 cm

Forest, c. 1937
oil on paper
91.4 × 60.9 cm

Alert Bay Burial Ground, 1937–39
oil on canvas
83.2 × 60.4 cm
(page 30)

Indian Church, Forest Edge, c. 1939
oil on canvas
68.6 × 53.3 cm

Young Arbutus, c. 1939
oil on paper
86.3 × 55.8 cm

Quiet, 1942
oil on canvas
111.8 × 68.6 cm
(page 21)

Summer, Mount Douglas Park, 1942
oil on paper
57.2 × 86.3 cm
(pages 154–55)

Dana Claxton
Paint Up #1, 2010
chromogenic print
182.9 × 182.9 cm
(page 8)

Reg Davidson
New Beginning, 2006
red cedar, cedar bark, acrylic
53.3 × 22.8 × 15.2 cm
(page 5)

Robert Davidson
Raven's Tail Mask, 1992
red cedar, cedar bark, human hair, opercula, copper, crow feathers
30.5 × 20.3 × 17.8 cm
(page 73)

This is Crazy (Eagle and Mouse Woman) Drum, 1995
acrylic on hide
76.2 cm (diameter) × 10.2 cm

Blind Justice, 1996
red cedar, cedar bark, opercula, horse hair
71.5 × 40.5 × 19 cm

Tulgyaa Hlangngee (Tell Me a Story), 2002
red cedar, acrylic
185.4 × 94 × 5.7 cm

Relaxed Symmetry, 2003
red cedar, acrylic
116.8 × 58 × 4.7 cm
(each panel)
(page 26)

Beau Dick
Tsonokwa Mask, 2007
red cedar, horse hair, acrylic
78.8 × 66.1 × 35.6 cm
(page 76)

Christos Dikeakos
Windfall, Hornby Island, 1994
chromogenic print
36 × 82.1 cm
(pages 110–11)

250 Northern Street, 2009
lightjet print
121.9 × 63.7 cm

Stan Douglas
Downtown Eastside, 2002
chromogenic print
65.2 × 115.5 cm (sight)

McLeod's Books, Vancouver, 2006
chromogenic print
103.5 × 260 cm (image)
(pages 108–9)

Charles Edenshaw (Tahagen)
Painted Spruce Root Hat, late 19th century
spruce root, pigment
20.5 × 37.8 cm (diameter)
Promised Gift of Michael Audain and Yoshiko Karasawa
(page 57)

Gathie Falk
22 Apples, 1997
oil on canvas
183.7 × 168.2 cm
(page 93)

Graham Gillmore
Ploy, 2003
collage, acrylic on canvas
284.4 × 345.2 cm
(page 95)

Greg Girard
Shanghai View 4, 2002
chromogenic print
178.2 × 216.6 cm (sight)
(page 112)

Gitk'san Artist
Portrait Mask, c. 1800
wood, pigment, tin
40.7 × 33 × 15.2 cm
(page 56)

Guardian Figure, c. 1900
red cedar, pigment
121.1 × 32 × 25.5 cm
(page 58)

Rodney Graham
Schoolyard Tree, Vancouver, 2002
chromogenic print
128.9 × 160.7 cm
(page 113)

Nautical Scene with Loudhailer, 2004
transparency in lightbox
85.7 × 68.6 × 14 cm
Collection of the Vancouver Art Gallery, Gift of Michael Audain and Yoshiko Karasawa
(page 156)

Philip Gray
Water Spirit Mask, 2009
red cedar, acrylic, horse hair
33 × 22.9 × 12.7 cm

Porcupine Hunter Mask, 2010
red cedar, acrylic, porcupine quills
67 × 38.1 × 25.4 cm
(page 72)

Angela Grossman
Musical Notes, 2007
oil, graphite on printed paper
70.2 × 50.3 cm
(page 94)

Haida Artist
Female Portrait Mask, early 1800s
wood, pigment
23.5 × 19.2 × 11.5 cm

Female Portrait Mask, 1840–60
wood, pigment
24 × 19.3 × 14 cm
(page 18)

Old Woman Mask with Labret, c. 1840–60
wood, pigment, abalone
25.6 × 22.2 × 12.4 cm
(back cover)

Model Totem Pole, 1860s
argillite
49.1 × 11 × 11 cm
Promised Gift of Michael Audain and Yoshiko Karasawa
(page 54)

Spruce Root Hat, c. 1870
spruce root, pigments
18.5 × 37.5 cm (diameter)
Promised Gift of Michael Audain and Yoshiko Karasawa

Shaman Platter, 1870s
argillite, bone
34 cm (diameter) × 4.8 cm
Promised Gift of Michael Audain and Yoshiko Karasawa

Model Totem Pole, late 19th century
yellow cedar, pigment
69 × 8.5 × 10.2 cm
Promised Gift of Michael Audain and Yoshiko Karasawa

Lawren Stewart Harris
Abstraction, c. 1945
oil on canvas
146 × 120 cm (sight)
(page 86)

Jim Hart
The Three Watchmen, 2001
bronze
22.8 × 12.7 cm (circumference)

Model Pole, 2006–09
yellow cedar
236.2 × 36.5 × 26 cm
(page 80)

Heiltsuk Artist
Articulated Mask, c. 1830–50
wood, pigments, hide
27.5 × 31 × 18 cm
(page 152)

Ancestor Mask, c. 1850
wood, pigment
26.5 × 23 × 16.5 cm
(page 51)

Frontlet, c. 1860–80
wood, pigments, abalone shell
21 × 19.2 × 12 cm
Promised Gift of Michael Audain and Yoshiko Karasawa
(page 53)

Fred Herzog
Bogner's Grocery, 1960
chromogenic print
71.1 × 96.5 cm
(pages 106–7)

Edward John Hughes
Echo Bay, 1953
oil on canvas
61 × 45.7 cm
(page 6)

Brady's Beach near Bamfield, B.C., 1960
oil on canvas
63.5 × 81.7 cm

Departure from Nanaimo, 1964
oil on canvas
80.5 × 121 cm (sight)

Ferry Passing Malaspina's Gallery, 1966
oil on canvas
63.5 × 81.7 cm

Dean Hunt
PK'vs: Wild Man of the Woods, 2009
red cedar, acrylic, horse hair, skunk hair, eagle and flicker feathers, Kerkimer diamonds
66 × 60.9 × 27.9 cm
(page 75)

Richard Hunt
Totem Pole, 2003
red cedar
167 × 53 × 35 cm
(page 66)

Tony Hunt, Jr.
Tsonokwa Mask, 2006
red cedar, acrylic, horse hair
71.1 × 50.8 × 22.8 cm
(page 69)

Charlie James
Sun Mask, late 19th–
early 20th century
wood, paint
44.2 × 37.3 × 17 cm
(page 63)

Philip Janze
Sun Mask, 1986
copper, acrylic
86.3 × 81.3 × 12.7 cm
(page 71)

Brian Jungen
Variant 1, 2002
Nike athletic footwear
132.1 × 108 × 21 cm
(page 85)

Kwakwaka'wakw Artist
Human Face Ridicule Mask, c. 1880
wood, pigment
29 × 29 × 23 cm
(page 17)

Model Canoe, c. 1880
wood, pigment
27 × 159 × 22 cm

Sun Mask, 19th century
wood, pigment
48 × 52 × 31 cm
(page 52)

Bookwus Mask,
late 19th century
wood, pigment
59 × 57.5 × 31 cm

Tim Lee
Upside Down Water Torture Chamber, Harry Houdini 1914, 2004
chromogenic print
132.1 × 106.7 cm
(page 100)

It Takes a Nation of Millions to Hold Us Back, Public Enemy 1988, 2006
chromogenic print
152.4 × 198.2 cm

Attila Richard Lukacs
Varieties of Love: Painting the Lovers' Portrait, 1991
oil, enamel, tar,
gold leaf on canvas
284 × 254 cm
(page 96)

Ken Lum
Nancy Nishi, Joe Ping Chau, Real Estate, 1990
chromogenic print
242.8 × 152.4 cm
(page 105)

James Williamson Galloway (Jock) Macdonald
The Black Tusk, Garibaldi Park, B.C., 1932
oil on canvas
71 × 90.8 cm
Collection of the
Vancouver Art Gallery,
Gift of Michael Audain
and Yoshiko Karasawa
(page 39)

Scott McFarland
Boathouse with Moonlight, 2003
chromogenic print
178.5 × 229.3 cm (sight)
Collection of the
Vancouver Art Gallery,
Gift of Michael Audain
and Yoshiko Karasawa
(page 103)

Marianne Nicolson
Tunic for a Noblewoman: In Memory of Wadzidalaga, 2009
acrylic, brass, copper, silver,
abalone shell on wood
129.5 × 124.4 × 7.7 cm
(two panels)
(pages 78–79)

Nisga'a Artist
Portrait Mask, c. 1880
wood, pigment
25 × 20 × 14 cm
(page 55)

Nuu-chah-nulth Artist
Bone Club, late 18th–
early 19th century
whalebone, abalone, hide
59.7 × 6.2 × 2.5 cm
Promised Gift of
Michael Audain and
Yoshiko Karasawa

Articulated Mask, c. 1840
wood, pigment
33.5 × 18.1 × 13 cm
(page 50)

Black Rim Hat, c. 1840
spruce root, cedar bark,
pigment
18.5 × 35 cm (diameter)
Promised Gift of
Michael Audain and
Yoshiko Karasawa

Speaker's Mask, c. 1890
wood, pigment
44 × 22 × 23 cm

Sisiutl Headdress with Articulated Feather Crown,
c. 1900
wood, pigment, cloth, string
44 × 16.3 × 76.5 cm
Promised Gift of
Michael Audain and
Yoshiko Karasawa

Nuxalk Artist
Raven Mask (Bella Coola),
c. 1860–80
wood, metal, mirror,
cord, pigments
25 × 72.4 × 23.5 cm
(page 2)

Earthquake Mask, c. 1880
wood, pigment
27.3 × 21 × 18 cm
(page 44)

Mask (Bella Coola), c. 1880
wood, pigment
41 × 34.5 × 20 cm

Norman Antony (Toni) Onley
Juno, 1962
oil, canvas collage on canvas
128.7 × 113.4 cm
(page 90)

José Clemente Orozco
Naturaleza Muerta (Autorretrato) [Still-Life (Self-Portrait)], 1944
oil on canvas
63.5 × 86.5 cm (sight)
(page 131)

Prometheus, 1945
ink, oil on paper
50.8 × 42.5 cm
(page 130)

Pedregal [Stony Place], 1947
oil on canvas
41.9 × 61.9 cm (sight)
(page 129)

Laurie Papou
She saw her fallen clothes as a charity, a homage, 2000
oil on panel
171.4 × 123.1 cm
(page 97)

Walter Joseph Phillips
Jim King's Wharf, Alert Bay, 1927
colour woodcut
30.8 × 23.4 cm (image)

Mamalilicoola, 1928
colour woodcut
33.3 × 38.2 cm (image)

Sharp's Dock, Pender Harbour, 1952
colour woodcut
22.8 × 35.6 cm (image)
(page 41)

Bill Reid
Killer Whale, 1984
bronze
132 × 48.5 × 69.6 cm
(page 70)

Diego Rivera
Naturaleza muerta en ovalo [Oval Still-Life], c. 1915–16
oil on canvas
92.5 × 79.5 cm (sight)
(page 123)

Niña con vestido rosa [Girl with Pink Dress], 1930
tempera on linen
51.2 × 38.7 cm (sight)
(page 124)

Luz hilando [Light Spinner], 1936
watercolour, ink on paper
55.6 × 51.6 cm (sight)
(page 4)

Autorretrato [The Firestone Self-Portrait], 1941
oil on canvas
60.9 × 43.2 cm
(page 120)

El curandero [The Folk Healer], 1945
watercolour on paper
46.2 × 60.7 cm (sight)
(page 127)

Retrato de Gladys March [Portrait of Gladys March], 1946
oil on canvas
76.2 × 70.8 cm (sight)
(page 126)

Maternidad [Motherhood], 1954
oil on canvas
92.6 × 156.9 cm (sight)
(page 128)

Larry Rosso
Beaver with Two Frogs, Eagle, Raven and Thunderbird, 1997
red cedar
134.6 × 195.6 × 9 cm
(page 62)

Salish Artist
Figure, late 19th century–early 20th century
wood, pigment
71 × 15 × 7.5 cm
(page 48)

Basket with Lid, 1930s
cedar root, cherry bark, grass
68.5 × 36 cm (diameter)

Jack Leonard Shadbolt
Butterfly Transformation Theme 1981, 1981
acrylic on canvas
160.3 × 122.5 cm each
(six panels)
(pages 28–29)

Against the Light, 1989
acrylic on canvas
170.6 × 124.6 cm

Steven Shearer
Guitar #5, 2002–03
chromogenic print
177.2 × 283.2 cm
(pages 118–19)

Jay Simeon
Seawolf and Killer Whale Mask, 2008
alder, cedar bark, horse hair, holly wood, paua shell, copper
58.4 × 35.6 × 25.3 cm
(page 74)

Danny Singer
Kinkaid, 2004
chromogenic print
57 × 295.5 cm (sight)

Calder, 2005
chromogenic print
47.3 × 235.7 cm (sight)
(pages 114–15)

David Alfaro Siqueiros
Hacia la cumbre! [Towards the Top!], 1960
pyroxilin on panel
78.3 × 58.2 cm (sight)
© Estate of David Alfaro Siqueiros/SODRAC (2011)
(page 132)

Los Dos Davides [The Two Davids], 1963
pyroxilin on masonite
59.1 × 43.8 cm (sight)
© Estate of David Alfaro Siqueiros/SODRAC (2011)
(page 133)

Sueño [Sleep], 1970
pyroxilin on novopan
88.9 × 121.9 cm (sight)
© Estate of David Alfaro Siqueiros/SODRAC (2011)
(pages 134–35)

Gordon Appelbe Smith
Winterscape, 1991
acrylic on canvas
170.2 × 254.4 cm
(page 43)

P4, 1994
acrylic on tarpaulin
210.8 × 170.1 cm

Henry Speck, Jr.
Hok Hok Headdress, 2004
red cedar, cedar bark, marine enamel
188 × 88 × 30.5 cm
(page 68)

Norman Tait
Mischievous Man Mask, 2008
alder, acrylic, opercula
90 × 32.5 × 17.5 cm
(page 77)

Rufino Tamayo
Bañistas [Bathers], 1930
oil on canvas
78.6 × 69.1 cm
© D.R. Rufino Tamayo, Herederos, México 2011, Fundación Olga y Rufino Tamayo, A.C.
(page 138)

Mujer llamando [Woman Crying Out], 1941
oil on canvas
91.4 × 60.9 cm (sight)
© D.R. Rufino Tamayo, Herederos, México 2011, Fundación Olga y Rufino Tamayo, A.C. (page 137)

La Constelación [Constellation], 1947
oil on canvas
54.2 × 102.6 cm (sight)
© D.R. Rufino Tamayo, Herederos, México 2011, Fundación Olga y Rufino Tamayo, A.C. (page 136)

Figura de pie [Pious Figure], 1959
oil, sand on canvas
130 × 97.2 cm
© D.R. Rufino Tamayo, Herederos, México 2011, Fundación Olga y Rufino Tamayo, A.C. (page 139)

Hombre contra un muro [Man against a Wall], 1975
oil, sand on canvas
95.2 × 128.9 cm (sight)
© D.R. Rufino Tamayo, Herederos, México 2011, Fundación Olga y Rufino Tamayo, A.C. (page 25)

Takao Tanabe
Strait of Georgia 1/90: Raza Pass, 1990
acrylic on canvas
139.7 × 183 cm
(page 42)

Rivers 01/01: Jordan River, 2001
acrylic on canvas
114.3 × 304.8 cm

Ron Terada
The Idea of North, 2007
wood, metal bucket, soil
91.8 × 60.2 × 27.3 cm
(page 10)

Art Thompson
Killer Whale Moon Mask, c. 1997
red cedar, acrylic, copper, abalone shell
134.6 × 104.1 × 35.6 cm
(page 67)

Tlingit Artist
Chilkat Blanket, c. 1870s
mountain goat wool, cedar bark
131 × 192 cm
(page 61)

Bear (Shaman's) Mask, c. 1880
wood, pigment
26.2 × 17.7 × 13.5 cm

Devil Fish (Octopus) Feast Dish, c. 1880
alder, abalone, horn
11.2 × 36 × 18.1 cm
Promised Gift of Michael Audain and Yoshiko Karasawa

Owl Mask, 1840–60s
wood, pigment, human hair, hide
26 × 25 × 11.5 cm
(page 59)

Tsimshian Artist
Chest, 19th century
wood, pigment
47 × 80 × 45.1 cm
(page 60)

Portrait Mask, c. 1860
wood, pigment
23.5 × 18.5 × 11 cm

Portrait Mask, c. 1860
wood, pigment, hair, hide
30.5 × 21 × 17.5 cm

Articulated Mask, c. 1880
wood, pigment, copper, fabric, lead, cedar bark
29 × 31.5 × 12 cm
(page 159)

Ancestor Portrait Mask (from Kitwankool, Kispiox area), late 19th century
wood, pigment, cedar bark
30.5 × 21 × 14.5 cm

Unknown First Nations Artist
Copper (belonging to Willie Seaweed), 18th century
copper, pigment
69 × 37 × 1.5 cm
(page 65)

Bent Wood Box and Lid, 19th century
red cedar, pigment
69.5 × 53.5 × 52.5 cm
(page 64)

Bent Wood Box and Lid, 1860s
red cedar, opercula
47 × 80 × 46.5 cm

Canoe Feast Dish, c. 1880
alder, brass tacks
78 × 35 × 17.5 cm

Unknown First Nations Artist (Haida or Tsimshian)
Corner Oriented Box, 1870s
wood, pigment
37.4 × 30.5 × 28 cm

Unknown First Nations Artist (Haida?)
Canoe Form Bowl, c. 1880
wood, pigment
20.6 × 98.5 × 26.7 cm
(page 62)

Frederick Horsman Varley
Misty Day, West Coast, c. 1928
oil on panel
30.4 × 38.2 cm

Dusk—Tantalus Range, c. 1929
oil on panel
30.4 × 38.1 cm
(page 160)

Stumps and Mountains, c. 1932
oil on panel
30.3 × 38.2 cm

Bridge over Lynn Creek, c. 1933
oil on panel
30.2 × 37.9 cm
(page 38)

All F.H. Varley works
© Varley Art Gallery, Town of Markham

Stephen Waddell
Stazione de Termini, 2008
chromogenic print
139.7 × 205.8 cm
(page 117)

Jeff Wall
From *Children*, 1988
transparency in lightbox
134.5 cm (diameter) × 22 cm
Collection of the Vancouver Art Gallery, Gift of Michael Audain and Yoshiko Karasawa

River Road, 1994
transparency in lightbox
90.5 × 119 × 22 cm
Collection of the Vancouver Art Gallery, Gift of Michael Audain and Yoshiko Karasawa
(page 13)

Basin in Rome, 2003
transparency in lightbox
42.2 × 42.2 × 11.2 cm
Collection of the Vancouver Art Gallery, Gift of Michael Audain and Yoshiko Karasawa

Ian Wallace
Times Square, NYC, 2003
acrylic, photolaminate on canvas
183.5 × 183.5 cm
(page 22)

John Webber
Nootka Prints, 1784
six engravings
27.9 × 40.7 cm (variable)
(*The Inside of a House in Nootka Sound*, page 47)

William Percival Weston
Jotunheim, 1932
oil on canvas
100.5 × 90.1 cm (sight)
(page 40)

Michael Nicoll Yahgulanaas
Fishing, 2008
acrylic, graphite on panel
61.1 × 50.7 cm
(page 140)

Don Yeomans
Raven and Frog Panel, 2006–07
red cedar, acrylic
122 cm (diameter) × 4 cm
(page 84)

Lawrence Paul Yuxweluptun
An Indian Game (Juggling the Books), 1996
acrylic on canvas
152 × 208 cm
(page 143)

Burying Another Face of Racism on First Nations Soil, 1997
acrylic on canvas
487.7 × 289.6 cm

New Age Indian, 1998
acrylic on canvas
243.8 × 198.1 cm

Etienne Zack
Innerworks, 2007
acrylic and oil on canvas
198.5 × 229 cm
Collection of the Vancouver Art Gallery, Gift of Michael Audain and Yoshiko Karasawa
(page 91)

PHOTO CREDITS

All photographs are by Vancouver Art Gallery photographers Trevor Mills (back cover, pages 2, 5, 17, 18, 26, 41, 43, 44, 48, 50–56, 58, 59, 61–64, 66, 68–73, 75–77, 80, 82/83, 84, 85, 89, 95–97, 98–99, 105–7, 152, 159); Rachel Topham (front cover, pages 6, 8, 14, 22, 35, 38, 39, 40, 42, 47, 65 (copper), 86, 90–94, 113, 129, 131, 140, 143, 154–55); or Trevor Mills and Rachel Topham (page 81), with the exception of the following: Roy Arden, page 116; Christos Dikeakos, pages 110–11; Stan Douglas, pages 108–9; Greg Girard, page 112; Fred Herzog, pages 106–7; Tim Lee, page 100; Ken Lum, page 105; Scott McFarland, page 103; Marianne Nicolson, pages 78, 79; Steven Shearer, pages 118–19; Danny Singer, pages 114–15; Stephen Waddell, page 117; Jeff Wall, pages 13, 101; Christie's, New York, pages 4, 25, 120, 124, 127, 130, 132, 133, 134–35, 136–39; Donald Ellis, page 57; Heffel Fine Art Auction House, pages 3, 21, 30, 33, 34, 36–37, 160; Scott Massey, courtesy Catriona Jeffries Gallery, page 10; Kenji Nagai, pages 67, 74; Royal British Columbia Museum, page 65 (photograph); Sotheby's, New York, pages 60, 123, 126, 128; University of British Columbia Library, Special Collections, pages 28–29; Donald Young Gallery, Chicago, page 156.

IMAGE CREDITS FOR COVER AND OPENING SEQUENCE

Front cover: Emily Carr, *War Canoes, Alert Bay,* 1912 (detail)
page 2: Nuxalk Artist, *Raven Mask (Bella Coola),* c. 1860–80
page 3: Emily Carr, *Arbutus Tree,* c. 1913–20
page 4: Diego Rivera, *Luz hilando [Light Spinner],* 1936
page 5: Reg Davidson, *New Beginning,* 2006
page 6: E.J. Hughes, *Echo Bay,* 1953
Back cover: Haida Artist, *Old Woman Mask with Labret,* c. 1840–60

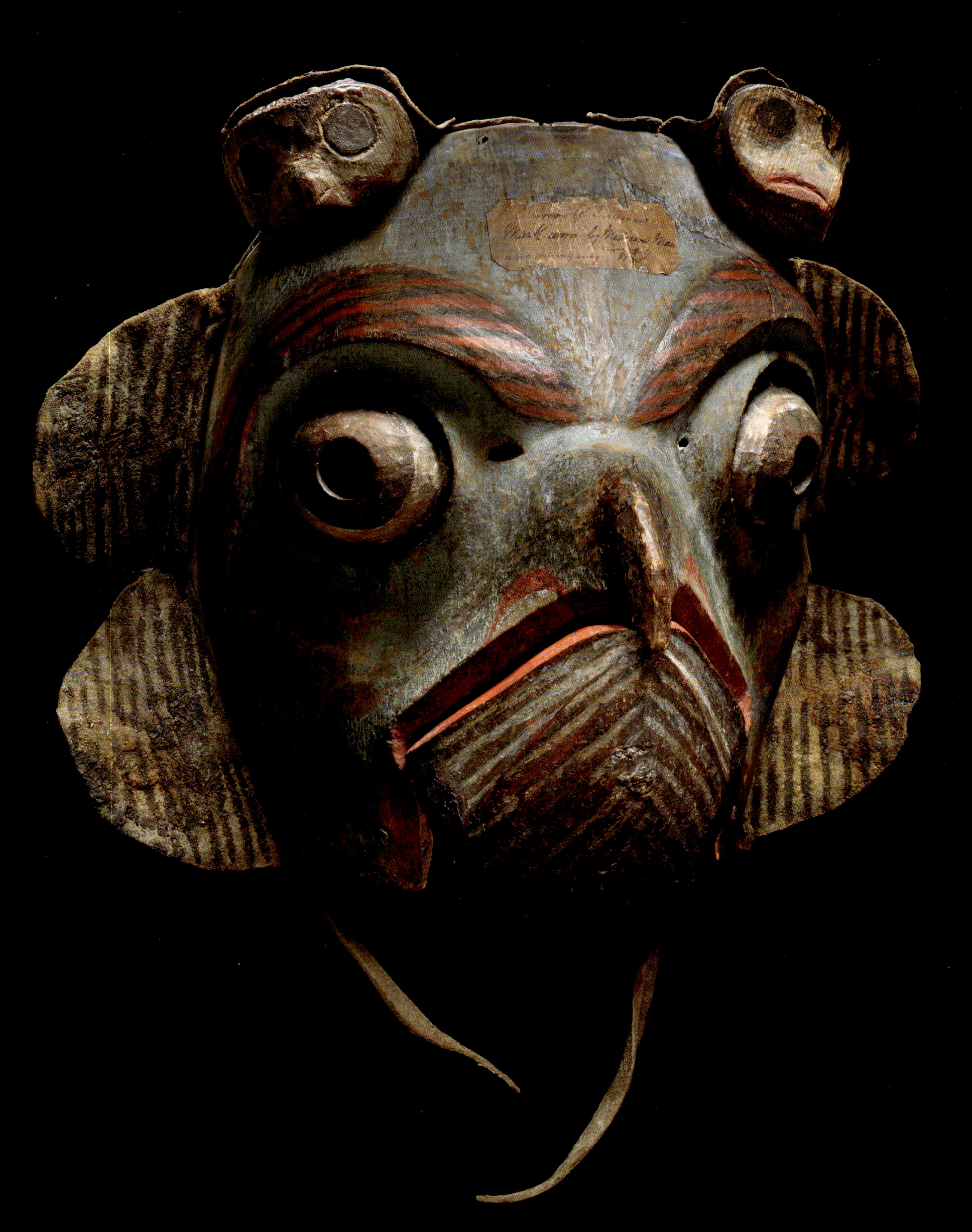
Mask worn by Medicine Man

CONTRIBUTOR BIOGRAPHIES

GRANT ARNOLD, the Audain Curator of British Columbia Art, has worked at the Vancouver Art Gallery for nearly two decades. He has published widely on photography and the art of the region.

MICHAEL AUDAIN, a prominent business leader in Vancouver, is one of the leading cultural philanthropists in Canada. He has supported the artistic life of this province and country for many years through his own activities and those of the Audain Foundation for the Visual Arts.

THE HONOURABLE GORDON CAMPBELL was recently appointed Canadian High Commissioner to the Court of St. James, London. He served as Premier of the Province of British Columbia from 2001–11 and is a long-time friend of Michael Audain and Yoshiko Karasawa.

JESSICA BERLANGA TAYLOR is an independent art critic and curator, based in Montreal, who specializes in Mexican modern and contemporary art; she was advised by Julia Soto Martínez, a scholar of Mexican Modernism based in Cuernavaca, Mexico.

IAN THOM has worked as Senior Curator—Historical at the Vancouver Art Gallery since 1988. He is the author of numerous publications on Canadian and British Columbian art.

CHARLOTTE TOWNSEND-GAULT is a Professor in the Department of Art History, Visual Art and Theory at the University of British Columbia, where she specializes in First Nations cultural studies; she has published extensively in this field.

facing
Heiltsuk Artist
Articulated Mask c. 1830–50

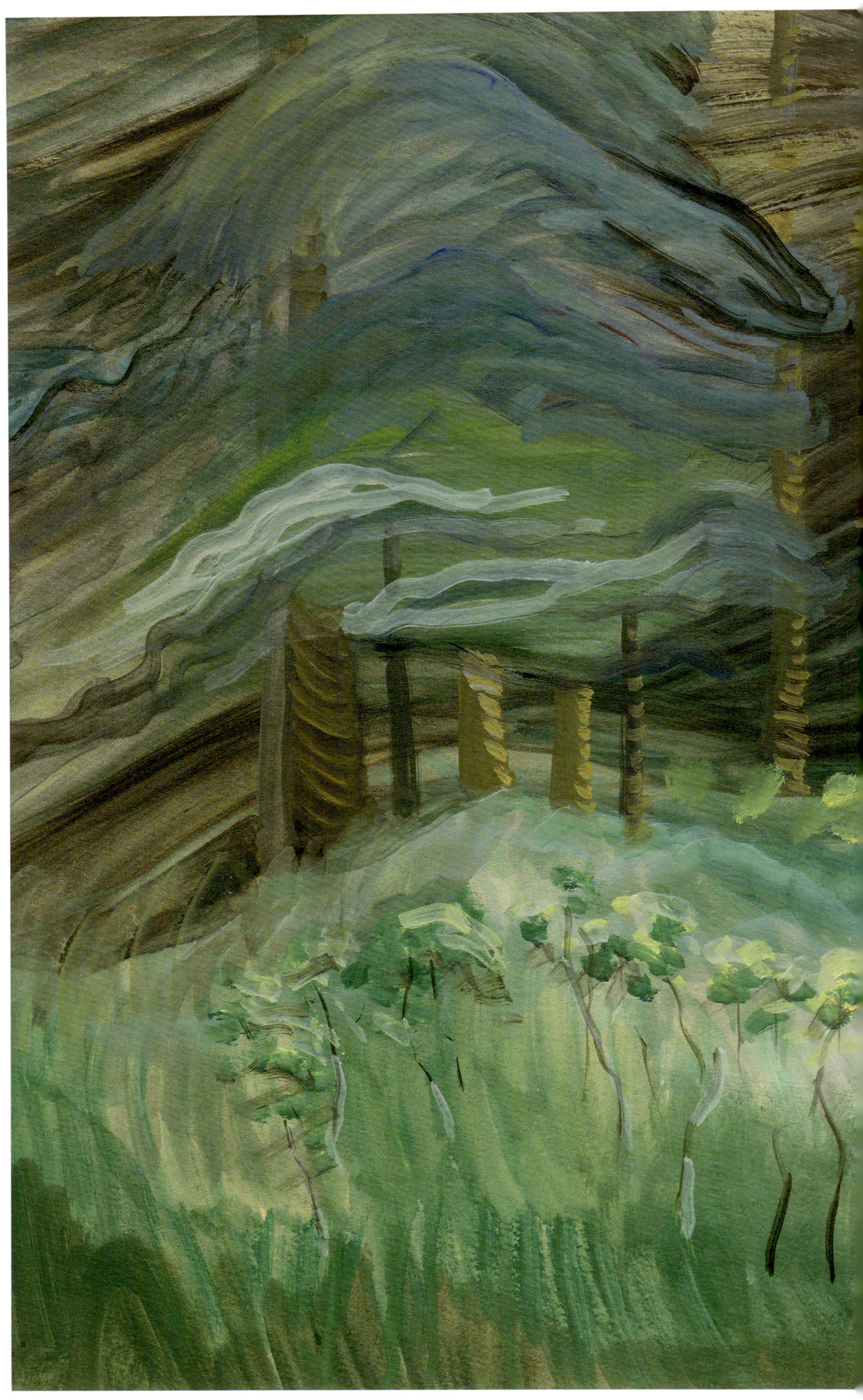

Emily Carr
Summer Mount
Douglas Park 1942

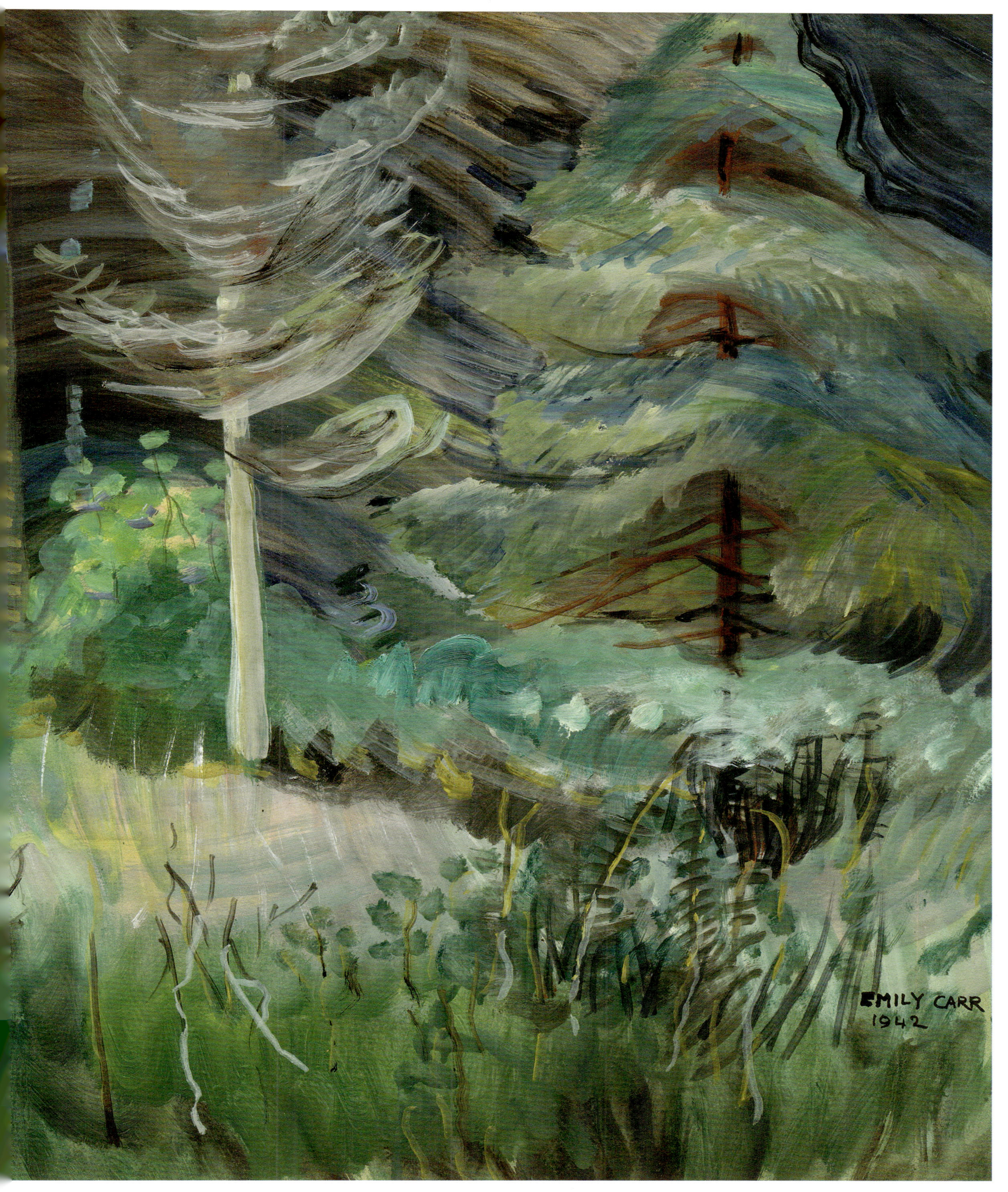
EMILY CARR
1942

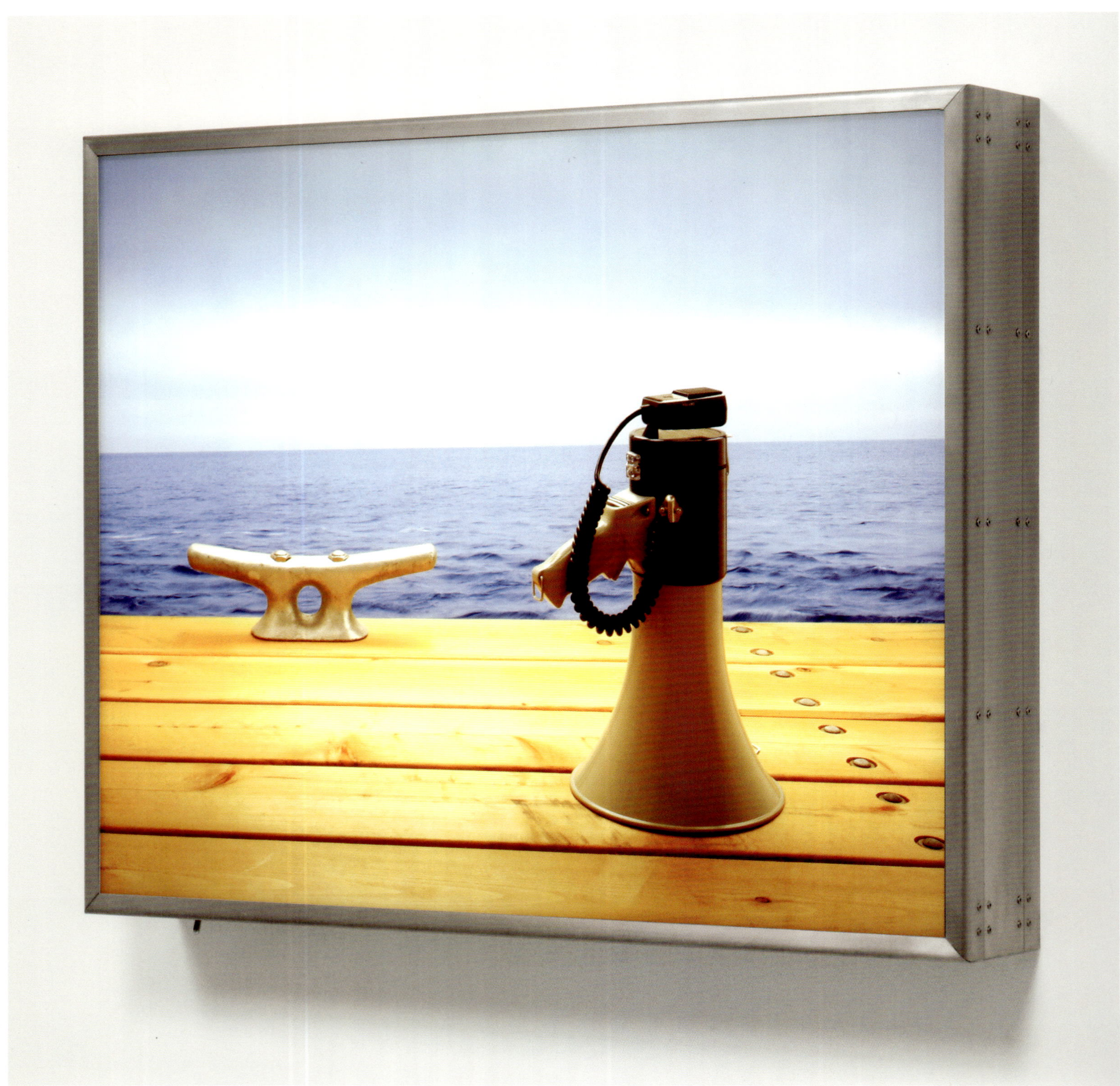

Rodney Graham
Nautical Scene with
Loudhailer 2004

ACKNOWLEDGEMENTS

OUR FIRST THANKS are to Michael Audain and Yoshiko Karasawa, who have generously agreed to allow us to denude the walls of their homes and borrow many of their most prized possessions. We are also grateful to Mr. Audain's assistants, Barbara Binns and Georges Dordor, who have helped enormously every step of the way. Many dealers and auctioneers have been extremely helpful in providing images of works in the Audain collection, and particular thanks are owed to Sotheby's, New York; Christie's, New York; the Heffel Fine Art Auction House, Vancouver; Donald Ellis, Dundas, Ontario, and New York; Douglas Reynolds Gallery, Vancouver; and the many other dealers and auctioneers throughout Canada, the United States and Europe who were also generous with assistance. We extend our deepest thanks to all.

At the Vancouver Art Gallery, we are grateful to the entire staff, but particular mention must be made of Glen Flanderka, Rory Gylander and the entire Preparation staff; Trevor Mills, Rachel Topham and Danielle Currie in Photo Imaging; Registrar of Collections Susan Sirovyak and Assistant Registrar Kim Svendsen; and Conservators Monica Smith and Kathy Bond. Within the Senior Management team we are particularly indebted to Director of Operations Tom Meighan; Director and Curator of Public Programs Heidi Reitmaier and, on her staff, Interpretation Coordinator Kimberly Phillips; and to Chris Nicolls, Director of Finance. Dana Sullivant, Director of Marketing and Communications, and Communications Manager Carolyn Jack have also contributed immensely. Scott Elliott, Deputy Director, Development, and his team have greatly assisted in securing sponsorship for this project. The exhibition has been enthusiastically supported from the beginning by the Gallery's Director, Kathleen S. Bartels, and Chief Curator/Associate Director, Daina Augaitis. Karen Love, Manager of Curatorial Affairs, has been instrumental throughout, particularly in the production of this book. Finally, Bruce Wiedrick, Exhibition Coordinator, has managed the exhibition budget. To all, our sincere thanks.

At Douglas & McIntyre, Publisher Scott McIntyre has been a constant supporter of this project, and we have benefited from the skills of Lucy Kenward and Art Director Peter Cocking. We were also blessed by the editing skills of freelancer Judith Penner. Most importantly, we value enormously the insightful contributions to this volume by the essayists, Charlotte Townsend-Gault, Jessica Berlanga Taylor with Julia Soto Martínez, and the Honourable Gordon Campbell.

GRANT ARNOLD AND IAN THOM, *Exhibition Curators*

First U.S. edition 2012

11 12 13 14 15 5 4 3 2 1

Douglas & McIntyre
An imprint of D&M Publishers Inc.
2323 Quebec Street, Suite 201
Vancouver BC Canada V5T 4S7
www.douglas-mcintyre.com

Vancouver Art Gallery
750 Hornby Street
Vancouver BC Canada V6Z 2H7
www.vanartgallery.bc.ca

Cataloguing data available from Library and Archives Canada
ISBN 978-1-55365-929-7 (cloth)

Published in conjunction with *Shore, Forest and Beyond: Art from the Audain Collection*, an exhibition organized by the Vancouver Art Gallery and presented from October 29, 2011 to January 29, 2012.

Publication coordination by Karen Love, Vancouver Art Gallery
Editing by Judith Penner
Book design by Peter Cocking
Photography and digital image preparation by Trevor Mills and Rachel Topham, Vancouver Art Gallery
Front cover image: Emily Carr, *War Canoes, Alert Bay*, 1912 (detail)
Back cover image : Haida artist, *Old Woman Mask with Labret*, c. 1840–60
Printed and bound in Canada by Friesens
Text printed on acid-free paper
Distributed in the U.S. by Publishers Group West

Every effort has been made to trace ownership of visual material used in this book. Errors or omissions will be corrected in subsequent printings, provided notification is sent to the publisher.

The Vancouver Art Gallery is a not-for-profit organization supported by its members; individual donors; corporate funders; foundations; the City of Vancouver; the Province of British Columbia through the B.C. Arts Council and Gaming Revenues; and the Canada Council for the Arts.

Douglas & McIntyre gratefully acknowledges the financial support of the Canada Council for the Arts, the British Columbia Arts Council, the Province of British Columbia through the Book Publishing Tax Credit and the Government of Canada through the Canada Book Fund for our publishing activities.

Shore, Forest and Beyond: Art from the Audain Collection is funded in part with proceeds from the Vancouver Art Gallery's Jack and Doris Shadbolt Endowment for Research and Publications.

PRESENTING SPONSOR:

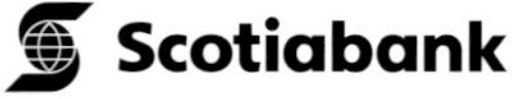

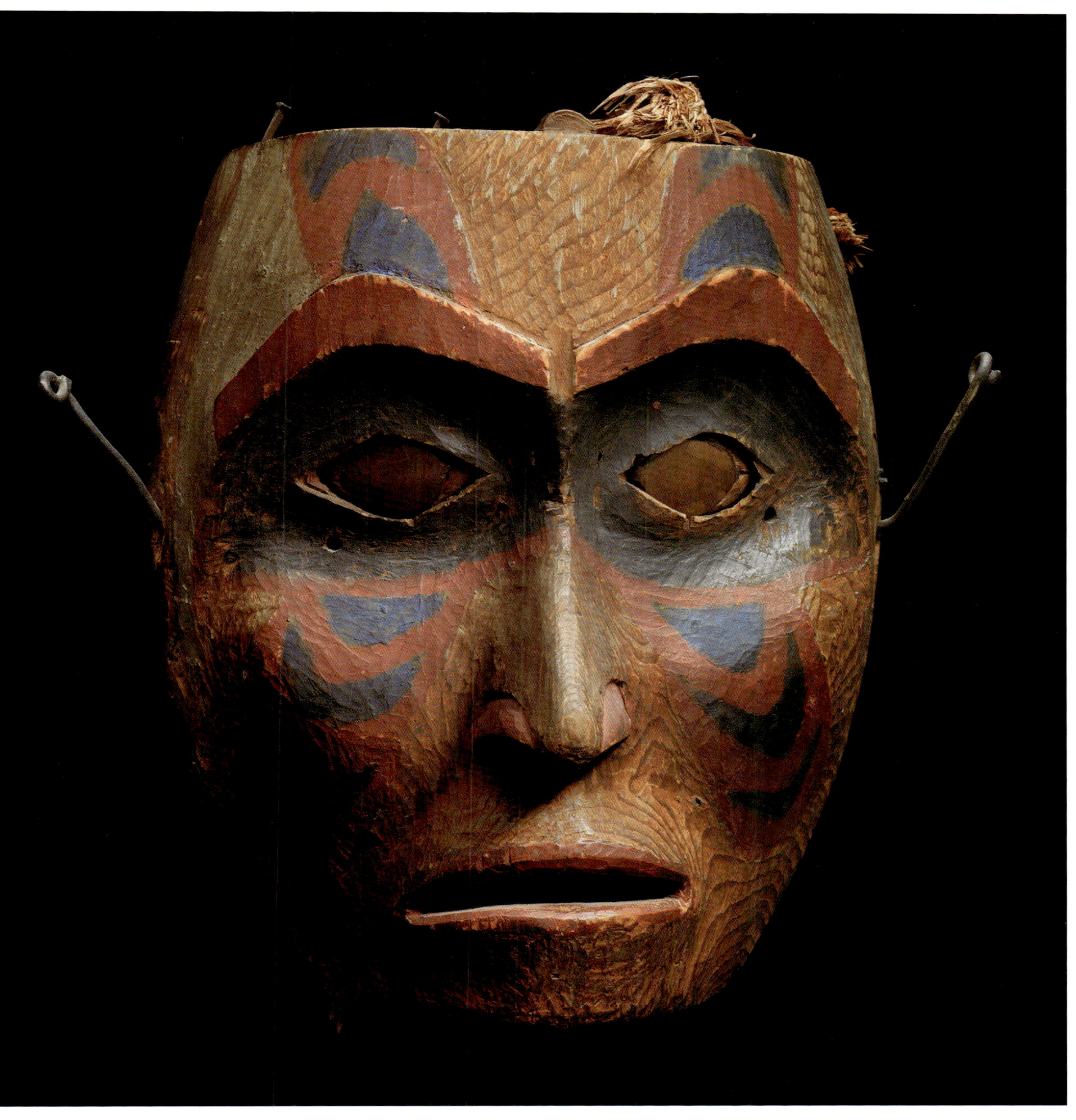

Tsimshian Artist
Articulated Mask c. 1880

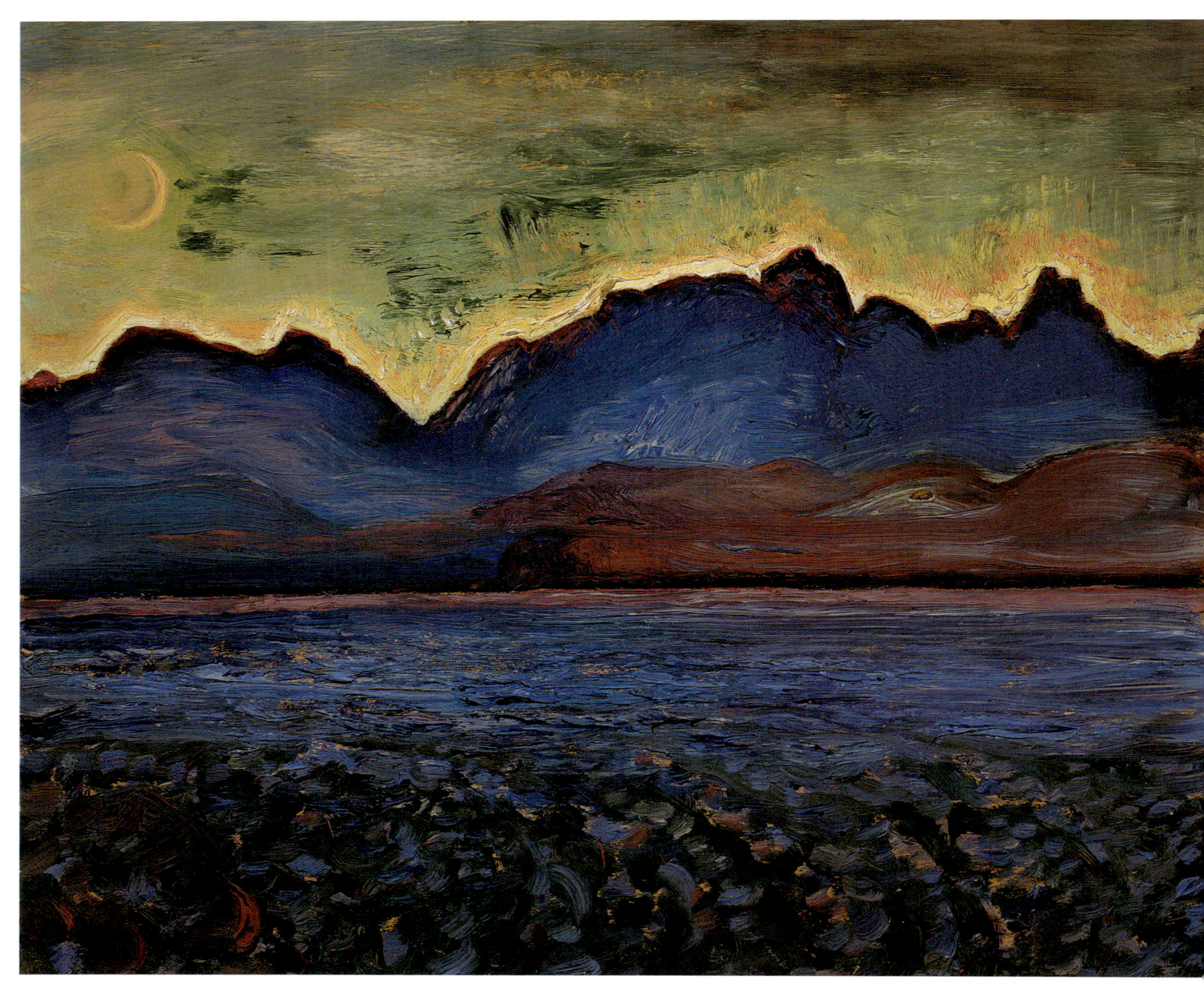

Frederick Horsman Varley
Dusk—Tantalus Range
c. 1929